"Tim Morgan is frank   d the allure
of atheism. This book   hat the best
minds in atheism have u   way   d wanting."

Josh McDowell
Author of *Evidence That Demands a Verdict,*
#13 on *Christianity Today's* list of
"The Top 50 Books That Have Shaped Evangelicals"

"Ever wondered if we can be skeptical about skepticism and what its history is? Then Tim Morgan's *Thank God for Atheists* is for you. Here is a walk through the terrain of skeptical arguments with a former skeptic who knows how they think. It is a fascinating and important tour of a world many people do not understand. A careful read will equip you for meaningful conversation with anyone that doubts and says, 'Why would you believe that?' Turnabout is fair play and this book shows why."

Darrell Bock
Professor of New Testament Studies
Dallas Theological Seminary

"Sometimes faith needs to get shaken in order to be rebuilt stronger than before. Tim Morgan's spiritual and intellectual journey to rediscovering his faith (with the unlikely help of Dawkins, Hitchens, and Harris) will help anyone searching for solid ground to build from."

Justin Brierley
Host of radio show *Unbelievable?*
Senior Editor *Premier Christianity* magazine

"While I disagree with much of Tim's arguments in his book as many atheists like myself will relate to, I did find this to be an insightful and easy to read book. A must-read for atheists who are interested in the struggles and triumphs that religion can cause in the mind of a believer."

Mike Mello
President of F.A.C.T.S.
(Florida Atheists, Critical Thinkers & Skeptics)

"This is a must-read book for Christians—it's an excellent, concise look at the atheist worldview that is becoming increasingly influential in our culture. Tim has done a fantastic job of boiling the issues down to the most pertinent points every Christian should understand. *Thank God for Atheists* is an especially valuable guide for Christian parents who want to be equipped to discuss those points with their kids."

Natasha Crain
Author of *Keeping Your Kids on God's Side*
Blogger at ChristianMomThoughts.com

Thank  for Atheists

TIMOTHY MORGAN

HARVEST HOUSE PUBLISHERS
EUGENE, OREGON

THANK GOD FOR ATHEISTS

Copyright © 2015 Timothy Morgan
Published by Harvest House Publishers
Eugene, Oregon 97402
www.harvesthousepublishers.com

Library of Congress Cataloging-in-Publication Data
Morgan, Timothy, 1972-
Thank God for Atheists / Timothy Morgan.
    pages cm
ISBN 978-0-7369-6628-3 (pbk.)
ISBN 978-0-7369-6629-0 (eBook)
1. Apologetics. 2. Atheism. 3. Christianity and atheism. 4. Morgan, Timothy, 1972—Religion.
I. Title.
BT1212.M67 2015
239'.7—dc23

                                                              2015008068

Printed in the United States of America

        15 16 17 18 19 20 21 22 23 / BP-JH / 10 9 8 7 6 5 4 3 2 1

Foreword

My work in New Testament has often dealt with the skepticism that comes from discussing the gospels and issues tied to the historical Jesus. Skepticism about Jesus and the Bible runs deep for many. But all of this is moot if God does not exist. That also is a popular current take on life and reality. Without God, there is no possibility of divine revelation, no possibility of God sending a Son to die for sin and give life, no possibility that we as humans are special creatures in the creation made in the image of God, accountable to him as our creator and designed to know him in this life and the one to come.

In *Thank God for Atheists,* Tim Morgan speaks as one who has trekked with doubts like an atheist. He has read the texts, listened to the arguments, and has a respect and appreciation for the questions atheists have raised over the centuries, many of them questions bred in honest query and others in a hostility to anything that suggests purpose or design to our world. Whether we consider the atheists of old or the newer, more glitzy version that has worked hard to market themselves much as those of the faith have, Morgan interacts on familiar ground. This book is not an ordinary study and critique of atheism. It is a journey through the history of its arguments, one significant atheist at a time. Starting in classical times and ending up with the modern "Four Horsemen" of atheism, this book works through the labyrinth of skepticism, pointing out the places where queries have made good points, as well as where the objections come up shallow and short.

I am often asked what book I would recommend that faces up to the kind of questions atheism raises. In the past I have just as often found myself suggesting that there is no single book that does this well. That is no longer the case. Here is a work that puts atheism to the test in ways all of us can follow. It is clear about both atheism's strengths and weaknesses. It often gives the reader the opportunity to pause and ask if atheism is all it is sometimes said to be. It questions the questioners with great observations. So I commend this book because it engages atheism with honesty, openness, and skill, answering questions many have asked. In its directness, it shows that a world of design is not a delusion, but the product of a purposefulness that gives humanity a rationale that extends existence beyond the void where atheism leaves us. To show that this is where atheism ultimately takes us does people a favor and reflects a humanism that actually gives worth to us all. When we appreciate where atheism ultimately truly takes us, we can see why humanity and life matters when contrasted with the shadow atheism casts over meaning in life.

—**Darrell L. Bock**
Professor of New Testament Studies, Dallas Theological Seminary

Acknowledgments

There is a saying in the Somali language, "Omwana taba womoi," which translates to "A child belongs not to one parent." While my name appears on the cover, I am indebted to the following people who helped birth this book.

A huge thank-you goes to Daniel Haddad for the late nights spent around his kitchen table reviewing early stages of the manuscript. His feedback regarding which subjects engaged him helped shape what content made the final cut. If you find the syntax smooth and flowing, thank Travis Hearne. Before his brilliant red pen, the manuscript was very verbose.

Thank you to my literary agent, Leslie Stobbie, who believed in this project from the outset and found a home for the book at Harvest House Publishers. I am grateful to Linda Nathan for editing the sample chapters we shopped with publishers. A big thank-you to Terry Glaspey at Harvest House for his acquisitions role and for still believing in first-time authors when many publishers are reluctant to take a risk with fresh voices. I am grateful to Harvest House editor Steve Miller for being an effective liaison offering strategic suggestions and invaluable help narrowing the book's focus.

Thank you to Dr. Darrell Bock for affording me the opportunity to collaborate with him on *Jesus and the Restoration of Israel* and for generously writing the foreword to this book. Gracias to Dr. Robert Choun for taking in graduate students like they were his own children.

I appreciate the members of F.A.C.T.S. (Florida Atheists, Critical Thinkers & Skeptics), who came to numerous meetings of my book club. Their participation helped me understand the atheist mindset as well as demonstrated that not all atheists fit the "angry atheist" stereotype.

Thanks to my loving parents, Mike and Eva Morgan. Mom gave up her career to be home with us kids, and dad worked endless overtime in a hot, smelly, dirty paper mill to provide his children a college education.

Last but certainly not least, I wish to thank my best friend and wife, Megan Morgan. Thank you for your continued love and support even on the days your husband is a bit of a turkeyhead.

Contents

1

My Journey into Disbelief

*"If only I knew where to find [God]...
if I go to the east, he is not there;
if I go to the west, I do not find him."* [1]

JOB

*"That's me in the corner. That's me in the
spotlight, losing my religion."* [2]

MICHAEL STIPE, R.E.M.

In a recent Pew Research Center poll, 31 percent—nearly a third of respondents—expressed doubts about the existence of God. [3] How about you? When you watched news coverage of a weeping mother pulling the body of her dead infant from the rubble following the 2010 Haiti earthquake or saw an entire village swept away in the 2011 tsunami in Japan, did you wonder, just for a moment, *Where is God in this?*

Perhaps your doubt is more an intellectual hurdle than an emotional objection to suffering. Intellectual obstacles might include reconciling how ice cores drilled from Antarctica appear to indicate the South Pole is at least 800,000 years old, which conflicts with the biblical age of the Earth. [4] Another issue might be how kangaroos, wombats, and Tasmanian devils made the journey from the final resting place of Noah's ark all the way to Australia. [5] They are, after all, not known for their skill at swimming.

Maybe introducing these questions just raised the number of doubters to 31.01 percent. Of the two-thirds of believers who never doubt, some may have strong faith. Others may be well-read and already have answers to these questions. However, a lot of the nondoubters simply surround themselves with like-minded people to shield themselves from challenges to their beliefs. Fair enough, but odds are one day you will be confronted by a child, a friend, or maybe even a spouse with doubts that you cannot ignore by simply walking away. Just like it is better to keep the fire going in your marriage than it is to attempt to relight an extinguished flame, the best time to tackle doubt is in the calm, not during the storm.

This is not a book of easy answers. This is a book for people who like to think. I will present arguments both for and against belief in God. Both theists and atheists will find some parts disturbing and other parts comforting. This is not a book for people whose response to conflicting views is to bury their heads in the sand. It is not a book for intellectual cowards.

Fair warning: You are going to hear an honest presentation of the atheist worldview. However, the whole point of my story is how and why I found the atheist view so unconvincing that it drove me back to faith, something which cannot be explained unless you know what that view is.

Thus, if you like books that challenge your thinking and not just "yes" books designed to make you feel better about believing something you already wanted to believe in the first place, this is the book for you. Welcome, brave and inquisitive reader, hungry for knowledge.

One caveat for the atheist reader: This is your book too! I have walked the proverbial mile in your shoes. I was a card-carrying agnostic atheist when I started researching this book. You will not find watered-down caricatures of the atheist position here. At the end of this chapter, I document the measures I have taken to present both positions fairly.

What follows is a series of four mini-debates with the greatest minds of atheism, from atheist forerunners like Friedrich Nietzsche to the New Atheists. In addition to copious reading, I watched innumerable debates while researching this book (which began as a personal search for the meaning of life). One of my favorite debates was a discussion between Richard Dawkins and John Lennox from Oxford University's Museum of Natural History,[6] not only because of the content but because it was a great example of how even those who deeply disagree can still maintain respect and civility. The remarkable part was that when people from the audience were interviewed afterward, the reaction was nearly evenly split over whether Dawkins or Lennox had made the most persuasive argument. These people heard the same set of facts, yet some found them persuasive while others thought them to be spurious.

Aristotle best explained this phenomenon. He said people evaluate truth on the basis of three factors: an intellectual factor that he called logos, an emotional factor called paythos, and a social factor, ethos. In sharp contrast, almost 300 years later in his speech "Pro Milone," Cicero gave us *Res ipsa loquitur,* or, in its modern form, "The facts speak for themselves." Aristotle had it right. Consider how often people hear the same facts yet arrive at substantially different conclusions regarding their meaning. If the facts truly speak for themselves, why do the resulting interpretations vary so greatly? How is it that of two college students taking the same philosophy class, one punts his lifelong faith while the other embraces belief in God for the first time in his life? Something beyond facts alone must be involved.

Clearly Aristotle was on to something in observing there are considerations beyond the facts that influence how we attempt to fit those facts into our worldviews. If you expect a completed puzzle to look like Leonardo da Vinci's painting *The Last Supper,* you will arrange the puzzle pieces differently than someone who expects the completed puzzle to resemble the gray rectangle that appears on the reverse side. It is fascinating how our presuppositions guide how we fit the pieces together. Both the person who envisions a colorful, meaningful end result and the person who thinks the final image should be devoid of color and meaning can make all the pieces fit.

When Facts Keep Us from Finding Truth

Anyone who reads this book just for its facts is unlikely to find anything persuasive here. Unless we are willing to consider the emotional and social factors behind our beliefs, we are merely looking for ways to force facts to fit our preconceived models. I will highlight several examples of such forced fact manipulation throughout the book. Facts can be twisted. Facts can be selectively ignored. No one builds a worldview solely on facts.

In fact (pun intended), a series of studies in 2005 and 2006 by researchers at the University of Michigan found that when misinformed people were exposed to corrected facts in news stories, they rarely changed their minds. To the contrary, they often became even more strongly convinced of their erroneous beliefs. Facts, the researchers found, were not curing misinformation. Instead, like an underpowered antibiotic, facts can actually make the bacteria of misinformation even stronger.[7]

Brendan Nyhan, the lead researcher on the Michigan study, said, "The general idea is that it's absolutely threatening to admit you're wrong."[8] He explained how the phenomenon of being confronted by facts leads to a known psychological reaction called "backfire," whereby someone would rather double down on wrong beliefs than acknowledge making a bad bet.

Thus, my challenge to you is to not let this book "backfire" on you. I implore you, if you have the courage, to not read the four debates with the mindset of "your position" and the "response to your position." Try, if at all possible, to read both sides as if you had no opinion on the matter. Granted, this is incredibly difficult to do. Perhaps it may help to visualize the proverbial man shipwrecked on a desert island since childhood who is hearing these arguments for the first time. Try imagining the reaction of someone who has never heard any arguments on this subject. If you can achieve a mindset of neutrality, this book may be eye-opening. Otherwise, the huge number of facts may just further entrench your current beliefs, regardless of whether they are right or wrong.

A Preacher's Deconversion

Be wary of anyone who presents "just the facts" on theism or atheism. It is my belief that any fair and honest discussion on such matters should include an open disclosure of the speaker's background. This chapter is mine.

My story is that of a former Southern Baptist preacher who lost his faith, became agnostic, and embarked on a path to fully embrace atheism. I attempted to rid myself of the baggage of my childhood religious indoctrination that had influenced my career, my relationships, and even my personality, only to leave me disappointed with what became of my life as a result.

Immediately some irreligious readers are going to doubt the veracity of my story. After all, skeptical writing is replete with claims that belief in God is merely wishful thinking. The general sentiment is that someone simply needs enough courage to face the stark reality that we are here alone in order to embrace the end of faith. Anyone sincerely willing to give up the comfort inherent in the premise "God loves you and has a wonderful plan for your life"[9] will find ample scientific evidence to explain our origin and existence without the need for God, right?

Radical German philosopher Ludwig Feuerbach posited that idea two centuries ago. He argued that God was merely an invention dreamed up by human beings to provide metaphysical consolation.[10] Sigmund Freud later popularized that position.[11] Is it possible for someone to sincerely explore the origin and nature of the cosmos without concluding that we live in a closed mechanical system wherein science has explained away the old man in the sky playing dice with the universe?

Skeptics may question the sincerity of someone who claims to have studied atheism with an open mind, even a positive disposition toward it, yet found it intellectually unfulfilling. That was certainly the case for me. When I turned to the great skeptics like Nietzsche, Russell, Freud, Dawkins, Hitchens, Dennett, Harris, Shermer, and Boghossian for answers, I found none that were cogent. Before you write off my quest as insincere, please extend me the courtesy of hearing why I sought an alternative model to faith and judge for yourself.

How I Came to Faith in the First Place

I once heard a speaker say even as a small child he had a drug problem. After a dramatic pause for effect, he continued, "Every Sunday morning my momma drug me to Sunday school, every Sunday evening she drug me to Sunday night services, every Wednesday she drug me to mid-week service." That was my upbringing; every time the church doors were open we were drug there. If you believe Richard Dawkins, I was brainwashed and abused. He claims early religious indoctrination leads to "the presumptuousness whereby religious people *know*, without evidence, that the faith of their birth is the one true faith, all others being aberrations or downright false."[12]

Since I have met people like that, I cannot fault Dawkins for making that observation. However, it is not universally true and certainly was not for me. Growing up in Baton Rouge, Louisiana, the variety of people and views I was exposed to were just fine shades of redneck culture. Mind you, they were great people who would give you the shirts off their backs, but I felt like I was trapped in an endless episode of *Duck Dynasty*. It was not until college that I was exposed to international students, foreign professors, and a marketplace overflowing with new worldviews.

As I contemplated my own views in the context of the beliefs of Muslims, Hindus, atheists, and others I interacted with in the dorms and around campus, I could not escape the offensive quality of my belief that these people were destined for hell. It was easy to believe the exclusivity of Christianity in church youth group where I was surrounded by people of similar persuasion while nonbelievers were nameless, faceless foreigners and outsiders. It was tougher to stomach this idea when the Muslim was the nice guy sitting next to me in sociology class who had a wife and kid and just wanted to get an education and a small slice of the American dream. It was too convenient, suspiciously so, that I just so happened to be born into the "right" faith while he was constrained to hell, primarily because of where he was born and raised. Quite to the opposite of Dawkins' claim, my upbringing caused me to seriously doubt my serendipitous luck of emerging from the right womb.

I was envious of those who converted from agnosticism to faith in college because they had a certainty I lacked in knowing they had not simply adopted the faith of their parents. It was at that time that I started looking for reasons that validated my beliefs. I wanted to know if my beliefs were worth believing. Interestingly enough, I found that almost every author who wrote on the subject had converted from atheism to theism in adulthood. There were scientists like Francis Collins and Alister McGrath, journalist Lee Strobel, and authors C.S. Lewis and Josh McDowell. Although I continued to wrestle with whether I was being presumptuous, I did feel some validation in that even hardened atheists like Antony Flew experienced late-life conversions.

I explored the evidence Dawkins accuses religious people of accepting *a priori*, like the historicity of the Gospel writers' accounts, the validity of the biblical canon, and extrabiblical corroboration of Jesus' life and teaching, and grappled with historical considerations such as the theory that Constantine invented Christianity to unite the Roman empire around a common religion.[13] I found the evidence for Christianity quite compelling. It is worth noting, however, that at this stage in my life I was reading Christian writers whom I expected to validate my views. I was not yet reading any skeptical writers, a fact that I will return to shortly.

It was during college that I sensed God calling me to be a pastor. After graduating valedictorian of my class with a Bachelor of Science from Louisiana Tech, I completed a Master's program at Dallas Theological Seminary, the largest nondenominational seminary in the world. To contextualize my theology, Dallas Seminary would have been a Presbyterian seminary at its founding but remained independent over the lone issue of dispensationalism.

My First Major Disappointment with God

After graduating from seminary I was invited to be an associate pastor at a church in Florida. I came into the position with all the eager expectation of someone hoping to change the world, or at the very least one hot, sunny little corner of it. However, I soon found all the wonderful, nationally proven programs I wished to implement were met only with resistance if not open opposition. The status quo was so deeply entrenched in that traditional community church that I was vilified for challenging it.

On several occasions I was reprimanded by members of the deacon board for usurping authority from the senior pastor. He was a nice fellow with whom I enjoyed working and with whom I had no personal qualms, but I did have trouble adopting his vision, not because I disagreed with it, but simply because it seemed nonexistent. He was quite content with the church just like it was. Once when I pressed him on his future vision for the church, he responded, "The only person who likes change is a wet baby." While he was content to just punch the clock and collect a check, I was working too hard for too little pay to be satisfied by the status quo. Therefore I pushed for some new programs, like a Saturday night service with contemporary music, more community outreach, and the possibility of a satellite campus. However, I soon learned the meaning of the Japanese proverb "The nail that stands the tallest receives the blow" when I was fired for insubordination.

I was not just terminated, but run out of town in the most unbecoming manner, being paid two months of hush money if I voluntarily resigned and saved the deacons any embarrassment over an otherwise controversial termination. There had been a small minority in favor of the changes I advocated. If the leader were to fall on his own sword, well, who could blame the deacons for that? Finding myself in the tough position of choosing between having food in the fridge or taking the moral high road, I took the buyout and bit my tongue. The experience was a decided disappointment and window into the dark side of church politics.

Shortly thereafter, new information shed light on why the senior pastor always kept to himself and avoided stepping on toes. A few months after my departure, it came to light that he, a married man, had engaged in a lengthy affair with a married parishioner. It all immediately made sense; the man was so racked with guilt that he did not feel like a leader and, even if he had the motivation to lead, he could not afford to step on anyone's toes and invite scrutiny of his personal life.

In a nutshell, my first foray into Christian church work was to go where I thought God had directed me, only to be subjected to two years of wall-beating skullduggery due to a pastor's extramarital affair that indirectly cost me my job. That was strike one for God.

Further Frustration with God

I accepted a position as a Baptist church planter for my second pastoral job. I left my friends in Florida to start a new church in California. The denomination promised me a salary for two years in order to launch a new church and grow it to financial self-sufficiency. Still licking my wounds from my first foray into Christian vocational work, I prayed long and earnestly, "God, guide me to the right place. Please deliver me from another mess."

California, however, would prove to be another debacle. After packing everything I owned and moving coast-to-coast, I was immediately greeted by disappointment when I learned that the pastor who was supposedly coordinating this church plant had overpromised the available support structure. Though he had not secured a firm commitment from the denomination, he nonetheless assumed that they would commit funds. He did not warn me the plan was based on presumptions, not promises. Once I arrived, the denomination was not sympathetic to the project, the funding was not given, and I found myself alone in a strange new city. I had a job in title only with only a fraction of the promised income, which was not enough to live on.

The pastor felt bad about the situation and gave me free room and board in his guest room, but it did not seem like the rest of his family agreed, so I quickly found my living conditions quite awkward. Living in someone else's full house, I had nowhere to store my personal belongings and no money to pay for storage, so a local youth pastor, Paul, allowed me to store my things for free in his recently condemned rental house.

Eventually the denomination allocated some funds to the project, and I was able to rent a small studio apartment. When I returned to Paul's rental house to retrieve my things, I found the door kicked in and my valuables pilfered by unscrupulous thieves.

Despite the rocky start, I poured my heart and soul into the church plant endeavor for the next two years. Things never got much easier, however. If there was a central theme to that period of my life, it was Matthew 5:45: "[God] causes his sun to rise on the evil and the good, and sends rain on the righteous and the unrighteous." I was sacrificing everything for God, but not finding any more sunshine for it. If anything, it seemed like storm clouds constantly darkened my life while things were sunnier in the lives of nonbelievers around me.

At the time, I had the best Chevy Camaro money could buy, a grad school graduation gift from my family that was my pride and joy. It was my lone nice possession. It had an aftermarket body kit and custom grill that made it truly one of a kind, a real head-turner. I sold it to buy a used SUV that we desperately needed so we could move gear for our weekly church service that met in a rented space. I survived on ramen noodles to free up more funds for marketing and promoting the new church. Each decision was bathed in prayer. Though I strongly felt it was God's will and would not fail, it all came to naught.

The SUV was broken into and the church's sound system, keyboard, laptop, video camera, and projector were stolen. The promo pieces we mailed did not bring in any new people, although I did receive some hate mail explaining that churches are bad for the community because they remove valuable property from the tax base and "isolate people in holy huddles that do nothing for their community." The angry atheist's letter complained that churches remove people from "legitimate service organizations" like the Rotary Club or Kiwanis that actually better the community. What kind of person takes the time to write hate mail to churches?

As if being robbed twice in the first year, the financial struggles, and the church's slow start were not frustrating enough, my continued singleness haunted me personally and professionally. The church plant struggled because a single pastor lacked legitimacy in the eyes of our target demographic. Statistics show unchurched people join churches primarily after they get married and start families. What did a single pastor who knew nothing of their lifestyles have to offer? Moreover, I felt lonely in the irreligious county I had moved to, where it was rare to meet women who shared my religious faith.

I eventually did meet one gal who was passionate about God. She also wanted to be in full-time Christian work. Our goals were so much aligned that it seemed like we would make a great team. I prayed fervently, "God, I can handle being broke and the church faltering, if I just had someone like Christelle in my life so I don't have to do this all alone." It was just another unanswered prayer, though. Strike two for God.

I was not upset with God that Christelle did not take a romantic interest in me. It would be supremely selfish to pray for that. No, the frustrating thing was that she did not take an interest in any Christian guy. She told me she was quite content with "just her and Jesus." In fact, when I looked her up more than a decade later, she was still plucking along single in her late thirties. While I knew Jesus loved her, I also knew he had no plans to marry her. If he was not going to take her to the altar, I thought it rude that he would stand in everyone else's way.

All this time I was burning the candle at both ends, working 80-plus-hour weeks trying to facilitate a church coming together within our allotted time frame. However, being young and single, the church was attracting people of similar circumstance. Weekend service attendance peaked at 30 or so, but many were students, unemployed, or underemployed. At the end of two years of toil, the church was not financially self-sufficient. When the denomination pulled the plug financially, everything I had worked so hard for began to unravel.

I tried to tough it out and stay on without pay. I looked for secular work to pay the bills so I could keep working at the church as an unpaid, volunteer pastor. However, Agilent, the largest employer in our relatively small city, had just made massive layoffs. Even when I tried to get hired as a Starbucks barista I found myself competing against engineers with master's degrees.

I was running out of money and the church plant was in an agonizing and inevitable downward spiral. With profound disappointment and sadness, I took the only job I could find, one all the way across the country, using my skills as a flight instructor. I gave up on California. Moreover, as this was strike three, I gave up on God.

Why I Wanted God to Go Away

Trying my best to serve God had left me broke, alone, and disenchanted. If this was what loving and serving God were like, then

I wanted nothing to do with Him. I gave away my massive library of theological books and left for Massachusetts intending to hit the reset button on my life for a fresh, godless start. I had given God nearly a decade of fervent, sincere service and had nothing to show for it. It only seemed reasonable to try life without him for a change. I felt I could not do any worse.

Unfortunately, the idea continued to haunt me that God was still "out there" and I was merely ignoring him. I had not yet stopped believing, only caring. I had experienced enough years of frustration trying to please God. I was through fretting over that. However, it bothered me that He might be silently watching in disappointment, taking notes like some hall monitor in the sky. The possibility remained that I may still have to answer to him one day. I did not merely want to live with indifference to God; I wanted God to go away. I did not just want God to leave me alone; I wanted God to disappear entirely. I wished to live my own life without the interference of my childhood religious indoctrination. As C.S. Lewis wrote in *Surprised by Joy*,

> No word in my vocabulary expressed deeper hatred than the word INTERFERENCE. But Christianity placed at the center what then seemed to me a transcendental Interferer. If its picture were true then no sort of 'treaty with reality' could ever be possible. There was no region even in the innermost depth of one's soul (nay, there least of all) which one could surround with a barbed wire fence and guard with a notice "No Admittance." And that was what I wanted; some area, however small, of which I could say to all other beings, "This is my business and mine only."[14]

That decade of disappointment opened my mind to atheism. It offered an escape, an out, from a belief system that I had found to be nothing but problematic. I picked up atheist authors like Richard Dawkins, Christopher Hitchens, Sam Harris, Bertrand Russell, and Friedrich Nietzsche for the first time. I trust I have adequately laid out my sincere, eager expectation and willingness to believe them. I "read not to contradict and confute...but to weigh and consider," as Francis

Bacon said in *The Essays*. These books on atheism to me were Bacon's "few [books] to read wholly, and with diligence and attention." Coming full circle to my earlier comment, in college I read books by theists in order to embrace theism. Now I was reading books by atheists in order to embrace atheism. My heart was over God. My head sought a good intellectual reason to dismiss Him permanently.

Why Atheism Proved Intellectually Unfulfilling

I was astoundingly disappointed by what I read. The arguments were so poor that the greatest authors of atheism did more than any Christian apologist to push me toward belief in God. Christian writers had made some good arguments, but nothing that equated to incontrovertible proof. If an indisputable argument for God's existence were so hard to erect, I expected the other side would have an unassailable counterargument that addressed the Christian apologist and, even more importantly, provided a positive case against belief in God.

I kept reading more and more books on atheism, each time thinking, "Surely this cannot be the best argument for it." I kept hoping the next book would present a better case than the prior only to find each new book just as disappointing as the last. I expected to hear a strong argument for why there is no God. Instead, atheists like Russell candidly admitted, "I do not pretend to be able to prove that there is no God."[15] I was deeply disappointed.

When atheists engaged apologists with rebuttals, they often merely attacked caricatures of their positions. When they advanced a positive case, such as an argument for philosophical materialism, their rationales suffered from serious logical flaws.

I implore the skeptical reader not to brand my experience balderdash. I acknowledge I have made a bold and brash statement, but I believe it is one I have backed up in this book. I challenge both skeptic and Christian alike to read through to the end and evaluate whether my findings are unfair or insincere. I am not arguing *for* anything, but simply relaying my experience of reading this literature with an open mind and the reasons I found it intellectually unfulfilling.

In each chapter I will explore one book on atheism. I felt the four books included here best represent atheistic thought because they are either well-known *New York Times* bestsellers, have had a significant influence in the discourse of nonbelief, show the development in atheists' views over time, or are some combination of all of those. I have purposely included a wide spectrum of atheist authors ranging from Enlightenment era, like Nietzsche, to the current modern leaders of the New Atheists, like Richard Dawkins. I did so in order to represent the whole position. I do not want to be accused of targeting weak links like early, undeveloped writings or later writings of more confrontational tone. It is my goal to summarize the arguments each author advances with the same impartiality of CliffNotes summarizing *Hamlet*. Believers who read this book will gain a good grasp on the issues skeptical authors are raising and will hopefully gain insight, even empathy, into why nonbelievers see things differently.

Have I fairly summarized the atheist position? Richard Dawkins thinks so. Upon reading my summary of his book, he wrote that it "strikes me as an admirably fair and thorough summary of my book."[16] I made the same offer to Sam Harris to review the summary of his book, but he did not respond. It is worth noting, however, that Dawkins asked me to modify only one point in the entire summary, and I attempted to be equally fair to Harris' work.

Being fair to Nietzsche and Russell obviously presented a larger challenge since they are deceased. I posted the summary of their books in the atheist forum on Reddit.com to solicit feedback from the more than two million atheist members of the forum. I also invited members of the F.A.C.T.S. (Florida Atheists, Critical Thinkers & Skeptics) to attend my book club for face-to-face dialogue. I am indebted to the members of F.A.C.T.S. who attended and the individuals who commented in the Reddit forum for their suggestions, which led to numerous revisions to the summaries of the atheists' positions in order to fairly represent their arguments. I wanted to present the best each author offers, not some watered-down caricature of their positions.

While some skeptics may not agree with some or any of my critiques, it is my goal to make a fair summary of each author's position before critiquing it so that no one may accuse me of setting up a straw man. Only after I have fairly summarized each book's position will I share my personal observations about the issues I found with the arguments that, for me, presented insurmountable obstacles to adopting the view. Beginning with chapter 3, I present a chapter summarizing an atheist's seminal work, such as Nietzsche's *Beyond Good and Evil*, followed by a response chapter. Cross-references are given for each significant point because you may occasionally desire an immediate response to a particular issue. However, I encourage you to consider the cumulative weight of the full argument whenever possible in order to perceive how the individual points are interconnected.

In all this, I am simply sharing my own journey. It is not my goal to hard-sell either worldview. You are free to draw your own conclusions based on the evidence.

As I began my journey into disbelief, I read these works in the order that they were brought to my attention. I picked up books because atheist friends recommended them or, in the case of Hitchens, because his articulate debating skills impressed me. Sometimes I read whichever book Amazon delivered first. However, the speed of the US postal service hardly makes for a logical book outline, so I have arranged the material here chronologically ranging from ancient atheism through the most recent books of the New Atheists. The chronological order also highlights how atheism first distanced itself from Nietzsche before digging into the trenches it has guarded since the early 1900s.

While this order allows a logical progression, I acknowledge I was further into my journey of disbelief while reading certain books. Therefore, I have tried to disclaim each chapter with a short introduction describing my disposition toward disbelief at that stage of my journey.

My goal is both modest and monumental. For the theist unfamiliar with atheist writing, I have summarized more than 100 years of atheists' arguments. I hope believers finish this book with a better understanding and appreciation of the mindset of the unconvinced. For the unbeliever, I have sworn myself to be fair to the best of my ability in representing the views that I formerly favored. Ideally, an unbeliever who has not read any books on atheism will finish this one with an accurate overview of the arguments atheists are presenting and the particular nuances each individual author offers that would aid the reader in determining which author he may wish to further explore.

I hope to go beyond just presenting a good overview of the subject to actually challenging people's thinking, never by condemning or criticizing, but by pointing out the full implications of some arguments and the fallaciousness of others through logical, dispassionate dialogue that appeals to the mind, not the emotions. I hope to stretch and even challenge readers' thinking, but never to attack, slander, or satirize.

2

The Early Skeptics (A Brief History of Atheism)

"Those who cannot remember the past are condemned to repeat it."[1]

GEORGE SANTAYANA

Cookie caused this chapter. He is one of the most well-read, intelligent, and articulate, albeit outspoken, atheists I have ever met. He is a brilliant fellow, so the nickname fits him in the manner an NFL linebacker might adopt the tongue-in-cheek nickname *Tiny*.

I was living in Orlando, Florida, when I created a spiritual book club and advertised it on MeetUp.com and at local coffee shops. I encouraged people with skeptical viewpoints to meet me at the Drunken Monkey Coffee Bar to exchange ideas and challenge my thinking. I kept finding apparent problems in the arguments of atheist writers, so I reached out to see how others had resolved the problems I encountered.

That particular evening Cookie passionately interjected, "In this day and age how can you believe..." and proceeded to refer to belief in the supernatural as "Bronze Age superstition" rendered obsolete by skepticism. I challenged him about his proposition that skepticism was unique to the post-Enlightenment era. My intent was not to rebuff his conclusion, but to question the historical accuracy of its underlying basis. I was under the impression skepticism had been around for ages. I vaguely remembered a podcast discussing how Epicurus had challenged Plato's ideas of forms and belief in life after death hundreds of years before the advent of Christianity. Cookie was aware of Epicurus but thought he was ahead of his time: The world was not yet ready for skeptical thought. Cookie then cited Galileo as an example of how free thought was still being oppressed only 200 years before the Enlightenment.

I had never studied the history of skepticism, so I conceded the point. That conversation, however, stuck with me and sparked my interest in the origin and history of skepticism. As I began to study the history, I was amazed how global, widespread, and ancient it was. Not only was Epicurus not at all unique, he had numerous predecessors.

The structure of this chapter must by necessity differ from the remainder of the book because it reaches so far back. In many cases, we are discussing mere fragments and quotations by later thinkers rather than complete works that can be summarized and critiqued. As Peter Adamson describes ancient philosophy in his excellent podcast *The History of Philosophy Without Gaps*, "For all of these figures our knowledge is really based on nothing more than tantalizing scraps. People who work in the field call these scraps fragments."[2] Therefore, numerous fragments covering several skeptical thinkers are covered in this single chapter in rapidfire, point-counterpoint manner.

Why bother addressing these ancient skeptics at all when little is known of their views? Why not simply begin with full-length works like Nietzsche's 1886 *Beyond Good and Evil*? The answer is simple. The fallacious idea that atheism is a post-Enlightenment belief has become so entrenched that it is taken for granted. I include the works of the ancient skeptics to refute the mistaken assumption that atheism is the progression of reason and science conquering ancient fears and superstitions. To the contrary, I discovered that skepticism has co-existed alongside every major world religion. Whether it is Hinduism, Christianity, Islam, you-name-it, skepticism is found right alongside it.

The Term *Atheist*

The term *atheist* originated pre-Enlightenment. It appeared in English books as early as 1566.[3] To claim that the ideology was a product of

Enlightenment thought is as misleading as claiming that Henry Ford was responsible for the automobile.* While Ford opened the door to making automobiles affordable, the first modern car was running 56 years before he was born.[4] Just like automobiles were around before Ford, atheism was around long before the Enlightenment. As we shall see, philosophical thinking clearly identifiable as atheistic began to appear in Europe and Asia in the fifth or sixth century BC, many millennia before the view was rebranded "atheism."[5]

Primitive Atheism

Before we get into the individual adherents and their teaching, we should also address the fallacy that that belief in God and/or gods was merely primitive mankind's only manner of explaining the universe. A common fallacy is that religion was merely a stand-in until science arrived. To the contrary, historian William Durant, in his comprehensive eleven volume *The Story of Civilization*, shows how African pygmy tribes in the fifth century BC were observed to have no identifiable cults, religious rites, totems, deities, spirits, or special burial ceremonies.[6] The Carvaka School evidenced a materialistic movement in ancient India around the sixth century BC.[7] The isolated Veddahs of Ceylon, a tribe in Sri Lanka, are a modern example of a people group devoid of scientific understanding who do not seek to explain the world through myth and fable. They live in caves, cannot count past two, are "but a degree removed from wild beasts,"[8] and yet are agnostic at best. Despite their primitive culture, they have no prayers, sacrifice, or other religion.[9] Instead of a linear progression from "primitive" religious beliefs to "better" scientific beliefs, when we look at history as a whole, in every period we see exactly the same balance we see today—a skeptical minority coexisting with a faithful majority. Below are highlights from some of these ancient skeptics.

---

* Steam-engine automobile prototypes preceded Ford's Model T by more than 130 years. Ford was not even responsible for bringing modern, engine-driven automobiles to the world. That distinction belonged to Karl Benz.

Skepticism and Greek Mythology

According to atheist Bertrand Russell, "Western philosophy begins with Thales."[10] Even Aristotle agreed. It is interesting, therefore, that Thales attempted to explain natural phenomena without reference to mythology.[11] From the inception of philosophy, we already see skepticism of religious myths. Skepticism predated Christianity by 500 years. Rejecting stories of Zeus, Thales believed water was the origin of the cosmos. Though only fragments of his reasoning remain, we see him attempting an early scientific explanation of cosmology more than 2500 years ago. No source has survived to explain how he arrived at his theory. We can imagine Thales observing water boiling off and noting that salt and other residues were left behind, which appear to have been "created" by the water boiling away. Incomplete and inaccurate as it was, it was nevertheless an attempt to describe the world through observation of evidence.

Thales' understanding of natural causes allowed him to make a fortune by cornering the olive market.[12] His understanding of weather patterns allowed him to predict a bumper crop of olives. Knowing this would, in turn, create a huge demand for olive presses, he cornered the market on olive presses in Miletus in advance, allowing him to charge whatever he wished for people to use his presses once they came into high demand.

Despite his wisdom, he was not an atheist. He believed, among other things, that gods were in magnets. Once again we lack the explanation why. Perhaps absent a physical explanation, Thales reverted to a gods-of-the-gap explanation.

Right on his heels (c. 570–475 BC) was Xenophanes, a skeptic critical of mythology. While the atheist argument that God is a human invention is usually attributed to Ludwig Feuerbach in the Enlightenment, Feuerbach was merely borrowing Xenophanes' 1300-year-old observation that the gods were merely men's projections of how they saw themselves. As Xenophanes wrote, "Ethiopians say their gods are snub-nosed and black. Thracians [who were themselves pale and red-haired] that they are pale and red-haired."[13] In language reminiscent of

Christopher Hitchens, Xenophanes argued that if cows or horses could paint, they would paint god in the image of a cow or a horse.

> But if cattle and horses and lions had hands
> or could paint with their hands and
> create works such as men do,
> horses like horses and cattle like cattle
> also would depict the gods' shapes and make their bodies
> of such a sort as the form they themselves have.[14]

Xenophanes did not stop with questioning anthropomorphic projections of God. He was skeptical of using stories of gods to explain natural phenomena as well. While the Greeks had a goddess named Isis who was identified with the rainbow, Xenophanes thought the rainbow was nothing more than clouds with some color in them. As for the sun, he doubted it was a god named Helios but rather thought it was just a bunch of fire that was gathered together.[15] Xenophanes is a great example of how the ancient world was not merely a collection of gullible boobs credulously willing to swallow any mythological explanation, waiting in ignorance for the light of science to reveal all truth. Skepticism was alive and well 500 years before Christianity. It certainly is not a child of the Enlightenment.

Skepticism and Hinduism

What about Hinduism? Could it spring up only in a pre-Enlightenment world where gullible people were willing to accept the unscientific premise of an immaterial reality? No. Yet again we find skepticism entrenched right alongside spiritual beliefs. The Carvaka School of materialism in India in the sixth and fifth centuries BC "only accepted perception as valid evidence. They considered other evidence like testimony, analogy, and inference as unreliable."[16] Thus, the existence of soul and God were rejected *because they could not be proved by perception.*[17] This statement could just as easily come from any of the four New Atheists' books. There simply is nothing new about the New Atheism.

Skepticism and Confucianism

Shortly following the birth of Confucianism, Xunzi (c. 312–230 BC) taught a doctrine centered on realism and materialism. He asserted, "Heaven is simply the natural world; thus people should focus on the human, social realm, rather than dealing with heavenly ideas." In addition to challenging people to focus on the earthly realm, Xunzi rejected belief in nonhuman agencies. For example, he said rain sacrifices had no effect on the weather because they did not influence spirits.[18] He taught that ethical norms were not absolute but invented to rectify man's co-existence.[19] His argument about focusing on the social realm instead of heavenly ideas is exactly the argument an atheist challenged me with, almost word-for-word when I appeared on the Garin Hoover radio show.[20] She had no idea she was touting a 2300-year-old ideology.

Skepticism and Philosophy

It is interesting that though modern skeptics dismiss beliefs based on holy books, they never interact with Plato's philosophical texts, which proposed immaterial reality, the soul, and the afterlife *based on reasoned arguments alone.* Plato raised these arguments 350 years before a single verse of the New Testament was written.

Nietzsche was one of the few skeptics to acknowledge the connection between Plato and Christianity, claiming "Christianity is Platonism for 'the people.'"[21] Yet his argument that Christianity is Platonic has fallen into disfavor because it suggests that the soul and the afterlife could be deduced on a purely rational basis. Apart from Nietzsche, most skeptics prefer to ignore the fact that Plato arrived at these beliefs without an appeal to any religious text.

In the Allegory of the Cave in Plato's *Republic*, he argues his famous Theory of Forms according to which people live their lives in a cave, forced to face a blank wall where shadows are projected by things passing in front of a fire behind them. If they are not enlightened, Plato argues, they will mistake the shadows for the unseen but real forms that cause them.

Based on this belief that what we see is only a reflection of deeper reality, Plato relates in Book X of *Republic* the story of Er, a Greek soldier who dies in battle. While his body is laid upon a funeral pyre to be burned, Er has a soul that leaves his body and joins another group of spirits who go with him to a passageway that leads to the afterlife. Before that, they are stopped and judged by divine beings.

I would not base any argument for God on Plato's philosophy simply because there are more scientific ways to make the argument. However, I find it fascinating that Plato, perhaps the greatest philosopher of all time, arrived through reason at a view of the afterlife very similar to that of the New Testament, penned 350 years later. By reason alone, Plato delineated a worldview so compatible with Christianity that Christian apologists Justin Martyr, Clement of Alexandria, Origen, and Augustine all cited him.[22]

Like every other period in history, there were skeptics. Contemporary with Plato's Christian-friendly teaching, we find Epicurus (341–270 BC). While his school of philosophy is officially known as Epicureanism, every one of his core teachings could come straight from any book on atheism:

- Pleasure and pain are the measure of good and evil
  (compare to Sam Harris' *The Moral Landscape*).

- Death is the end of the body.

- Gods neither reward nor punish humans.

- The universe is infinite and eternal
  (Bertrand Russell's position before Edwin Hubble).

- Events in the world are ultimately based on the motions
  and interactions of atoms moving in empty space.[23]

Just like atheism today, Epicurus' skeptical philosophy had a small but devout following. It is worth noting that his belief in the finality of death *preceded* Jesus' death and resurrection by more than 200 years. There is a profoundly mistaken notion that people in the first century were all still caught up in superstition and mythology, all too unquestioningly willing to accept reports of miracles and stories of people rising from the dead. To the contrary, we see how skepticism of such claims was well entrenched long before Christianity. For example, in Acts 17, the people of Athens were willing to consider what Paul had to say about God until he mentioned Jesus' resurrection from the dead, at which point the crowd began to ridicule him for suggesting the possibility of such an event.

Nietzsche was aware of the ideological battle between Epicurus' materialism and Plato's belief in a reality that transcends what we see with our eyes. Nietzsche quotes Epicurus: "they [Platonists] are all actors, there is nothing genuine about them."[24] The New Atheists are reluctant to highlight such conflicts, perhaps because drawing attention to the fact that the same talking points were already being debated 2200 years ago would preclude them from using the moniker "New" Atheists.

Was Epicurus an isolated example of reason in an otherwise superstitious ancient world? Not at all. We find his philosophy alive and well 200 years later within one lifetime of Jesus' birth in Lucretius' Latin poem *De Rerum Natura* ("On the Nature of Things"). The poem reflects a mechanistic philosophy that "all that exists is matter and void, and all phenomena result from different motions and conglomerations of base material particles called 'atoms.'"[25] Lucretius, like Bertrand Russell, who was still espousing his view 2000 years later, seeks to convert his Roman audience to Epicurus' worldview that "the universe described in the poem operates according to these physical principles, guided by *fortuna*, chance, and not by the divine intervention of the traditional Roman deities."[26] Russell acknowledges his "own view on religion is that of Lucretius" in a 1930 essay, but after Russell we almost never find an honest admission that the New Atheists are citing 2000-year-old viewpoints. The exception is Peter Boghossian, who acknowledges the ancient nature of skepticism, but only once in a passing comment.[27]

Skepticism and Christianity

How about the first century? Was Christianity able to begin only because people were nothing more than credulous, unenlightened simpletons? Certainly not. To the contrary, we find Jesus' story was met with exactly the same kind of skepticism still being expressed 2000 years later. Writing around AD 175, a Greek intellectual skeptic named Celsus wrote *True Doctrine*, in which he attempted to explain the phenomenon of Christianity in purely naturalistic terms. He doubted the virgin birth. Instead he said (without evidence) that Jesus was the illegitimate product of Mary's affair with the Roman soldier Pantera and that she fabricated the virgin birth to cover her tracks. Celsus dismissed Jesus' apparent miracles as magic tricks he learned in Egypt. In Celsus' words, "having tried his hand at certain magical powers, Jesus returned from there [Egypt], and on account of those powers gave himself the title of God."[28]

The New Atheists are fond of pointing out parallels between the resurrection of Jesus and the story of Osiris (while glossing over significant differences), as if archeology has only recently discovered material that suggests the creators of Christianity plagiarized their stories. In reality, this is an old, tired argument that has been around since the inception of Christianity. In Justin Martyr's second-century text, his antagonist, Trypho, raises the accusation that the story of Jesus' virgin birth is borrowed from mythology about Zeus. Quite contrary to the New Atheists' claim that early Christians were duped by old reinterpreted stories, the truth is that this objection was raised from the outset and rejected.

When we look at the reception Paul received while preaching in Athens in Acts 17, we see exactly the kind of reception we would expect today. Paul opened his sermon the way William Lane Craig might open a debate with Richard Dawkins, by claiming that God made the world. At that point, he had not lost his audience. The Athenians were familiar with Epicurus' teaching (à la Bertrand Russell) that the world was not created but infinite, as well as with Thales' teaching (à la Richard Dawkins) that the world had material causes and was not made by gods. Despite these beliefs, the crowd was willing to consider Paul's argument. However, they sneered and walked away the moment Paul mentioned resurrection from the dead. They were willing to consider cosmological arguments, but the idea of dead people rising was a deal breaker. You can easily imagine this scenario playing out with a street preacher on any college campus today. Skepticism is patently not a product of the Enlightenment.

Far from being superstitious and credulous, the early Christians who became convinced that Jesus had risen from the dead were so skeptical that the Roman authorities thought they were atheists. Yes, you read that right. The earliest Christians were so skeptical of supernatural claims they were accused of being atheists! For example, Justin Martyr defended Christianity against Caesar by saying, "For not only among the Greeks did reason prevail to condemn these things through Socrates, but also among the Barbarians were they condemned by Reason...*Hence, are we [Christians] called atheists*. And we confess that we are atheists, so far as gods of this sort are concerned, but not with respect to the most true God."[29]

Ignatius of Antioch was born just five years after Jesus' death. He was a disciple of the apostle John, one of Jesus' 12 disciples. His belief that Jesus had risen from the dead was not based on any gullible predisposition to believe in fairies, unicorns, or even gods, but rather on the firsthand eyewitness testimony of John, who had seen the post-resurrection Jesus with his own eyes. In fact, Ignatius was so adamantly skeptical of humans being divine that he was willing to die for it. Brought to Rome by Emperor Trajan, Ignatius was given the option to either acknowledge that the emperor was divine or be fed to wild animals. Ignatius was condemned *for the charge of atheism* because he refused to believe the popular superstition that the emperor was divine. Ignatius was thrown to lions in the Colosseum because of his skepticism.

When the New Atheists claim that Christianity spread only because gullible first-century people lacked post-Enlightenment skepticism, they demonstrate their ignorance of history. In order to spread, Christianity needed evidence sufficient to compel people like Ignatius, who were so skeptical about claims of divine human beings that they were willing to die for their beliefs. Compared to Bertrand Russell, who stated that he was not skeptical enough to die for his beliefs, Ignatius' hardcore skepticism is enough to make the New Atheists look like faith-heads.[30]

Skepticism in the Roman Empire

I found no shortage of blame placed on religion in the New Atheist writings for everything from the spread of AIDS to the perpetuation of war. Sam Harris boldly asserts that religion is "antithetical to our survival."[31] What is interesting about historical claims that Christianity will bring "eminent doom" is that these claims are as old as Christianity itself. For example, there are numerous accounts, some contradictory, about the Great Fire of Rome on July 19, 64. The popular legend that Nero sang and played the lyre during the fire seems doubtful.[32] Nero may have sent men to intentionally start the fire, and Tacitus records indisputably that Nero scapegoated Christians.[33] He ordered some to be thrown to the dogs and others to be crucified to deflect rumors of his own responsibility.[34] Within 30 years of the advent of Christianity, Nero was able to convince the pagan populace that killing Christians would safeguard Rome. Although the real danger lay within their own government, Roman citizens were more prepared to accept the idea that Christianity was dangerous.

The argument that Christianity is bad for society is so old that Augustine refuted it back in the fifth century. He wrote *The City of God* following the sack of Rome by Gothic king Alaric. At the time, Roman intellectuals were lamenting the unraveling of the Roman Empire, which many interpreted as a punishment for adopting Catholic Christianity. In response, Augustine pointed out how the moral unraveling of the Roman Empire had begun before Christ was even born. The fact that Augustine had to defend Christianity against the same criticism raised by Harris 1600 years later—that it was "antithetical to our survival" (in Augustine's case the Roman Empire's survival)—proves that this charge against Christianity is nothing new.

One would think that if Christianity threatened to undo the world as the New Atheists claim, it would have done so by now. Skeptics have been crying wolf for nearly 2000 years.

Skepticism and Islam

How about in the Muslim world, among the people Dawkins says can "believe absurdities" that make them "commit atrocities"?[35] Surely

Islam spread because the Middle East was devoid of reason and skepticism. Perhaps if the New Atheists' post-Enlightenment rationalism had been around back then, many religious wars could have been avoided—maybe even the Crusades, perhaps even 9/11? No, yet again no. Have we learned nothing yet?

Once again we find skeptics in the midst of a major religion's birth. Outspoken Arab rationalists and atheists included Muhammad al Warraq (fl. seventh century), Ibn al-Rawandi (827–911), Al-Razi (865–925), and Al-Ma'arri (973–1058). Al-Ma'arri wrote and taught that religion was a "fable invented by the ancients."[36] His sayings were so similar to the New Atheists' that his zingers would seem at home in a Christopher Hitchens book. For example, with Hitchens' flair for hyperbole, Al-Ma'arri wrote there were only two sorts of humans: "intelligent men without religion and religious men without intelligence."[37]

Arab rationalist Ibn Tufail (c. 1105–1185) followed in this lineage of Arab skepticism. Some consider his book *Hayy ibn Yaqzon* ("Alive, Son of Awake") "one of the most important books that heralded the Scientific Revolution."[38] His medieval book shares views "in different variations and to different degrees [with] the books of Thomas Hobbes, John Locke, Isaac Newton, and Immanuel Kant."[39]

In his allegory, the main character, Hayy, is raised by a gazelle alone on a desert island where he discovers ultimate truth *through systematic reasoned inquiry*. When he finally comes in contact with civilization and religion, Hayy determines that while religion is ultimately necessary for the multitude to have decent lives, it is also a distraction and ought to be abandoned by the reasonable. Tufail advanced these ideas during the early centuries of Islam, way before the Enlightenment.

Again and again we see alongside *any* major religion's origin, no matter how far back we go, that skepticism is right there in the mix. There is absolutely nothing new about skepticism. Skepticism is neither a product of the Enlightenment nor required by it. It is as old as religion itself. If there is one central truth I uncovered by studying the history of skepticism, it was that whatever reason one can give for being an atheist, it cannot be that the Enlightenment necessitates it. That logic simply cannot stand. Skepticism clearly predates the Enlightenment by millennia. The argument that Enlightenment thought requires skepticism reflects delusions about the history of skepticism.

Skepticism in the Post-Enlightenment

Does this historical survey prove anything? Even if we concede for argument's sake that there is nothing new about atheism (even the "New" Atheism), that does not mean that skeptical thinkers have not finally gotten it right. Maybe science has only recently vindicated the ancient phenomenon of skepticism. Many atheists would argue that we have finally experienced the dawn of atheism, like Kant being awoken from his "dogmatic slumber" by the recollection of Hume.[40] I am skeptical (no pun intended) of this claim since, historically, the various events and epochs that are frequently referred to as the "dawn" of atheism are invariably followed by a "sunset."

The Enlightenment is frequently referred to as the dawn of atheism. New practices of testing conclusions, using the scientific principle, opposing superstition, and questioning the authority of institutions, especially the church, seemed the beginning of the end for religion. However, let us not forget that the Enlightenment gave way to Romanticism as thinkers challenged reductionistic Enlightenment thinking.[41] Romanticism was a reaction against physical materialism that had failed to provide an adequate explanation of the whole of reality.[42] The sun had set on the fanciful idea that science could explain everything.

The publication of *On the Origin of Species* in 1859 was another potential "dawn of atheism." Darwin's book finally provided an alternative, scientific explanation for the diversity of life, countering the "mythology"* of Genesis and allowing for intellectually self-fulfilled atheism. However, the dawn quickly turned to twilight again when science raised unforeseen problems. Darwin consciously avoided discussing the origin of life problem in *Origin of Species,* but his correspondence

---

* Augustine pointed out that the word used in Genesis for a day (*yom*) can either be used to describe a 24-hour day or a period of time. He wrote, "What kind of days these were, it is difficult or perhaps impossible for us to conceive" (*The City of God* XI.6., see also *The Literal Meaning of Genesis*). He held that Genesis was allegorical in AD 426, 1433 years before Darwin published *On the Origin of Species.*

with friends and colleagues showed that he simply assumed a natural cause for the emergence of life. He was convinced that "the intimate relation of Life with laws of chemical combination and the universality of the latter render spontaneous generation not improbable."[43] He was blissfully unaware that electron microscopy, which was not to be developed until the 1930s, would prove that the spontaneous generation of the first single cell was mind-bogglingly harder than he could ever have imagined. During the brief period between Darwin and Einstein, atheists could dismiss the biblical account of Genesis for *both* the origin of the universe and the diversity of life, since the default position at the time was that the universe was simply eternal and therefore needed no explanation. However, this argument was based only on the absence of contrary evidence.

Unfortunately, during the 1900s, as science began eroding atheism's once-strong position, the sun set forever on the eternal universe argument and discussion of "In the beginning, God created..." was suddenly back in the observatory and the academy. In 1916, Albert Einstein proposed his theory of general relativity, which, if true, meant that the universe was not eternal but had a beginning. In 1919, British cosmologist Arthur Eddington conducted an experiment during a solar eclipse, which confirmed that general relativity was indeed true; the universe had a definite beginning after all. Eddington later wrote, "Philosophically, the notion of a beginning of the present order of nature is repugnant to me...I should like to find a genuine loophole."[44] Why was it repugnant? Because a creation would point to a Creator. Bertrand Russell had argued for an eternal universe in *Why I Am Not a Christian,* but science was eroding Russell's perfect argument.

Like British science writer Sir John Maddox, editor of *Nature* for 22 years, Eddington seemed to realize that the Big Bang gave "ample evidence" to creationists, just as Maddox had argued in his editorial "Down with the Big Bang."[45] Eddington and Maddox realized that, instead of eliminating God, continued scientific advancement was actually yielding ground back to the theists.

Perhaps the 2000s will offer another dawn of atheism, although initial indicators have not been encouraging. The complete draft of the human genome, completed in 2003 by the Human Genome Project under the direction of Christian physician-geneticist Francis Collins, revealed an eye-opening amount of information within the genome. According to Collins,

> Such is the amazing complexity of the information carried within each cell of the human body, that a live reading of that code at a rate of three letters per second would take thirty-one years, even if reading continued day and night. Printing these letters out in regular font size on normal bond paper and binding them all together would result in a tower the height of the Washington Monument.[46]

This finding has theists grinning ear-to-ear as they add the argument of specified complexity* to their arsenal. As atheist Carl Sagan illustrated in his novel *Contact*, a message as simple as a series of prime numbers points to an intelligent source. Eighteen years later, Dr. Collins demonstrated that the message embedded in DNA is vastly more specific and complex than a series of prime numbers. Therefore, even by an atheist's logic, it requires an intelligent source.

Meanwhile, the ever-elusive explanation of biogenesis is providing powerful talking points for biochemists like Fazale Rana, author of *The Cell's Design: How Chemistry Reveals the Creator's Artistry*, who, thanks to science, can now debate atheists like Adam Rutherford with arguments from the laboratory instead of from Genesis.[47]

A purely material explanation of life's origins to replace the discredited Miller-Urey experiment would be another significant dawn for atheism.[48] Whether it would usher in a lasting age of atheism is a different question. Any credibility atheism might gain in the laboratory could be overshadowed by negative exposure from current events. With his nuclear ambitions combined with his human rights violations, atheist dictator Kim Jong-un could do for atheist public relations what Hitler did for the reputation of eugenics.[49]

---

* Because the purpose of this book is not to advance theists' arguments but to interact with atheist literature, I refer the reader interested in specified complexity to Frank Turek and Norman Geisler's book *I Don't Have Enough Faith to Be an Atheist* (Wheaton, IL: Crossway, 2004).

Instead of the cliché "two steps forward, one step back," the two centuries since the Enlightenment have been more like "one step forward, one step back" for skepticism. Having gained ground with Darwinism, shortly thereafter skeptics were forced to abandon the argument that the universe is eternal; it now demands an explanation.* The explanatory power of natural selection is, unfortunately, entirely dependent on the origin of the first living cell, a phenomenon whose explanation still eludes scientists. This is not to say that science will not find a natural origin for life. The problem, rather, is that science's answers invariably spawn new questions.

The Toll of Science on Antony Flew's Atheism

A tangible example of how scientific advancements are undermining atheism is the conversion of famous atheist Antony Flew. Long before Richard Dawkins, Christopher Hitchens, and Sam Harris rose to notoriety, Flew was arguably the best-known atheist since Bertrand Russell. His conversion was not the result of the emotional and irrational appeal of a preacher's sermon, or of reading the work of a Christian apologist, or even of a religious friend's urging. According to Flew, it was *science itself* that led him to belief in God. Here is Flew's account in his own words. Note the strong influence of science per the italicized portions:

> There were two factors in particular that were decisive. One was my growing empathy with the insight of *Einstein and other noted scientists* that there had to be an Intelligence behind the integrated complexity of the physical universe. The second was my own insight that the integrated complexity of life itself—which is far more complex than the physical universe—can only be explained in terms of an Intelligent Source. I believe the origin of life and reproduction simply cannot be explained from a biological standpoint despite numerous efforts to do so. With every passing year, *the more that was discovered* about the richness and

---

* The eternal universe was Bertrand Russell's position and the default position of atheism until the early 1900s.

inherent intelligence of life, the less it seemed likely that a chemical soup could magically generate the genetic code.[50]

> Why do I believe this, given that I expounded and defended atheism for more than a half century? The short answer is this: this is the world picture, as I see it, *that has emerged from modern science.* The enormous complexity [of DNA]...looks to me like the work of intelligence.[51]

While Flew found materialism and atheism to be tenable views during the twentieth century, he concluded that scientific advancement rendered them unsustainable in the twenty-first century.

Another example of a skeptic led by new scientific discoveries to a biblical worldview is Dr. Dean Kenyon, Professor Emeritus of Biology at San Francisco State University. Dr. Kenyon received his PhD in biophysics from Stanford University and became a biology professor at San Francisco State University in 1966. In 1969 he coauthored *Biochemical Predestination,* in which he argued that DNA developed naturally. Based on his scientific understanding of DNA through the 1960s, Dr. Kenyon felt that the science of the origin of life left no room for a Creator. He even wrote the textbook used to teach students that view.

However, continued scientific study forced Dr. Kenyon to change his mind. New discoveries about the complexity of cells led him to this conclusion:

> No longer is it a reasonable proposition to think that simple chemical events could have any chance at all to generate the kind of complexity that we see in the very simplest living organism. We have not the slightest chance of a chemical evolutionary origin for even the simplest of cells *with the new knowledge that has accumulated in this century.*[52]

A deeper understanding of molecular biology led Kenyon to recant his position on evolution. The above quote comes from a television program about DNA. I encourage the reader to follow the endnote to a short excerpt from the show in which Dr. Kenyon explains in his own words how science changed his mind.

The point is not to assemble a head count of those who have lost their faith in the laboratory versus those who found it there. The point is *science*, not holy texts or apologists' arguments, is leading atheists like Antony Flew and evolutionists like Dr. Kenyon to belief in God. However, the New Atheists persist in denial, clinging to the myth that science is eroding the last footholds for belief in God.

Some atheists are so entrenched in denial that they simply cannot accept the fact that science caused Flew to abandon atheism. For example, I intentionally ignored stronger quotes about the scientific reasons for Flew's conversion from his book in favor of his own words from an interview following its publication. Why? Because rather than admit the role science played in Flew's conversion, some skeptics have falsely claimed Flew's coauthor Roy Varghese misrepresented him.[53] Therefore, I cited the words from the lips of their own prophet to show it was science that induced Flew's conversion. No one should be so blindly committed to atheism as to think it is mandated by science.

If we have established only one thing about skepticism, it is that chronological arguments for it fail. We have not reached a point where the evidence demands atheism—2500 years of the same argument coupled with a recent history of one step forward, one step back "advances" should make us skeptical that day is anywhere around the corner.

3

Friedrich Nietzsche—
Enlightenment Atheism

*"We must first settle whether to believe
Christ or Nietzsche."*[1]

BERTRAND RUSSELL,
THE MYSTERIES OF LIFE AND DEATH

After Richard Dawkins' *The God Delusion,* Friedrich Nietzsche's *Beyond Good and Evil* was the second book I read about atheism. I was disappointed by Dawkins for reasons elaborated in chapter 11, but at the time I was still searching for a reason to dump my childhood indoctrination. Dawkins came across as "preaching to the converted" to sell books. I thought I might find a more honest platform in a classic atheist who was writing from passion, not for profit. I heard Nietzsche published *Beyond Good and Evil* at his own expense; it seemed like a message he was passionate to convey. Plus, he coined the famous atheist slogan "God is dead," which *Time* magazine parodied on a cover in 1966.

I read that Nietzsche had a bit of a dark side. I was aware he challenged social norms and traditional morality. That seemed intriguing at that stage in my life. I had dedicated the whole of my twenties to morally upright living only to face a string of setbacks and frustration. I was all too keenly aware of the familiar saying, "Nice guys finish last."

I came to the conclusion that clean living had been a train wreck, so I was ready to try not playing by the rules for a change.

Mind you, I did not swing from trying to do good to intentionally trying to be evil. It is not like I aspired to chain women up in my basement like Hannibal Lecter. It was just that years of clean living left me nothing to show for it, which turned me morally ambivalent. I was doing whatever I thought would make me happy, and I did not fret about labels like *right* and *wrong*.

I expected Nietzsche to affirm this lifestyle, since he and Christopher Hitchens shared a rebellious reputation. Hitchens struck me as rather cynical and, after Dawkins, I wanted to read a classical atheist for a fresh perspective. For these reasons, I chose to dig into Nietzsche.

Nietzsche's Biography

Friedrich Nietzsche was born October 15, 1844 to Carl Nietzsche, a Lutheran pastor, and his wife, Franziska, in the small German town of Rocken. He experienced considerable loss in his formative preteen years. His father died when Nietzsche was only five, and his brother, Ludwig, died at age two when Nietzsche was only six. The family moved to Naumburg to live with Nietzsche's maternal grandmother, who died only six years later.

Nietzsche also suffered disruptive illnesses throughout his childhood, including vision problems, migraine headaches, and violent indigestion. Within two years of publishing *Beyond Good and Evil,* Nietzsche had a complete mental breakdown ending in dementia.[2] Doctors from Ghent University Hospital who studied Nietzsche through personal correspondence and biographical papers concluded that he suffered from psychiatric illness and depression.[3] Nietzsche never publicly commented on how his family tragedies and personal health affected him, so we can only speculate. His story, nonetheless, fits a common pattern of people becoming disillusioned with God due to the loss of a loved one or exacerbating painful experiences.

As a teen, Nietzsche's talents in poetry and musical composition helped him get admitted to the prestigious Schulpforta boarding school. After studying theology and philology (the study of languages) at the University of Bonn for just one semester, he dropped out and announced to his sister Elisabeth that he had lost his faith and was following his favorite professor to the University of Leipzig, where he would study philology.[4] His doubts had started at least two years prior, at age 18, when he had argued that historical research discredited Christianity.[5] After completing his studies at the University of Leipzig, he became a professor of classical philology at the University of Basel when he was only 24.

At 38, Nietzsche's proposal to Lou Salome, who was 17 years his junior, was rejected. Nietzsche never married and was accused by his friend, famed German composer Richard Wagner, of being too intimate with his male friends.[6] Wagner also suggested that Nietzsche's altered moods were due to "unnatural debauchery with indications of pederasty," allegations which Nietzsche flatly denied.[7] Joachim Kohler wrote a book advancing the hypothesis Nietzsche was secretly gay based on anecdotes and suggestive comments from Nietzsche himself.[8] The allegation seems consistent with Nietzsche's strong misogynistic opinions (see "Epigrams and Interludes" on page 58). However, *The New York Times* review of Kohler's book questioned Kohler's hypothesis,[9] and his anecdotal evidence clashes with stronger indications of Nietzsche's heterosexuality, like his love letters to Cosima Wagner.[10]

While highly speculative, if it were true Nietzsche was homosexual, that could partially explain his rejection of Christianity, which some consider homophobic. It seems possible Nietzsche had a personal grudge against Christianity because he spoke more kindly of other religions, even praising Buddhism for fostering critical thought.[11]

Nietzsche's philosophy has been labeled "life-affirmation," meaning he embraced rather than ignored the harsh realities of the world in which we live. He radically questioned the objectivity of truth and advocated a complete re-evaluation of Judeo-Christian values.[12] Nietzsche's left-wing German supporters clashed with German conservatives who sought to ban his books as subversive.[13] Though his supporters have tried to downplay Nietzsche's influence on Hitler, 150,000 special durably designed copies of his book *Thus Spoke Zarathustra* were distributed to German soldiers during World War I.[14] Hitler also paid homage to his memory,[15] was a frequent visitor to the Nietzsche museum in Weimar, used Nietzsche's expressions in *Mein Kampf,* and publicized photos of himself staring in rapture at a bust of Nietzsche.[16]

Atheist philosopher Michel Onfray has argued that the first modern book on atheism was Catholic priest Jean Meslier's posthumously published essay *Thoughts and Feelings of Jean Meslier: Clear and Evident Demonstrations of the Vanity and Falsity of All the Religions in the World,* which rejected both God in the Christian and Deistic senses and the existence of the soul and miracles. However, it was not translated into English, which limited its global impact.

English poet Percy Shelley gets credit for the first atheistic publication in English, an anonymous pamphlet entitled *The Necessity of Atheism,* which got him expelled from Oxford University in 1811.[17] The first full-length philosophical works from authors whose names are widely known outside the academy belong to Ludwig Feuerbach, Karl Marx, and Friedrich Nietzsche. Because Marx is more a political economist and Feuerbach commands less name recognition than Nietzsche, I chose Nietzsche's *Beyond Good and Evil* to represent classic atheism. Who better to choose than the philosopher who gave us the famous aphorism "God is dead"?

Nietzsche's Argument

Nietzsche's subject matter is unique among the books I have reviewed here. Conspicuously absent from his title are the words *God* or *faith.* His primary focus was on morality and how it should be viewed in light of Darwinism. His secondary focus was on man's meaning and purpose post-Darwin. Although he originated ideas recycled by the New Atheism, such as religion's culpability for fights and suffering, he wrote very little about God and only a bit more about religion, but a lot about man and morality. While his theme should emerge on its own by the end of this chapter, in order to provide a useful framework, I would like to suggest that Nietzsche is best understood as defining, or perhaps redefining, the nature and role of man in a post-Christian world.

On the Prejudices of Philosophers

From the onset, Nietzsche acknowledged the ancient roots of atheism. He observed, "It took a hundred years until Greece found out who this garden god, Epicurus [341-270 BC], had been."[18] Nietzsche referred to Epicurus as a god for advocating tenets of atheism like the finality of death and the absence of divine justice. Hundreds of years before Christianity, Epicurus opposed Plato's popular view that the visible world was a reflection of higher forms.[19] Nietzsche echoed Epicurus when he attacked "Plato's invention"[20] with the quip "belief which regards the soul as something indestructible, eternal, indivisible...ought to be expelled from science!"[21] Nietzsche claimed such things were superstitions, but did not provide any supporting arguments.

[response on page 63]

Free Will

In a rather cryptic paragraph called "Freedom of the Will," Nietzsche seemed to argue that we have the ability to make free choices. He said the person exercising free will "identifies himself with the executor of the order" and delights in commanding his own outcomes, boldly proclaiming "I am the effect." He said, "A philosopher should claim the right to include willing as such within the sphere of morals."[22] Nietzsche argued that we must have free will in order to make moral judgments. While this was largely taken for granted in Nietzsche's day, later scientific discoveries would increase Nietzsche's relevance by raising the question of determinism: Are we just chemically programmed machines dancing to the tune of our DNA?

[response on page 64]

Living by Nature

Nietzsche observed the inherent despair of living a life modeled after nature. It was a dim life, in his view:

> "According to nature" you want to live?...Imagine a being like nature, wasteful beyond measure, indifferent beyond measure, without purposes and consideration, without

mercy and justice, fertile and desolate and uncertain at the same time; imagine indifference itself as a power—how could you live according to this indifference?[23]

[response on page 65]

Atheism's Dark Side

Nietzsche wrote 27 years after Charles Darwin published *On the Origin of Species*. Nietzsche embraced the full implications of Darwin's evolutionary model frankly and fearlessly. Where Darwin provided a biological explanation of life, Nietzsche provided a psychological model of how life works in Darwin's model.

According to Nietzsche, self-preservation is the primary and preeminent human instinct. He said, "Physiologists should think before putting down the instinct of self-preservation as the cardinal instinct of an organic being."[24] Altruism, self-denial, and self-sacrifice, to Nietzsche, were signs of weakness:

> There is no other way: the feelings of devotion, self-sacrifice for one's neighbor, the whole morality of self-denial must be questioned mercilessly and taken to court…There is too much charm and sugar in these feelings of "for others," "not for myself" for us not to need to become doubly suspicious at this point and to ask: "are these not perhaps—seductions?"[25]

For Nietzsche, hunger, sexual lust, and vanity were not base desires inferior to altruism and self-denial. To the contrary, they were actually the essence of mankind:

> Whenever anyone sees, seeks, and wants to see only hunger, sexual lust and vanity as the real and only motives of human actions; in short, when anyone speaks "badly"— and not even "wickedly"—of man, the lover of knowledge should listen subtly and diligently.[26]

[response on page 65]

The Free Spirit

I appreciate Nietzsche's candid admission that "nobody is very likely to consider a doctrine true merely because it makes people happy or virtuous."[27] This came right on the heels of Ludwig Feuerbach's famous claim in *The Essence of Christianity* that religion is merely wishful thinking. Nietzsche recognized the absurdity of the proposition. Yet later atheists from Sigmund Freud onward, realizing the power of Feuerbach's argument, have made it one of their core arguments. They conveniently fail to mention that it was challenged from the onset by Nietzsche himself.

In his second chapter, Nietzsche argued that our suppressed desires are our essence. He continued building his case that base impulses like force, slavery, and tyranny actually serve to enhance man.

> We [the new philosophers] think that hardness, forcefulness, slavery, danger in the alley and the heart, life in hiding, stoicism, the art of experiment and devilry of every kind, that everything evil, terrible, tyrannical in man, everything in him that is kin to beasts of prey and serpents, *serves the enhancement of the species "man"* as much as the opposite does.[28]

Whereas actions of love and generosity should be concealed and awarded with a good beating:

> There are occurrences of such a delicate nature that one does well to cover them up with some rudeness to conceal them; there are actions of love and extravagant generosity after which nothing is more advisable than to take a stick and give any eyewitness a sound thrashing: that would muddle his memory.[29]

For Nietzsche, materialism and atheism went hand-in-hand, since reality was nothing more than the material world. The higher virtues of love, kindness, and gentleness were mere illusions in a mechanistic world propelled by human passions:

Suppose nothing else were "given" as real except our world of desires and passions, and we could not get down, or up, to any other "reality" besides the reality of our drives—for thinking is merely a relation of these drive to each other: is it not permitted to make the experiment and to ask the question whether this "given" would be sufficient or also understanding on the basis of this kind of thing the so-called mechanistic (or "material") world?[30]

[response on page 71]

What Is Religious

Chapter 3 does not get any prettier. I should stress that, though many people will find Nietzsche's views troubling, I am sincerely attempting to accurately and fairly represent him in this section, not just to cherry-pick his worst quotes. If anyone doubts this is Nietzsche's essence, I invite them to read him themselves; every atheist should grapple with Nietzsche.

In this chapter Nietzsche explained the meaning of his title *Beyond Good and Evil*: Because morality is mere delusion, we need to look *beyond* "meaningless" concepts like good and evil. While Richard Dawkins gave us *The God Delusion*, an alternative title for Nietzsche's book could be *The Morality Delusion*. For Nietzsche, good and evil were just meaningless labels we place on things to try to make them hallowed even though they are really hollow.

> Whoever has really...looked into, down into the most world-denying of all possible ways of thinking—beyond good and evil and no longer, like Buddha and Schopenhauer, under the spell and delusion of morality—may just thereby, without really meaning to do so, have opened his eyes to the opposite ideal: the ideal of the most high-spirited, alive, and world-affirming human being.[31]

Lest we miss Nietzsche's point that evil is illusory, consider his allusion to Buddhism. In Buddhism, suffering and evil are also illusory. As explained by Dilgo Kyhentsa, Buddhist Vajrayana master, "It is like seeing a rope and mistaking it for a snake. When we think that the rope is a snake, we are scared, but once we see that we are looking at a rope, our fear dissipates. We have been deluded by our thoughts."[32]

To Nietzsche, morality is a similar delusion. Anyone who refrains from doing evil because it is "evil" is as foolish as the man startled by the rope: The danger is really only in his own mind.

In this chapter, Nietzsche also raised the same point touted today by the New Atheists, that the concepts of God and sin are responsible for human conflict.

> Perhaps the day will come when the most solemn concepts which have caused the most fights and suffering, the concepts of "God" and "sin," will seem no more important to us than a child's toy and a child's pain seem to an old man.[33]

Ironically, only a few paragraphs later, he acknowledged that "to love man *for God's sake*—that has so far been the noblest and most renown feeling attained among men."[34] While he seemed to affirm that some religious people have sought to love others rather than to cause suffering, he nonetheless went on to argue against this "ulterior intent" for loving people. Whatever reason man has for acting, it should not be based on a fictitious old man in the sky.

For Nietzsche, the American Declaration of Independence's contention that it is "self-evident that all men are created equal" and "endowed by their Creator with certain inalienable rights" was nonsense. His claim "the democratic movement is the heir of the Christian movement" was meant as an insult.[35] He believed men were inherently unequal. A few were "strong and independent" and thus "predestined to command,"[36] but the vast majority only existed for servility, and religion was a useful placebo that helped them justify their lowly existence.

> To ordinary human beings, finally—the vast majority who exist for service and the general advantage, and who may exist only for that—religion gives an inestimable contentment with their situation and type…something

of a justification for the whole everyday character, the
whole lowliness, the whole half-brutish poverty of their
souls…men not noble enough to see the abysmally different order of rank, chasm of rank, between man and man—
such men have so far held sway over the fate of Europe,
with their "equal before God." [37]

Stalin recognized this pacifying effect of religion. That is why he
agreed with Marx that atheism's rejection of reward or punishment
beyond this life was an essential foundation for society. [38] Thus, while
Stalin did not kill millions because of his belief in atheism per se, his
belief that atheism was critical for the success of Communism was sufficient justification in his mind for mass executions to eradicate religion. Stalin did not kill 2-3 million people due to atheism alone. [39] His
atheism was compounded with the belief that Communism would not
function without it.

[response on page 72]

Epigrams and Interludes

Nietzsche's writing style is atypical. Though he wrote chapters,
he wrote in numbered paragraphs that allowed him to jump freely
between topics. In chapter 4, some paragraphs are as short as a single sentence, giving the chapter the feel it is comprised of wise, pithy
proverbs.

Certainly the biggest concept Nietzsche raised in this chapter is,
"All credibility, all good conscience, all evidence of truth comes only
from the senses." [40] The New Atheists share this belief in the primacy of
sensory evidence. Revelation, testimony, and faith cannot be trusted if
they conflict with our senses. All of this goes back to Nietzsche.

In addition to that key point, he continued asserting the idea that
mankind is not inherently good. "The great epochs of our life come
when we gain the courage to rechristen our evil as what is best in us." [41]

Richard Dawkins claims that Christianity is misogynistic [42] and
complains about "the loathing of women for 2000 years in those

countries afflicted by the sky-god and his earthly male delegates."[43] Given that Dawkins speaks so despairingly about how women fare in Christianity, it is interesting to note what Nietzsche had to say about women:

> Science offends the modesty of all real women.

> Whatever women write about "woman," we may in the end reserve a healthy suspicion whether woman really wants enlightenment about herself—whether she can will it.

> When a woman has scholarly inclinations, there is usually something wrong with her sexuality.

> What is truth to woman? From the beginning, nothing has been more alien, repugnant, and hostile to woman than truth—her great art is the lie, her highest concern is mere appearance and beauty.

> Woman wants to become self-reliant...this is one of the worst developments of the general uglification of Europe.

> Woman has much reason for shame; so much pedantry, superficiality, schoolmarmishness, petty presumption, petty licentiousness and immodesty lies concealed in woman.

> Comparing man and woman an on the whole, one may say: woman would not have the genius for finery if she did not have an instinct for a secondary role.

> A man, on the other hand, who has depth...must always think about woman as Orientals do: he must conceive of woman as a possession, as property that can be locked, as something predestined for service and achieving her perfection in that.[44]

[response on page 74]

Natural History of Morals

Morality was considered the domain of priests and pastors for so long that Nietzsche felt compelled, as any atheist should, to provide a rational explanation for a godless morality. An atheist acts good in Nietzsche's estimation not in the sense of doing something that could be absolutely good, like an act of pity, but in the sense of working for the preservation of the community and choosing actions serving the utility of the herd.

> As long as the utility reigning in moral value judgments is solely the utility of the herd, as long as one considers only the preservation of the community, and immorality is sought exactly and exclusively in what seems dangerous to the survival of the community—there can be morality of "neighbor love." Supposing that even then there was a constant little exercise of consideration, pity, fairness, mildness, reciprocity of assistance...they are still extra-moral. An act of pity for example, was not considered either good or bad, moral or immoral, in the best period of the Romans.[45]

Or, putting it more concisely...

> Morality in Europe today is herd animal morality.[46]

"Step upon step, the herd instinct draws its conclusions. How much or how little is dangerous to the community," said Nietzsche. Though he previously argued against the "delusion of morality,"[47] I do not think Nietzsche was flip-flopping on the issue. Rather, he seemed to be suggesting that no individual action is morally right or wrong *in and of itself*. However, actions do impact the community and, as such, actions which further the "utility of the herd" are deemed moral. In essence, the proverbial man stranded alone on a desert island cannot be either moral or immoral because morality is nothing more than the impact of our actions on the community.

Nietzsche observed the moral problem was not about finding a morality that served the utility of the community. It is rather easy to see what actions help or hurt a community. Rather, the problem was demonstrating that morality had any real, rational basis. In his words,

> The fundamental proposition on whose contents all moral philosophers are really agreed—hurt no one; rather, help all as much as you can—that is really the proposition for which all moralists endeavor to find the rational foundation…the real basis of ethics for which one has been looking for thousands of years.[48]

In other words, the fact it works does not make it *moral*, only *practical*. If one is content with the premise that this is all morality is—mutually agreed-upon rules that make society work better, like everyone driving on the right side of the road—then there is no dilemma. However, that model does not answer the objections of those who expect a rational explanation for why they should refrain from "wrong" actions.

[response on page 75]

Our Virtues

Nietzsche continued the discussion of morality in his chapter on virtues, observing that the fundamental problem with an atheistic explanation of morality is that it cannot build a moral system from the ground up; it must start with a predisposition toward English morality based on the fact it has proven its utility over time, then go looking for ways to "prove" the truth of these conventions.

> Ultimately they all want English morality to be proved right—because this serves humanity best, or "the general utility," or "the happiness of the greatest number"—no, the happiness of England. With all their powers they want to prove to themselves that the striving for English happiness…is at the same time also the right way to virtue.[49]

[response on page 77]

4

A Response to Friedrich Nietzsche

*"I dislike Nietzsche
because he likes the contemplation of pain,
because he erects conceit into a duty,
because the men whom he most admires are conquerors,
whose glory is cleverness in causing men to die."* [1]

BERTRAND RUSSELL,
A HISTORY OF WESTERN PHILOSOPHY

Bertrand Russell wrote, "[Nietzsche's] followers have had their innings, but we may hope that it is coming rapidly to an end." [2] To the contrary, it seems to me that Nietzsche's views are the most consistent with Darwinism. If anything ends with Nietzsche, it is the harmony he achieved with materialism and morality. After Nietzsche there is disconnect between how atheists view the world and how they relate to it. Nietzsche was courageous enough to write with unparalleled honesty. More importantly, he lived in harmony with his beliefs.

On the Prejudices of Philosophers

I applaud Nietzsche's integrity in acknowledging the pre-Enlightenment, pre-Christian roots of atheism as well as Plato's rational arguments for the soul. Nietzsche is the only atheist I have read who acknowledges that Plato rationally arrived at the idea of souls and life after death apart from special revelation. In fact, Peter Boghossian

erroneously counts Plato as a skeptic who advanced atheism! The claim
is incredibly misleading; early Christian apologists frequently appealed
to Plato's writing as an argument for the immaterial and the afterlife.[3]
Nietzsche is in the minority because he did not pretend his atheism was
post-Enlightenment thought. Boghossian gets at least this much right
when he notes that skepticism goes back to Lucretius, Sextus Empiri-
cus, Epictetus, Marcus Aurelius, and others.[4]

[original argument on page 53]

Free Will

Nietzsche correctly understood that free will is essential to morality. We cannot deem any action right or wrong if we are merely slaves
to our chemistry. However, Nietzsche never even attempted to prove
how free will could exist in a purely material world. He merely took it
for granted without evidence.

For that matter, I have not read any atheist writer who defends
free will. It is simply taken for granted even though anyone who posits materialism must question it. None less than Nobel Prize-winning
atheist molecular biologist and neuroscientist Francis Crick said, "You
are in fact no more than the behavior of a vast assembly of nerve cells
and their associated molecules."[5] These are the kinds of issues materialism raises: Is free will possible in a purely materialistic universe?

A Christian worldview that includes an immaterial mind apart
from the matter of the brain has no problem defending the concept of
free will. The atheist, on the other hand, must demonstrate how free
will arises from nothing but matter. It is especially ironic that atheists
have largely adopted the moniker "freethinkers" because the possibility of free thought is highly suspect in materialism. How can a person's
choices be truly free rather than chemically determined, including the
choice to be an atheist?

How can Nietzsche claim that "I am the effect" that freely chooses
my actions? Here again I find him being intellectually honest in not
merely taking it for granted. Nietzsche lived during a time when the
Judeo-Christian concept of a natural conscience was dominant. The
Catholic Church's teaching on this was underpinned by Romans 2:15,

in which the apostle Paul characterizes conscience almost as an imma-terial third person alternately accusing and defending its subject.[6] Alternative explanations of conscience, like Freud's, would not be pub-lished until 1923.

When Nietzsche embraced materialism, that ruled out immaterial concepts of conscience like Paul's. So how could free will be employed to decide between right and wrong choices? It seems that people would simply follow their natures. For example, we would not label the irre-sistible urge birds have to migrate as a right or wrong choice. Nietzsche rejected the idea of irresistible impulses and concluded that we must have free will, although he never articulated an explanation as to how. The insufficiency of this explanation continues to be the Achilles' heel of materialistic moral worldviews. How can you say anyone is wrong when we are just molecules in motion following our chemical pro-gramming and dancing to our DNA?

[original argument on page 53]

Living by Nature

Once again I find myself agreeing with Nietzsche. Nature is with-out purpose, justice, and mercy, just as he describes it. If nature is all we have as the basis for a moral framework, then humanity has every reason to despair. I appreciate Nietzsche recognizing this and speaking honestly on it, unlike Dawkins, who cherry-picks isolated cases from nature to extol (see page 209).

[original argument on page 53]

Atheism's Dark Side

Nietzsche embraced the idea that, far from being noble, man is merely the highest-evolved animal. Therefore, man should recognize that, like an animal, he is driven by base desires like hunger and sexual lust. The lion is not king of the jungle because he is kind to other lions, gentle-hearted, or meek. The lion is king because he is willing to kill all would-be usurpers.

Richard Dawkins can argue that we are better off following the model of Arabian babbler birds (see page 210), but he cannot justify *why* that is a better model beyond merely practical considerations. He cannot say Nietzsche is *wrong* for advocating might-is-right, nor can he defend pursuing justice against thieves and murderers if they are simply obeying nature's dictates.

For example, when a lion escapes a zoo, we tranquilize it and return it because letting lions roam the streets does not work very well in our society. If the lion were to eat a child before it is caught, you would not say it is a murderer or that justice must be served on the lion by executing it for its "crime." Nietzsche questioned whether similar labels are appropriate for humans if we are merely the highest of the animals.

[original argument on page 54]

Atheism versus Materialism

This is as good a place as any to interject the discussion of atheism's relationship to materialism. While the terms are sometimes used interchangeably, they are not quite equivalent. The general definition of *atheist* is "a person who disbelieves or lacks belief in the existence of God or gods." However, that definition is a bit dated. According to Christopher Hitchens, atheists are increasingly dropping the concept of disbelief and adopting a definition focused on the lack of belief, something along the lines of "no credible evidence has been presented for belief in God."*/7 Dropping disbelief from the definition of atheism fortifies the bulwark for defending the position.

If someone claims "there is no God," that is a positive truth claim affirming he knows something about God. That opens the door for someone to ask, "On what evidence do you know this?" However, narrowing the position simply to "no credible evidence has been presented" is not claiming to know anything. Therefore, it shifts the burden of proof entirely to the other party. By recasting the position as a request for evidence rather than a truth claim, all the work of making a case now falls on the theist. The atheist can deny the validity of theists'

---

* Hitchens' exact words were "No persuasive argument for the existence of God has ever been advanced...No argument in favor stands. We cannot say that we know that there could be no such entity."

arguments on a case-by-case basis and attack the theist's position at will. Meanwhile, he never has to defend his own position.

It is a brilliant strategy, but it seems to betray an underlying motive because taking the time to make a position more defensible implies a *desire* to defend the position. If it were only a position held dispassionately while remaining open-minded to other options, why bother to rewrite the definition to make it more defensible? We build forts only around land we want to keep.

The new definition of atheism as simply "a lack of belief" is completely illogical. The only way to lack belief in something is to have never heard of it. From the moment you are presented with an idea, you have a belief about it one way or another.

For example, no one lacks a belief in Leprechauns. You either believe tiny elfish men who spend their days stashing their gold at the end of rainbows exist or you do not. Even if you remain agnostic about Leprechauns, a position of uncertainty is still a belief because it requires a concept about which you remain uncertain. Being unconvinced about the existence of Leprechauns is not the same thing as lacking a belief in Leprechauns.

By contrast, consider someone living in a primitive, isolated Amazon tribe who has no access to books or the Internet and therefore has never heard of Irish folklore. That tribesman actually *lacks* a belief in Leprechauns. He lacks a belief because he has no concept of a Leprechaun. However, the moment an Irish tourist visits his remote village and tells him about Leprechauns, the tribesman has a belief—be it for, against, or undecided. It is simply impossible to lack a belief in something you have heard of, unless you have diminished mental capacity and cannot grasp even the concept. Until their mental capabilities develop, babies can be properly said to lack a belief in God. However, the claim makes no sense for even the dullest adult.

Moving past the absurd definition of a lack of belief, the statement "no credible evidence has been presented for belief in God" at least makes a coherent claim. However, one obvious problem with the definition is the question "Presented to whom?" To the atheist making the claim, obviously: "No evidence has been presented *to me* that *I* find convincing." However, that fails to acknowledge the fact that others are convinced by the same evidence.

Take the example of someone serving on a jury for a murder trial. It is certainly a valid position to believe that the prosecutor has not presented credible evidence of the defendant's guilt. Our interpretation of the evidence is affirmed when other jurors see the evidence the same way. The whole point of having a jury is to mitigate personal bias by seeing whether others come to the same conclusion. Therefore, a problem arises if the other 11 members of the jury interpret the same evidence differently. When this occurs, it is no longer sufficient to merely claim "No credible evidence has been presented *to me*" and shift the burden of proof onto the majority who were convinced by the same evidence. The person making the claim owes the rest an explanation. Simply taking the position "All of you don't get it" is not acceptable.

In matters of spiritual beliefs, consensus on the evidence is not required. However, when 87 to 98 percent of the world arrives at a different conclusion based on the same evidence, clearly people are applying different definitions of *credible*.[8] This is where the "no credible evidence" definition of atheism breaks down for being too simplistic.

It reminds me of a cartoon I saw in which two men dressed like Mormons are standing at a man's door. The man is looking at a blank pamphlet the two visitors have just handed him. Perplexed, he says, "This is blank," to which the two visitors reply, "We are atheists." Outside of cartoons, atheism is more than a belief in nothing. The "lack of belief" and the "no credible evidence" claims fail to adequately define what constitutes credible evidence. For example, it does not address issues like what role materialism plays in determining what evidence is deemed credible.

Materialism is defined as "the doctrine that nothing exists except matter." If someone is a materialist it follows *ipso facto* they are an atheist because disbelief in anything nonmaterial, God included, is intrinsic to materialism. Once someone takes the position that nothing exists except matter, they have by default taken a position on God.

While materialism is synonymous with atheism, atheists are quick to point out that being an atheist does not *ipso facto* make someone a materialist. They point out, for example, that an atheist might still believe in ghosts. That is a fair point.

Hypothetical atheist ghostbusters aside though, I question whether atheism and materialism are truly distinct. The atheist says, "I need credible evidence in order to believe in God." By "credible" evidence, he means *scientific* evidence. He is aware of the claims of Matthew, Mark, Luke, and John. He is aware that more than two billion people believe in Jesus.[9] He is aware of miraculous claims and stories of life-after-death experiences. He is aware of an internal moral compass that seems to defy materialistic explanation. However, none of these are considered credible evidence because they are not scientific evidence. Fair enough, I say. Demanding scientific evidence is certainly a reasonable claim in the twenty-first century.

What exactly is scientific evidence? According to American geologist Dr. Steven Schafersman, an atheist, it is evidence produced by three tools: empiricism, rationalism, and skepticism.[10] While these may be the tools of science, we need to understand that these tools are only applied within the philosophical framework of naturalism. In a paper on naturalism featured on famed atheist Stephen Jay Gould's website, Dr. Schafersman argues that "*naturalism is a methodological necessity* in the practice of science by scientists."[11] He conspicuously admits that while "naturalism does not necessitate a commitment to materialism…methodological materialism is probably universally adopted among scientists today." Regarding the possibility that "supernaturalistic explanations are preferable to some scientific naturalistic explanations, particularly concerning questions of origins," he says, "these suggestions sound preposterous (and I think they are preposterous)."

In other words: (1) whatever science finds, *by necessity* it must be a naturalistic explanation; (2) science is searching for materialistic causes only; and (3) when science comes across a case where a supernaturalistic explanation might seem preferable, it just dismisses it as preposterous and keeps looking for a naturalistic explanation. It is a specious argument for an atheist to claim that though he demands scientific proof, he is not a materialist. The only kind of proof science offers is materialistic! It is entirely self-contradictory to deny being a materialist while simultaneously affirming that only materialistic explanations count.

To illustrate, it is like asking for a fighter plane to roll off the Corvette assembly line in Bowling Green, Kentucky. It is not entirely implausible: Automotive assembly lines are certainly capable of assembling planes. In fact, Ford's factories produced bombers, aircraft engines, and military vehicles during World War II. So while the tools in Bowling Green could *hypothetically* produce a plane, they are currently *restricted* to producing Corvettes. The assembly line simply will not produce a plane until fundamental constraints are altered. In similar fashion, while science could hypothetically produce evidence for the supernatural, the framework is currently restricted to rolling out naturalistic causes and explanations.

Claims that atheism is strictly the restrictive position that "no credible evidence has been presented for God" are undercut by the demand that all evidence be filtered through naturalistic sciences which, by design, preclude supernatural causes. This couples atheism firmly to materialism. To claim otherwise makes as much sense as demanding someone prove they cannot speak English using only English words.

The claim that atheism is synonymous with materialism (a.k.a. naturalism) does not originate with theists. The idea has been embraced by members of the atheist community. In a recent debate with William Lane Craig, atheist cosmologist Sean Carroll described the two major worldviews as not atheism and theism but naturalism and theism. In Dr. Carroll's words:

> It comes down to a conflict between two major, fundamental pictures of the world. What philosophers would call ontologies: *naturalism and theism*. Naturalism says that all that exists is one world, the natural world obeying laws of nature that science can help us discover. Theism says that in addition to the natural world there is something else, at the very least God, perhaps there are other things as well. [12]

Note that atheist Carroll uses naturalism synonymously for atheism. The claim does not originate with Craig. At an absolute minimum, there is a strong correlation between atheism and materialism, if not a direct causal relationship.

Why does it matter? For Nietzsche, it determined how we should live our lives in light of naturalism. Whenever I point out the problem with naturalism, atheists simply dismiss it as not being part of atheism, as if atheism has nothing to do with naturalism. They revert back to the very narrow "no credible evidence" definition of atheism. They simply brush off Nietzsche's frightening neo-Darwinist views by saying, "That is not atheism." I found that the term *atheism* was surprisingly elastic whenever atheists wanted it to be, but razor-focused whenever that better suited their needs. When we consider how closely atheism seems to be entwined with naturalism, as in Nietzsche, the "no credible evidence" definition fails to adequately capture all that is involved.

When I investigated atheism, I found a double standard. A very broad definition was applied to Christianity, one that made it culpable for the actions of every religious nut job. In contrast, a very narrow definition was applied to atheism that essentially excused it from any wrong ever committed by any atheist. More controversial viewpoints like Nietzsche's were simply brushed off with "I simply lack belief in God." However, Nietzsche struck me as advocating a lifestyle consistent with materialism. His views demanded a response, but only received denial.

The Free Spirit

Nietzsche painted a frightening portrait of atheism. Can anyone embrace the ideas that slavery and tyranny enhance man? Love and generosity should be concealed? Only the strong have rights?

The Christian "baggage" I wanted to shed challenged all these awful views: If anyone kidnaps a man to sell him as a slave, he shall be put to death (Exodus 21:16). Love your neighbor as yourself (Mark 12:31). Be generous and ready to share (1 Timothy 6:18). The strong ought to bear the weaknesses of others and not just please themselves (Romans 15:1).

My problem with embracing atheism and dumping those absolutes was how I could respond to these ideas *as an atheist* or assert that I was right—that I had more than a difference of opinion with Nietzsche. I could side with Richard Dawkins and say we should be altruistic, like certain birds, but I could not say that those who side with Nietzsche are wrong, only that they see it differently. In fact, given the absence of any absolute basis for morality, it seems to me that Nietzsche had it right. If man were a beast, it seemed the benefit of the doubt went to Nietzsche's beastly view; Dawkins could not adequately refute him.

[original argument on page 55]

What Is Religious

I agree with Nietzsche that good and evil are meaningless concepts in a godless world. It seems to me Nietzsche got it right and the New Atheists, like Sam Harris, are merely deluding themselves when they try to justify godless ethical systems. When I say no one should be an atheist without first wrestling with Nietzsche, it is because he was one of the few to fully embrace all the implications of a naturalist worldview. If I were to embrace atheism, I think it would be Nietzsche's flavor of atheism because he seems to have understood what it means to be a hairless monkey. He does not pretend that humans are noble.

I find it ironic that though Nietzsche blamed the concepts of "God" and "sin" for human violence, mere paragraphs later he acknowledged that "To love man *for God's sake*"[13] has always been a core tenet of Christianity. I appreciate this frank admission that Christianity does preach love for all mankind. Although he argued that loving man for God's sake is, in his view, an improper motive, by arguing against the motivation he is making a frank admission that Christianity does teach love for mankind. One wonders why the New Atheists simply cannot seem to see this when it was so patently obvious to Nietzsche.

Nietzsche's view that the "vast majority exist for service"[14] becomes insightful juxtaposed with Christopher Hitchens' later dogmatic insistence that religion leads to servility. Nietzsche's view was that it is mankind's nature to serve, whether that takes the form of service to a religious institution or a secular state. It is mankind's nature, not the church, which is the cause of servility. Take away the church, and man will merely serve something else.

One of the biggest obstacles I had to fully embracing atheism was that it steals its ethics from Christianity. For example, I noticed that though Nietzsche rejected the concept "equal before God,"[15] atheists see no contradiction between enjoying life in America and rejecting the concept of God-given rights, *including the right to be an atheist,* that were the foundations of our Declaration of Independence. The justification for why America deserved to be independent to begin with was that our rights of "life, liberty and the pursuit of happiness" were *"endowed by [our] Creator."* Our Founding Fathers felt justified creating an independent nation based on such God-given rights by "appealing to the Supreme Judge of the world for the rectitude of [their] actions."[16]

I noticed also that while atheism rejects the concept of God-given rights, never have I heard any of the New Atheists suggest we need to go back and, as Nietzsche did, revisit whether liberty and the pursuit of happiness are innate rights in a godless society, whether everyone should equally enjoy these rights, or whether some basis underpins these rights. Sam Harris' *The Moral Landscape* comes the closest, but it is about explaining how a secular framework can define moral good. It stops far short of Nietzsche's more radical and apparently correct proposition that once we declare God dead we must reevaluate rights that were granted on the premise of His existence. A child may think his parents are extremely stingy, but once he learns that all his favorite toys did not come from Santa Claus, it is only appropriate that he reexamine his view.

Nietzsche raised the objection that not everyone has the same rights. However, because equality has proven itself in America, the New Atheism is content to leave it unchallenged, as if atheism offers a moral basis for those rights. Our freedoms are primarily rooted in ideas found in John Locke's *Two Treatises of Government*, wherein he argued men are by nature free and equal and that government is a social contract "where people in the state of nature conditionally transfer some of their rights to the government in order to better ensure the stable, comfortable enjoyment of their lives, liberty, and property."[17] Against this, Nietzsche argued authority is not voluntarily bestowed, but rather seized by the "strong and independent who are prepared and predestined to command."[18] He believed people are not by nature free and equal; they simply exist for service.[19] Why do the New Atheists hide Nietzsche in the closet? They conveniently ignore the voice of their own "prophet."

I have raised this objection with individual atheists and the response is always something along the lines of "Atheism is merely the belief no credible evidence exists for belief in God. It has nothing to do with government, law, or ethics." I do not find this answer adequate, nor should they. Without belief in God, the notion of a country with God-given rights is as preposterous as the notion of a country in which these rights come from Santa Claus or the Easter Bunny.

To hijack Nietzsche's own words, "This is my way; where is yours?"[20]

[original argument on page 56]

Epigrams and Interludes

The obvious problem with Nietzsche's claim that "all evidence of truth comes only from the senses" is that this statement itself did not come from the senses. It is as self-refuting as saying, "I don't speak a word of English." If all truth comes from the senses, which sense told Nietzsche this? Was it something that he saw in a microscope? Was it something he heard in a laboratory? Was it something he smelled in a test tube? Of course not. It is a philosophical premise deduced in his mind, which makes it unobservable by the senses.

We notice an important difference when we compare Dawkins' allegations of biblical misogyny with Nietzsche's misogynistic views. It can be easily and clearly demonstrated that Dawkins pulls verses out of context. The same word used for Adam's wife in Genesis 2:18 (the Hebrew word *ezer*) is used to describe God Himself elsewhere in Scripture (Psalms 30:10; 54:4; 104:14). Paul Copan has thoroughly refuted the claim that Christianity is misogynistic in chapter 10 of his excellent book *Is God a Moral Monster?* to which I refer my readers.

While Christianity can easily defend itself against allegations of misogyny, the same cannot be said for atheism. By whose definition is Nietzsche's atheist misogyny wrong while Dawkins' atheist philogyny is right? Should we follow Dawkins' example of the Arabian babblers and look for answers in nature? The dominant male silverback gorilla forcibly copulates with any female he chooses. He practices infanticide upon female gorillas' children that are not his own. Darwinism favors Nietzsche's position over Dawkins'. Dawkins' challenge is to formulate an argument for why Nietzsche is *wrong* that goes beyond a difference of *opinion*. I found this to be a big problem with atheism. It seems Nietzsche's misogyny is wrong, but wrong *according to whom*? It seemed to me "misogyny is wrong" was more than just my personal opinion, but atheism offered no absolute standard to make that claim.

[original argument on page 58]

Natural History of Morals

The question "Can atheists be good?" comes up frequently in debates. However, the question cannot be answered without a precise definition of *good*. As we see in Nietzsche's argument, anyone can be good if by "good" we simply mean acting in a manner that serves the herd and preserves the community. Yet this divorces *good* from caring about others: The man called "good" ultimately cares about himself alone. However, his own survival is contingent upon the survival of the herd. Therefore he will undertake actions that aid the herd's survival *for his own selfish reasons.*

The question of whether he is being good comes down to whether or not his motives count. If good means nothing more than "acting with the community's interest in mind," then sure, he can act good. But this definition has been severely diluted; it is hard to call it a moral claim. It is like saying someone is "good" when he drives on the right side of the road because this practice minimizes accidents. However, if by good we mean acting with the motives of altruism, generosity, and self-sacrifice, then no, he is not acting good. He acts out of selfishness because his own survival depends on the community.

Nietzsche failed to offer a viable explanation for morality. To me, this was a deal breaker in accepting his worldview. My problem with Nietzsche's suggestion that morality is determined solely by what is good for the community is this: Who defines membership in the community? While I obviously need more than just my neighborhood to survive and possibly more than the people in my city, do I need those outside my state? Countries smaller than my state have flourished. What then is my moral obligation to America?

Suppose a good case can be made that my survival depends on America's survival. Surely my moral obligation must end at the national level. I need nothing from a foreigner except perhaps his resources. Are tyranny, genocide, colonialism, and exploitation really wrong only if they hurt my own survival?

I grew up during the height of the Cold War. The vast majority of Americans believed that exterminating 291 million Soviet citizens[21] with a nuclear strike was wrong *in and of itself*, not merely because of the threat of the USSR's nuclear counterstrike capability. Suppose the Star Wars missile defense system had been successfully implemented before the collapse of the Soviet Union and there was zero possibility of a Soviet counterstrike. Would genocide become justified merely because it could be executed without risking our own survival? According to Nietzsche (see "Our Virtues" on page 61), who claimed nothing is wrong or evil unless it threatens your own survival, yes. It seemed to me that if that was the best rationale he could offer for morality, his worldview was inherently flawed.

According to Nietzsche, actions are judged solely based on what is good for the herd. However, this assumes that the good of society is in my interest. A sociopath does not care about the welfare of society because he either does not think he needs the herd to survive or does not care about his own survival. We incarcerate such people because, as Nietzsche says, they are "dangerous to the community"; but that does not mean they are *wrong*. They simply do not share our view that the welfare of the herd ultimately matters. An atheist cannot say they "should" care about the herd or "ought" to care how their actions affect others because "should" and "ought" imply a deontological moral obligation. The sociopath's view that society does not matter is simply a different way of looking at society. You cannot say it is "wrong" unless there is some absolute standard that makes the opposite view "right."

The problem with Nietzsche's view is it elevates an *opinion*—"the survival of the herd is the ultimate standard"—to the level of a *truth claim* without any rational basis for doing so. In atheism, if we ostracize or incarcerate someone for being a sociopath, we act with no more moral authority than if we incarcerated him because he preferred chocolate ice cream while the majority preferred vanilla. Similarly, the sociopath merely has a different opinion on the importance of society.

[original argument on page 60]

Our Virtues

Nietzsche hit the nail on the head. The problem is that an atheist moral philosophy equates striving for happiness with virtue. He observed English moral philosophers ultimately sought to justify actions which served the happiness of England. Likewise, the pursuit of German happiness justified Germany's exploitation of Poland, France, and Russia. Nietzsche's atheism offered Germans no reason for moral duty beyond their tribe.

[original argument on page 61]

Summary

I found I agreed with much of Nietzsche's writing. The way he viewed the world made sense and his conclusions were rationally derived—*if* you assume a starting point of a godless world. He had the keen insight that stripping man of his godly nature leaves behind a hairless monkey. In light of that, Nietzsche correctly reasoned that notions of good and evil are merely illusions. The lion is not king of the jungle because he is humble, but because he is strong and ruthless.

I commend Nietzsche for honestly addressing the problems within atheism. He admitted that atheists had a problem coming up with a "real basis for ethics"[22] and acknowledged that they were really just taking the "prevalent morality"[23] and seeking ways to justify it.

Such authenticity is completely absent from the New Atheists' writings. They have not solved these problems; they have simply learned to *pretend* they have solved them. For example, Dawkins may attempt to base a system of ethics on the behavior of Arabian babbler birds, but why should we prefer these birds' behavior over that of a violent species? Nietzsche tackles this problem head-on. His honest approach is more appealing than the smugness of the New Atheists, who fool no one but themselves when they glibly ignore these problems.

The New Atheists have a habit of portraying the fringes of Christianity as if they were the core. While it is tempting to take a play from their book and write a short polemic about Nietzsche's misogynistic side, it is not intellectually honest to represent the worst of a group as the best it has to offer. Thus, even though his misogyny makes for an easy target, highlighting it as representative of atheism would be a case of two wrongs not making a right.

Nietzsche is the perfect antithesis to Christ (I would say anti-Christ were that term not preloaded with symbolism). In contrast to Jesus emphasizing peace, patience, gentleness, self-control, and turning the other cheek, Nietzsche emphasized the will to power, physical strength, and embracing the beast within us. He offers a real but most importantly a complete alternative option to Jesus. In antithesis to Jesus' claim, "I am the way," Nietzsche says, "This is my way."[24] Bertrand Russell rightly observed that we must choose either Nietzsche or Jesus.[25] Nietzsche presented a complete, competing, viable atheist option to Christianity. It is a complete way of life, not just a denial of God.

I realized if I were to embrace atheism, Nietzsche's atheism made the most sense. Nietzsche is the only atheist who rejects Christianity without trying to borrow its ethics. I respect that he does not shy away from the implications of a godless world even though the world he sees is a nightmare. There is no evil; there are merely actions that are or are not useful to society. Women are possessions "predestined for service."[26] The Jews are "born for slavery."[27] The obstacle for me was, if all this were true, I would have to reject and oppose it because the implications are so barbaric.

This is not to say I rejected it because I did not want it to be true, but because it does not resonate as truth. I reject the notion that I simply inherit my morality from my parents, because people with radically different parents still manage to arrive at essentially the same morality. I reject that tyranny and power are the highest activities of man because, when I abuse others, I experience a guilty conscience, not intellectual concerns for social efficiency. I reject the idea we are hairless monkeys because I see dignity in people that materialism simply cannot explain. If I were to stab someone, describing the incident as "the bag of chemicals called 'Tim' poked a hole in the bag of chemicals called 'Bob'" doesn't fully capture the gravity of what happened. I had no choice but to reject Nietzsche because the world he described does not square with reality.

Nietzsche cited no evidence, but simply offered his statements about morality and God in matter-of-fact, take-it-or-leave-it fashion. Because he made his claims with minimal supporting arguments, there is not much to respond to in terms of evidence or logic. It simply comes down to whether his view seems to reconcile with reality. To me, reality is not so dark and foreboding. If Nietzsche meant to convince me that it truly is and that I am simply viewing it wrong, he should have supported his proposition.

In sum, I find Nietzsche courageous, honest, and consistent. I do not find him convincing because his view of reality is unrealistically dark. Even the New Atheists disagree with his perception of reality: They do not embrace cruelty, tyranny, and the evil inside them the way Nietzsche suggests. In that sense, Nietzsche is the great refuter of the New Atheism because he portrays the very dark world which appears logically consistent with materialism. While New Atheists like Dawkins and Harris may not agree with Nietzsche, the problem is that they lack a basis on which to truly refute him. Nietzsche challenges the New Atheists to prove that the kinder, gentler New Atheism is anything more than a difference of opinion.

In the next chapter you will see Bertrand Russell build on Nietzsche by offering supporting evidence and illustrations. Afterward, you will notice that the New Atheists offer little new material. They mostly just tweak Nietzsche and Russell's arguments.

Nietzsche's Key Concepts

Key Concepts*	Evidence Offered
Atheism is not a new belief.†	Epicurus believed it 300 BC.
Man has moral free will.	*None offered*
We cannot look to nature for guidance on how to live.‡	Nature exhibits no mercy, no justice, no purpose, and no concern. Who would want to live by those guidelines?
Hunger, sexual lust, and vanity are really the "only motives of human actions."	*None offered*
Denied "wishful thinking" argument against belief in God.	Personal opinion
Love and generosity should be concealed and punished.	*None offered*
"Independence is for very few; it is the privilege of the strong."	The concept of freedom for all is taken from Christianity, not from nature.
Personal morality is illusionary.	Buddhist analogies like jumping away from a rope because you think it's a snake when the danger is only in your mind.
Religion is responsible for fights and suffering.	*None offered*

Key Concepts*	Evidence Offered
Only evidence gained from personal observation is credible.	*None offered*
Women lack reason, hate truth, and have an instinct for subservience.	*None offered*
Morality is nothing more than what benefits the utility of the herd.	Roman Empire
The problem is not finding a morality that serves the needs of the community, but rather, justifying a real basis for any morality.	Moralists seem to just be looking for a justification for English ethics.
Enemies are a necessity, otherwise we take out our hostilities upon our peers.	*None offered*
"Life is simply will to power."	*None offered*
A healthy society accepts that "untold human beings" must be reduced to slaves and instruments for its sake.	*None offered*
Exploitation is not a quality of primitive society. It is the essence of life.	*None offered*

Key Concepts*	Evidence Offered
Self-centeredness is the nature of a noble soul.	*None offered*
"The democratic movement is the heir of the Christian movement."	Democracy was contrary to what he deemed to be the natural order of things; namely, that "Independence is for the very few; it is the privilege of the strong."

* only the concepts in bold have been retained in the New Atheism

† retained only by Peter Boghossian

‡ retained only by Sam Harris

Replies and Rebuttals to Nietzsche's Key Concepts

Arguments for Atheism/Against God	Rebuttal
Atheism is not a new belief.	*Agreed*
Man has moral free will.	*Agreed*—however, Nietzsche cannot prove this within his worldview.
We cannot look to nature for guidance on how to live.	*Agreed*
Hunger, sexual lust, and vanity are really the "only motives of human actions."	A gloomy assessment but consistent with materialism.
Denied "wishful thinking" argument against belief in God.	*Agreed*
Love and generosity should be concealed and punished.	If your worldview leads you to this conclusion, you need a better worldview.
"Independence is for very few; it is the privilege of the strong."	*Agreed, if* you believe in materialism. The alpha male lion is more privileged than the rest of the pride (pack). Equality is a concept from Creationism, not Darwinism.*
Personal morality is illusionary.	Only works in books and while philosophizing over coffee. When someone rapes your daughter, it is immediately recognizable as real evil.

84

Arguments for Atheism/Against God	Rebuttal
Religion is responsible for fights and suffering.	History gives ample evidence group hostility is inevitable with or without religion. Even when religion appears to be causal (i.e., Ireland), there are often underlying nonreligious causes.
Only evidence gained from personal observation is credible.	The argument is not based on personal observation and is therefore not credible based on the argument itself.
Women lack reason, hate truth, and have an instinct for subservience.	God describes himself using the same word used to describe Eve. In atheism, however, misogyny is simply a matter of opinion.
Morality is nothing more than what benefits the utility of the herd.	Elimination of the weak, the sick, or the outcast cannot be deemed wrong as long as it serves the majority interest.
The problem is not finding a morality that serves the needs of the community, but rather, justifying a real basis for any morality.	Agreed—atheism cannot offer anything beyond a pragmatic basis for ethics.
Enemies are a necessity, otherwise we take out our hostilities upon our peers.	In theism, there are enemies only as long as other groups align with evil. Enemies are not a necessity in and of themselves.
"Life is simply will to power."	Nietzsche's personal opinion. Would the world be better off if everyone lived by this or by Jesus' teaching to "turn the other cheek"? (Matthew 5:39).

Arguments for Atheism/Against God	Rebuttal
A healthy society accepts "untold human beings" must be reduced to slaves and instruments for its sake.	Here we see the mentality that prepared Germany to carry out the Holocaust.
Exploitation is not a quality of primitive society. It is the essence of life.	One of many dark conclusions Nietzsche drew from atheism. The problem is *in atheism* you can only disagree with this as a matter of personal opinion.
Self-centeredness is the nature of a noble soul.	Another dark conclusion of atheism. *See Exploitation* above.
"The democratic movement is the heir of the Christian movement."	*Agreed*

---

* The stated justification of America's Declaration of Independence was "that all *men are created equal*, that they are endowed by their Creator with certain inalienable rights." Darwinism offers no equivalent moral justification for equality.

5

Bertrand Russell—Classical Atheism

"It is difficult to overstate the extent to which Russell's thought dominated twentieth century analytic philosophy."[1]

NICHOLAS GRIFFIN,
THE CAMBRIDGE COMPANION TO BERTRAND RUSSELL

read Bertrand Russell's book *Why I Am Not a Christian* last. Reading him after the New Atheists demonstrated how oxymoronic the word *new* is in New Atheism. All the arguments about Darwin, religion's effects on society, miracles, the historicity of Christ, etc., were already in place a century ago in Russell's writing. The vast majority of the New Atheists simply try to improve Russell's concepts with better examples. Admittedly, the New Atheists do offer improved illustrations, which made reading Russell after the New Atheists a bit disappointing. In the spirit of fairness, I will occasionally save responses to some of Russell's arguments for later chapters where the arguments have been better presented by the New Atheists. After all, it was atheism's best and brightest that caused me to shed my disbelief.

Despite not finding anything new in Russell, I still heard him out. I was duly impressed that he articulated almost all of the New Atheists' arguments about 100 years before they did. The weakness or absence of Russell's supporting examples should not be held against him when the New Atheists had several decades to improve the illustrations he handed down to them.

Russell was, in fact, my favorite author of the bunch primarily because his arguments are so concise. I appreciate how he got directly to the point. Sam Harris and Nietzsche tied for my second favorite writers. I liked Harris' respectful and articulate demeanor. I loved Nietzsche for his blunt honesty. In terms of being succinct, though, none of them compares to Russell. He raised more valid points in just his preface and first chapter than other atheist writers covered in their entire books. His concise prose can be attributed to the fact these were originally standalone essays and were only later combined into one volume.

Despite my respect for his precise authorship, his content laid the last planks on my bridge out of disbelief by showing just how old the atheists' arguments were. To put the age of these arguments into context, Russell wrote on a typewriter—pre-Internet, precomputer and pretelevision. When he was born, Kitty Hawk was another 30 years away, Thomas Edison had not yet patented the light bulb, and no country allowed universal suffrage. That nothing significantly new has been advanced in favor of atheism since Russell's era completely decimates any notion that atheism is scientifically driven.

In terms of "breakthrough" moments, Darwin gave materialism a huge step forward with his suggestion that design in nature was not caused by a Creator. Edwin Hubble caused it to take a huge step backward when he demonstrated that the universe had a finite origin and exploded into existence without a material cause. But nothing truly revolutionary has been added to the debate since Russell pounded out his book on a typewriter in a room without air-conditioning.*

Russell's Biography

Bertrand was born in England on May 18, 1872 to an influential British noble family. His grandfather, John Russell, served as prime minister of the United Kingdom. The family was quite liberal for their time. His father, John Russell, Viscount Amberley by title, willingly consented to his wife's affair with their children's tutor. His mother, Katharine, Vicountess Amberley, advocated birth control at a time

---

* There are new issues like abiogenesis and DNA. However, no discovery since Russell's era has been an indisputable game changer. The focus of the arguments still remain on Russell's claims.

when it was still considered scandalous, and his grandmother was a campaigner for women's education.

Russell's father was a thoroughgoing atheist who even stipulated in his will that his children be raised agnostics. This takes the wind out of the sails of Russell's argument that "most people believe in God because they have been taught from early infancy to do it,"[2] since Russell likewise advocated what he was raised to believe.

Similar to Nietzsche and Freud, Russell experienced significant trauma in his formative years. His mother died from diphtheria when he was only two years old. Shortly thereafter, his older sister, Rachel, died. His father died of bronchitis following a long bout with depression when Bertrand was four. He was placed in the care of his grandparents, and his grandfather died in 1878 when Bertrand was six. Having experienced so much turmoil at an early age, Bertrand often contemplated suicide in his adolescence.

Bertrand's upbringing was not devoid of religious influence. Ultimately he ended up in the care of his grandmother, a countess from a Scottish Presbyterian family. Lest it be argued that Bertrand's upbringing was religious, we should note he wrote about remembering in detail his father teaching him to question God's existence.[3] Indeed, Bertrand was already reading atheist Percy Shelley in his preteen years with "much sympathy."[4] By age 15, he declared that he found Christian dogma unconvincing and that there was no free will. By 17, he concluded that there was no life after death, and a year later, while still a teenager, he became an atheist.

In August 1920, Russell traveled to Russia as part of an official British government delegation sent to investigate the effects of the Russian Revolution. He met Vladimir Lenin and had an hour-long conversation with him. Russell described him as disappointing in his "impish cruelty." He wrote a book about the trip, *The Practice and Theory of Bolshevism*, describing how he was the only one of the 25 delegates who came home thinking ill of the regime, despite his attempts to convince them otherwise. For example, he related a story about hearing shots fired in the middle of the night that he was sure were clandestine executions, but that the other delegates dismissed as backfiring cars. Russell's reaction is highly ironic, since New Atheists dismiss Soviet atrocities as the result of Marxism. Yet an atheist was the only member of the British government delegation to leave Russia with the impression that something evil was afoot.

Russell's private life was less than exemplary. After several passionate and sometimes simultaneous affairs with a number of women, he impregnated his lover Dora Black while still married to Alys Smith. He divorced Alys in 1921 and married Dora six days later. Some sources suggest that during his second marriage he had another affair with the wife of famous writer T.S. Eliot.[5] His second and third marriages also ended in divorce.

After serving six months in prison during World War I for pacifism, Russell did an about-face, supporting World War II under the justification of "relative political pacifism," claiming that Hitler's victory would permanently threaten democracy.[6] He would go on to claim in 1948 that a US nuclear first strike on the Soviet Union was acceptable because it would produce fewer casualties.[7]

One of the most famous moments of his life was when his appointment to the City College of New York in 1940 was annulled by a court judgment pronouncing him "morally unfit" to teach college. What got him barred from the post was not his atheism, but the views on sexual morality presented in his book *Marriage and Morals*.[8] Even Albert Einstein spoke in Russell's defense during the case.[9]

Between meeting Lenin, surviving a plane crash, being involved in the Cuban missile crisis, and being vouched for by Einstein, Russell is sort of the Forrest Gump of atheism. By that I only mean that he had a very interesting life, not that his intelligence was diminished.

Russell's Argument
Preface

Though Darwin's *On the Origin of Species* had already been in circulation for almost 30 years when Nietzsche wrote *Beyond Good and Evil*, it was Russell who first claimed that Darwin had refuted the theistic argument from design. With Russell, we see atheists begin to incorporate science into their objections to God. Previously, their objections were primarily philosophical.

Russell made the statement, "The question of the truth of a religion is one thing, but the question of its usefulness is another."[10] While he differentiated between truthfulness and effect, he still believed Christianity was both untrue and harmful. By separating the two, however, he raised the very valid point that the actions of religious people are separate from the validity of their beliefs. This went deeper than Nietzsche, who considered only the *effects* of the concepts of God and sin (fights and suffering) without addressing the merits of the concepts themselves.[11]

Still in the preface, Russell added something entirely new to Nietzsche's argument: he provided a definition of faith as "a conviction which cannot be shaken by contrary evidence."[12] Russell's definition has become the *de facto* definition of the New Atheists. For example, Richard Dawkins retains the premise while putting it in his own words: "Faith is belief in spite of, even perhaps because of the lack of evidence."[13]

To close his preface, Russell said, "The world that I should wish to see would be one freed from the virulence of group hostilities."[14] Dawkins echoes this wish in the opening pages of *The God Delusion*, wishing "with John Lennon" for "a world with no religion" that did not have the Northern Ireland Troubles.[15]

[response on page 105]

Why I Am Not a Christian

This chapter was originally a lecture delivered on March 6, 1927 to the South London branch of the National Secular Society. Russell first gave the term *Christian* a specific definition: two defining beliefs in God and immortality. He added that a true Christian must also believe Jesus was at the least the best and wisest of men, if not divine.

He then added:

> When I tell you why I am not a Christian I have to tell you two different things: first, why I do not believe in God and in immortality; and, secondly, why I do not think that Christ was the best and wisest of men, although I grant him a very high degree of moral goodness.[16]

This speech was unique in atheist writing in that it addressed Christianity exclusively. All the other books I have reviewed and critiqued end up lumping diverse beliefs into one pot and failing to consider the possibility that several religions could be wrong yet one could be right. Russell was more realistic in only trying to show how one religion, Christianity, is wrong.

[response on page 107]

The First-Cause Argument

Russell tackled the first-cause argument, which is the observation that everything we see in this world has a cause. Nothing is seen to cause itself. Therefore, if we go back up the chain of causes, we eventually arrive at a First Cause, whom we give the name God.

Russell questioned the need for a First Cause. In his words, "There is no reason to suppose that the world had a beginning at all."[17] An eternal world, according to Russell, eliminates the need for a First Cause.

Even if the world was not eternal, Russell claimed that postulating God to solve the First Cause argument was still problematic. He described the problem, "My father taught me that the question, 'Who made me?' cannot be answered, since it immediately suggests the further question 'Who made God?'...If everything must have a cause, then God must have a cause. If there can be anything without a cause, it may just as well be the world as God."

Even if the world had come into being, Russell still saw no need for a cause. In his words, "There is no reason why the world could not have come into being without a cause."[18]

[response on page 108]

The Natural-Law Argument

In his discussion of natural law, Russell made an interesting observation:

> There is, as we all know, a law that if you throw dice you
> will get double sixes only about once in thirty-six times,
> and we do not regard that as evidence the fall of the dice

is regulated by design; on the contrary, if the double sixes
came every time we should think that there was design.[19]

I find this interesting because Russell outlined what kind of odds
would suggest design long before scientists calculated the probability
of our universe occurring by chance. It turned out the odds against the
chance occurrence of our universe were far greater than Russell's odds
in favor of design. However, this fact has not fazed the New Atheists,
who continue to revise upward what odds would demand a design
hypothesis.

[response on page 109]

The Argument from Design

Russell then raised the argument of poor design, which is still popular today:

> It is a most astonishing thing that people can believe that
> this world, with all the things that are in it, with all its
> defects should be the best the omnipotence and omni-
> science have been able to produce in millions of years.[20]

He questioned what kind of God creates a world with the Ku Klux
Klan and observed that human life on this planet will die out in due
course.

Dawkins further develops Russell's argument by pointing to flaws
in organs. He says "evolved organs, elegant and efficient as they often
are, also demonstrate revealing flaws—exactly as you'd expect if they
have an evolutionary history, and exactly as you would not expect if
they were designed."[21] Christopher Hitchens adds to this what science
has since taught us about the entire universe's impending heat death.

[response on page 109]

The Moral Arguments for Deity

Russell then observed that Immanuel Kant, in *Critique of Pure Reason*, was convinced of God's existence due to a moral argument. Russell
claimed Kant's mistake was that he "believed implicitly in the maxims

that he had imbibed at his mother's knee."[22] Russell believed Kant mis-identified his moral inclinations as evidence of God because he failed to understand that they were not absolute truth, just the maxims his mother taught him.

[response on page 110]

The Argument for the Remedying of Injustice

Russell attacked the idea that God is required to remedy injustice in the next life since justice is often thwarted on Earth. He said that if you open a crate of oranges and find the top layer of oranges are bad, that does not mean the bottom oranges will "redress the balance" by being good.

He also raised the still-popular objection that "most people believe in God because they have been taught from early infancy to do it."[23] Immediately thereafter he said, "Then I think the next most powerful reason is the wish for safety, a sort of feeling that there is a big brother who will look after you. That plays a very profound part in influencing people's desire for a belief in God."[24]

[response on page 110]

Defects in Christ's Teaching

Russell was the first in this group to challenge "whether Christ ever existed at all."[25] Dawkins echoes this argument, but Harris and Hitchens do not, at least to the best of my knowledge.

Dawkins brings up several biblical passages in *The God Delusion*, but his understanding of the Bible has been called suspect even by the secular press, let alone apologists and theologians.* Thus, I personally agree with Terry Eagleton that atheists like Russell were the last to seriously consider Jesus' teachings.

It is a bit of a paradox that Russell would give consideration to Jesus'

---

* While Dawkins' book received accolades, his handling of biblical texts faced criticism. A particularly biting critic was Terry Eagleton, who wrote: "Imagine someone holding forth on biology whose only knowledge of the subject is the *Book of British Birds*, and you have a rough idea of what it feels like to read Richard Dawkins on theology...they [rationalists like Dawkins] invariably come up with vulgar caricatures of religious faith that would make a first-year theology student wince" (http://www.lrb.co.uk/v28/n20/terry-eagleton/lunging-flailing-mispunching).

teaching though he doubted his existence. He never explained this contradiction. Russell had two objections to Jesus' teaching: defects and moral problems. The sole defect Russell noted was that Jesus appeared to have been wrong about the timing of his second coming. The moral problem was that "[no] person who is really profoundly humane can believe in everlasting punishment...I really do not think that a person with a proper degree of kindliness in his nature would have put fears and terror of that sort in the world."[26] This argument has been expanded by the New Atheists. For example, Dawkins illustrates the same concept with the story of a woman who sought counseling to deal with fears of hell she learned in childhood.

[response on page 111]

The Emotional Factor

Regarding the role of emotion in faith, Russell said, "I do not think that the real reason why people accept religion has anything to do with argumentation. They accept religion on emotional grounds."[27]

[response on page 112]

Has Religion Made Useful Contributions to Civilization?

This chapter was originally an essay published by Russell in 1930. It was later bound into one volume. Russell wrote, "My own view on religion is that of Lucretius. I regard it as a disease born of fear and as a source of untold misery to the human race. I cannot, however, deny that it has made some contributions to civilization."[28] He listed two contributions: the Gregorian calendar, and the ability of Egyptian priests to predict eclipses. Regarding other useful contributions, he said, "I do not know of any other."[29]

In assessing the contributions of Christianity, Russell claimed we need to judge Christianity not by Christ but by the church. He said,

> Christ taught that you should give your goods to the poor, that you should not fight, that you should not go to church, and that you should not punish adultery. Neither Catholics nor Protestants have shown any strong desire to follow His teaching in any of these respects.[30]

Russell pointed out that when some religious orders tried to follow doctrines of poverty, they were condemned by the Pope and that
"judge not, that ye be not judged" (Matthew 7:1 KJV) was ignored during the Inquisition and by the Ku Klux Klan.

[response on page 112]

Christianity and Sex

In the section *Christianity and Sex*, Russell said, "The worst fea-
ture of the Christian religion, however, is its attitude toward sex." He
accused the church of wrecking sex by making sex dirty and doing
whatever it could to "secure that the only form of sex which it permitted should involve very little pleasure and a great deal of pain."[31]

Russell went on to say that the church's view on sex had led to awful
positions about sex education for young people. Said Russell, "The artificial ignorance on sex subjects which orthodox Christians attempt to
enforce upon the young is extremely dangerous to mental and physical health."[32] He compared it to taking a boy who is interested in trains,
telling him his interest in trains is wicked, keeping his eyes bandaged
whenever a train is on the railway, and even forbidding him to use the
word *train*. This would increase, not diminish, his interest in trains. In
addition, he would feel a morbid sense of sin because he was taught his
interest was improper.

Still in the section on sex, Russell raised a powerful albeit uncorre-
lated argument about the problem of God being both good and omnipotent. His omnipotence means that before he created the world, "he
foresaw all the pain and misery that it would contain." God is "therefore responsible for all of it," said Russell. He pointed out that if he
begat a child knowing that it would be a homicidal maniac, he would
be responsible for his child's crimes.[33]

Russell continued using the problem of pain to build a case against
God by saying, "I would invite any Christian to accompany me to the
children's ward of a hospital, to watch the suffering that is there being
endured, and then to persist in the assertion that those children are so
morally abandoned as to deserve what they are suffering."[34] Here he
was stating the problem of theodicy by example without articulating

all its points. In the spirit of fairness, I will strengthen Russell's argument by outlining the underlying theory, even though Russell himself did not outline these points.

The issue of theodicy utilizes three claims about God:

1. God is perfectly good.

2. God is all-powerful.

3. God does not prevent the existence of natural and moral evil.

The problem is that only two out of three can be true. For example, if there is evil in the world, God is either not perfectly good (since he would not then allow evil if he were all-powerful), or not all-powerful (since he apparently could not prevent evil if he were perfectly good). The third option, though rarely stated, is that God is perfectly good and all-powerful; therefore, evil is only illusionary (as in Buddhism). This is an extremely old argument that goes back to Plotinus, who lived about 150 years after Plato.[35]

[response on page 113]

The Soul and Immortality

In the subsection "The Soul and Immortality," Russell showed profound historical contemplation. He correlated the Christian emphasis on one's individual soul to Christianity's rise under the tyranny of the Roman Empire. Russell said the natural impulse of people with character is to try to do good in society. But when a group is deprived of political power—as the early Christians were—members of the group will shift their focus to personal holiness. Socially beneficial actions must be abandoned because

> holiness had to be something that could be achieved by people who were impotent in action. Social virtue came therefore to be excluded from Christian ethics. To this day conventional Christians think an adulterer more wicked than a politician who takes bribes, although the latter probably does a thousand times more harm.[36]

This idea is both profound and unique to Russell—the idea that Christianity started out inwardly focused because politics prevented it from enacting social change. Russell claimed it takes a "herd instinct" to force people not to focus on themselves as the early Christians did. In this we hear faint echoes of Nietzsche's idea that morality is exclusively defined by our relationship to society. If he was agreeing with Nietzsche, the implication is that Christianity ignores meaningful herd morality in favor of meaningless personal piety.

[response on page 116]

The Doctrine of Free Will

In this section, Russell touched on the problematic issue of free will. As we have already seen, Nietzsche claimed that humans have it, although he failed to substantiate the claim. He merely asserted it without evidence.

Russell took the challenge a bit more seriously, acknowledging that the concept of free will is hard to justify in a purely materialistic world. He said, "Materialists use the laws of physics to show, or attempt to show, that the movements of human bodies are mechanically determined."[37] The problem with this is plain. Said Russell, "If, when a man writes a poem or commits a murder, the bodily movements involved in his act result solely from physical causes, it would seem absurd to put up a statue to him in the one case and to hang him in the other."[38] Despite the problems raised by naturalism, he seemed to disagree that we are chemically programmed machines because he believed character could be trained.

He also commented on evolution in the midst of this section, echoing Nietzsche's assertion that Darwinism strips man of dignity. Russell said, "They [who believe in evolution] have seen that it will not do to make claims on behalf of man which are totally different from those which are made on behalf of animals." In the next chapter he said, "Man is a part of nature, not something contrasted with nature."[39]

Still in the section on free will, Russell made a comment about miracles. Although he merely mentioned this in passing, this statement is pregnant with meaning: "miracles are acts of God which contravene the laws governing ordinary phenomena."[40] He took this definition of miracles from David Hume, who interpreted miracles as "a transgression of a law of nature by a particular volition of the Deity, or by the interposition of some invisible agent."[41] Hume believed that weighing evidence was the only way to evaluate empirical claims such as "Jesus turned water into wine" or "the laws of chemistry are not altered by prayer." However, to claim that natural laws have been violated requires extraordinary evidence, because the evidence that the laws of nature are unalterable is "a firm and unalterable experience."[42] For example, while Jesus' "miracle" of turning water into wine may have been witnessed by perhaps a dozen or more people, the number of witnesses that H_2O does not spontaneously change chemical composition is in the magnitude of billions. Therefore, the eyewitness testimony of a few billion trumps the eyewitness testimony of the dozen. On this basis, Hume concluded miracles do not occur. This has been the de facto position of atheism ever since Hume. In fact, famous atheist Antony Flew wrote the foreword to a 1985 reprinting of Hume's *Of Miracles.*[43]

Miracles aside, coming back to the idea of making choices and whether we have free will, Russell pointed out that the morality of one choice over another is illusory. He again borrowed from Nietzsche the idea that we must look "beyond good and evil," as these are meaningless terms. Said Russell, "A man who is suffering from plague has to be imprisoned until he is cured, although nobody thinks him wicked. The same thing should be done with a man who suffers from a propensity to commit forgery; but there should be no more idea of guilt in the one case than in the other."[44] He expanded on this in the next chapter by saying, "The view that criminals are 'wicked' and 'deserve' punishment is not one which a rational morality can support."[45]

[response on page 117]

The Idea of Righteousness

This is yet another section where Russell echoed Nietzsche. Note that he adopted Nietzsche's descriptor for humanity: "the herd."

Now, what is "unrighteousness" in practice? It is in practice

behavior of a kind disliked by the herd. By calling it unrighteousness, and by arranging an elaborate system of ethics
around this conception, the herd justifies itself in wreak-
ing punishment upon the objects of its own dislike, while
at the same time, since the herd is righteous by definition,
it enhances its own self-esteem at the very moment it lets
loose its impulse to cruelty.[46]

[response on page 119]

Russell's Famous Reply to God

Russell is most often quoted for his celestial teapot analogy and for
his claim about what he would say were he to die and be confronted by
God for his disbelief. Dawkins quotes Russell, "Not enough evidence,
God, not enough evidence."[47]

That is not exactly what Russell said, although the gist is the same.
Those words were attributed to him by Emily Eakin in a May 11, 2002
article in *The New York Times*,[48] but she was misquoting an older interview of Russell by Leo Rosten. Here is the excerpt from the original
interview:

> I [Leo Rosten] asked, "Let us suppose, sir, that after you
> have left this sorry vale, you actually found yourself in
> heaven, standing before the Throne. There, in all his glory,
> sat the Lord—not Lord Russell, sir: God." Russell winced.
> "What would you think?"
>
> "I would think I was dreaming."
>
> "But suppose you realized you were not? Suppose that there,
> before your eye, beyond a shadow of a doubt, was God.
> What would you say?"
>
> The pixie wrinkled his nose, "I probably would ask, 'Sir,
> why did you not give me better evidence?'"[49]

[response on page 119]

Russell on Dachau

Russell never committed some of his most radical views to paper, and probably for good reason. One notable example was a comment he made in an interview shortly after World War II, claiming that "'Dachau is wrong' is not a fact."[50] He immediately went on to say he *felt* the Nazi concentration camps were wrong but he could not prove it was factually wrong in the same way he could prove gravity is a fact.

[response on page 120]

What I Believe

What I Believe was published as a pamphlet in 1925. It includes many themes we have already covered, such as the idea that man is not distinct from nature, fear causes religion, and criminals are not morally different from someone who catches a cold.

One of a few new ideas in this essay is the mind-body problem. As Russell described it,

> What we call our "Thoughts" seem to depend upon the organization of tracks in the brain in the same sort of way in which journeys depend upon roads and railways. The energy used in thinking seems to have a chemical origin; for instance, a deficiency of iodine will turn a clever man into an idiot. Mental phenomena seem to be bound up with material structure.[51]

In this same pamphlet, Russell explicitly stated, "I do not pretend to be able to prove that there is no God."[52]

Elaborating on his view that we cannot know anything to be ethical or not, Russell said, "I do not believe that we can decide what sort of conduct is right or wrong except by reference to its probable consequences," and that no one can tell us what we *ought* to desire because "what we 'ought' to desire is merely what someone else wishes us to desire."[53]

[response on page 120]

Our Sexual Ethics

Russell published *Our Sexual Ethics* in 1936. He wrote more about sexuality than the rest of these authors combined. Lest I open myself to the charge of using sex to sell books, I must point out that as much space as Russell devotes to sexual topics, I would not have accurately summarized his positions and priorities if I completely glazed over it. In fact, a search of his book on books.Google.com found more references to "venereal disease" in his writing than to "miracles," "Jesus," or "design."

One of Russell's more controversial notions was that virginity is undesirable because it is "unlikely that a person without previous sexual experience, whether man or woman, will be able to distinguish between mere physical attraction and the sort of congeniality that is necessary in order to make marriage a success."[54] He also believed "wives, just as much as prostitutes, live by the sale of their sexual charms."

Russell set a precedent that the New Atheists later adopt of offering alternative, nonreligious explanations for our sense of morality. Indeed, since theists have long argued that our moral sense comes from God, the best way to refute that argument is to demonstrate how God is not required for a sense of right and wrong. For example, Russell associated the taboo on adultery with "the desire of males to be certain of paternity."[55] He asserted it is hard to imagine that fatherhood, with all its responsibilities, could have become the basis of social institutions unless fathers were reasonably sure the child they were supporting was their own. On this basis Russell concluded, "It was, accordingly, wicked to have relations with another man's wife but not even mildly reprehensible to have relations with an unmarried woman."[56]

In closing, he said there are people who, by conventional standards, are sexually virtuous and therefore "often consider themselves thereby absolved from behaving like decent human beings."[57] He said moralists who are obsessed with sex emphasize it over other socially useful ethical considerations.

[response on page 122]

Can Religion Cure Our Troubles?

This final essay was published in two parts in a Stockholm newspaper in November 1954. In it, Russell addressed "the question whether societies can practice a sufficient modicum of morality if they are not helped by dogmatic religion."[58] Russell observed there are two kinds of morality: one which has "no basis except in a religious creed," and another which has "an obvious basis in social utility." He took the example of theft, acknowledging that "criminals are not always caught, and the police may be unduly lenient to the powerful. If people can be persuaded that there is a God who will punish theft, even when the police fail, it would seem like that this belief would promote honesty."[59] Having conceded this frank admission that belief in God's justice might have a restraining effect on society, Russell went on to argue that the "grave evils" committed by religion far outweigh the good which might be accomplished by associating morality with theology. Russell said, "I was concerned with the evils resulting from any system of dogmas presented for acceptance, not on the ground of truth, but on the ground of social utility,"[60] and "I can only feel profound moral reprobation for those who say that religion ought to be believed because it is useful, that whether it is true is a waste of time."[61]

[response on page 124]

6

A Response to Bertrand Russell

*"I would never die for my beliefs
because I might be wrong."*[1]

BERTRAND RUSSELL,
WHY I AM NOT A CHRISTIAN

I appreciate Russell's candid admission that he might be wrong. More recently, the debate has become more polarized, with neither side willing to make such magnanimous concessions. Russell once wrote, "The trouble with the world is that the stupid are cocksure and the intelligent are full of doubt." Nevertheless, he sounded cocksure in his speeches and essays. While Russell had some good insights, I doubt most of his conclusions. Judge the following for yourself.

Preface

Russell claimed that Darwin destroyed the Argument from Design. Since Russell mentioned this only in passing without offering any evidence, I defer replying till the chapter on Richard Dawkins, who better defends the position.

I find myself agreeing with Russell that the truth of religion and the effect of religion are two distinct and separate issues. This important distinction, although raised by an atheist, seems lost on the New Atheists. Harris seems to understand it when he says, "The fact that religious beliefs have a great influence on human life says nothing at all about their *validity* [emphasis his]."[2] However, he then proceeds along with the rest of the New Atheists to argue against religion based on the actions of religious people, as if religion's effect proved their beliefs untrue. That line of argumentation is as illogical as suggesting that parents cease to exist if their children turn out immoral. When Casey Anthony was charged with killing her daughter Caylee, did Casey's parents cease to exist? When the verdict came in that Casey was innocent, did her parents resume existing? The questions make no sense because the premise is illogical.

If we answer the question that religion causes harm in the affirmative, then we have arrived at nothing more than that religious people need to change their actions. We have not, however, offered any reason to not believe in God. Although Russell believed Christianity failed both the test of truth and of effect, he was at least discerning enough to acknowledge these as two separate issues. By contrast, the New Atheists devote entire chapters to the effect of religion on the flawed premise that the effect of religion has any bearing on its truth.

Russell committed a semantic fallacy when he misclassified Communism as a religion. He likewise twisted definitions when he tried to redefine faith as conviction despite contrary evidence. I had to dig through four dictionaries to find even a secondary definition that sounds even remotely close to Russell's uncommon use of the term *faith*. The primary and usual meaning that every dictionary listed first was trust.

I have faith that my wife is loyal. I trust she is sitting in a classroom at the University of Central Florida while I write this and not in the bed of another man. Can I prove that? No, but that does not mean my faith in her is *contrary* to evidence. When I trust my wife it is *because* of evidence. She has established a track record of loyalty and she goes out of her way to care for me. I have also witnessed how she responds when I get hurt. It is because of what I do know that I can trust her about the things I do not know.

I amassed a room-sized personal library while completing my master's at Dallas Theological Seminary, and not once did I ever come across a single Christian author who advocated believing despite evidence. Quite the contrary, I read entire volumes presenting evidence why it was reasonable to put trust in Christ.

My personal definition of faith is "choosing to believe the most plausible option even if it cannot be proved." For example, if I waited for proof my spouse loved me, I would never get married. It is always possible our spouse is just using us till someone better comes along. You could never, ever empirically prove your spouse's love, yet you choose to believe it. Contrary to evidence? Of course not. We believe because of evidence.

Faith is used even in science. Even Sam Harris acknowledges "that we never prove a theory right; we merely fail to prove it wrong."[3] It is always possible additional discoveries may show a scientific model is wrong, but we choose to believe it because it is the most plausible explanation of the evidence we currently possess. Likewise, after careful examination, I chose to believe in the resurrection not because it could be empirically proven, but because it is the best explanation of the evidence we possess.

Like Russell and Dawkins, I wish for a world free of group hostilities. I just find it naïve to believe eliminating religion would accomplish this. The source of "The Troubles" in Ireland, which both Russell and Dawkins cite as an example of the problem with religion, actually had nothing to do with religion.[4] The division was between the Unionists (who happened to be predominantly Catholic) who wanted a free, united Ireland and the Loyalists (who happened to be predominantly Protestant) who wanted Northern Ireland to remain within the United Kingdom. The background was that English settlers (who happened to be Protestants) were given land taken from native Irish people who, you guessed it, happened to be Catholic. If someone comes, takes your farm, and declares, "This belongs to me now," you do not need religion to despise that person. This is a basic fact of human nature that appears lost on Russell and Dawkins.

[original argument on page 90]

Why I Am Not a Christian

I find it commendable that Russell freely admitted it was incumbent on him to explain why he did not believe in God and why he thought Jesus was not a great man. The New Atheists have redefined their position to "No credible evidence has been presented for belief in God" and placed the burden of proof entirely upon theists. Russell was at least magnanimous enough to offer justification for his beliefs.

[original argument on page 91]

The First-Cause Argument

Russell claimed the universe did not need a cause because it could be eternal. Yet Russell contradicted himself in an essay published three years later when he acknowledged, "The second law of thermodynamics makes it scarcely possible to doubt the universe is running down."[5] He clearly understood this makes it impossible that the universe is eternal because it would have run down an eternity ago. He refuted himself by contradicting his own position.

Russell not only refuted himself, science also refuted him. The same year he delivered this speech, Edwin Hubble discovered the red shift in light that conclusively proved the universe did have a finite beginning at the Big Bang. Thanks to science, we now know the universe is not eternal.

Once science disproved Russell's eternal universe premise, rather than acknowledge his error, he simply changed his argument to claiming the universe could have spontaneously arisen without a cause. Theists posit the universe needs a cause because we never observe things spontaneously popping into existence without a cause. Russell, however, was content to assume the universe did exactly that.

I noted that atheists like Russell and Dawkins advance the argument that Jesus did not rise from the dead because resurrection is contrary to our observations today. They are logically inconsistent when they then turn around and assert that the universe is causeless, despite this being contrary to everything we observe about causes today.

Russell's question "Who made God?" commits the logical fallacy of a category mistake. A category mistake is when "things of one kind are presented as if they belong to another."[6] An eternal being does not have the property of a creator like numbers do not have the property of color. Asking "Who made God?" is as illogical as asking "What color is the number nine?"

[original argument on page 92]

The Natural Law Argument

It baffles me how an atheist like Russell can admit that a pair of dice which roll sixes every time should be regarded as designed, even though the odds of this occurring by chance are only one in thirty-six,[7] yet New Atheists like Dawkins can look at a universe whose odds of coming into existence by chance are 1 in 10^{138} and assume there is no design involved.[8] The rules of what constitutes evidence of design are certainly being applied inconsistently.

[original argument on page 92]

The Argument from Design

Arguing that something is poorly designed does not prove that it was not designed. Typewriters were less than optimally designed for writing books and are now "extinct." Nevertheless, typewriters were clearly designed.

Recent scientific discoveries have shown us how designs we thought were less than optimal can be far more elegant than they appear at first glance. When the full genome was sequenced, it was thought to be comprised of 98 percent "junk" DNA (DNA that does not encode protein sequences).[9] However, in 2012, after a decade of research, the ENCODE project found that 80 percent of the human genome serves some purpose after all.[10]

"Junk" DNA is not the only example of something scientists initially thought was poor design turning out to be good design after all. In his book *The Cell's Design*, biochemist Fazale Rana discusses the example of the enzyme RuBisCO. He says, "What we initially understand to be bad designs in nature actually turns out to be elegant designs as we learn more about how those systems operate. Often times the appearance of bad design stems from poor or incomplete understanding of a system."[11] RuBisCO is an enzyme involved in the first major step of carbon fixation, a process by which atmospheric carbon dioxide is converted by plants to energy-rich molecules such as glucose. Ecosystems are dependent on this enzyme in terms of photosynthesis and carbon fixation. While some enzymes can carry out thousands of chemical reactions each second, RuBisCO was thought to be very sloppy in terms of its catalytic activity, being able to fix only three to ten carbon dioxide molecules each second per molecule of enzyme.[12] As Dr. Rana describes it, "It turns out the enzymes in nature are actually operating optimally."

Perhaps the biggest problem with the poor design argument is you must know the *intent* of the designer to judge whether something is optimally or poorly designed. My iPad is elegantly designed for reading this book on an airplane. It is very poorly designed for running NASA Mission Control. You cannot deem the design good or bad until you know whether the designer's intent was portability or massive computing capability.

Take Hitchens' example of the future heat death of the universe. If the universe were intended to last into perpetuity, then yes, it was badly designed. But if it was designed to last for a fixed period after which God plans to intervene, then the design is perfectly fine.

[original argument on page 93]

The Moral Arguments for Deity

Russell dismissed our internal moral compass as merely our mother's moral teaching. He failed to consider the possibility that things our parents teach us could *also* be absolutely true. I learned math from my parents. That does not mean math is not absolutely true.

[original argument on page 93]

The Argument for the Remedying of Injustice

Russell made a good point that injustice in this life does not prove that God must exist in order to remedy injustice in the next life. However, this is a straw-man attack. I could not find any Christian who has ever advanced it.

When Russell suggested people believe in God simply because of their parents' teaching, he committed the same error he offered regarding our moral sense. In my early infancy I was taught the order of the alphabet is A, B, C, D, E, F, G... My teachers taught a catchy song to help me learn it. There is no logical reason to question the order of the alphabet simply because I learned it in infancy.

The irony of Russell's argument is that he himself was taught atheism by his parents, yet Russell nowhere suggested that his atheism should be questioned for that reason. Apparently skepticism is necessary only if one's parents were monotheists. Once again, I'm unimpressed by how hypocritically and unevenly the standard is applied.

In similar manner, Russell suggested people choose to believe in God because it comforts them. However, he never acknowledged the comfort atheists take from the belief that no one can hold them accountable beyond this life. Nietzsche was the last atheist to honestly admit, "Nobody is very likely to consider a doctrine true merely because it makes people happy."[13] From Russell onward, however, atheists have maintained this assertion that people choose to believe in God merely because it makes them happy. It cannot be a very good argument if even an atheist like Nietzsche can see the fallacy.

[original argument on page 94]

Defects in Christ's Teaching

Russell was the first of these authors to question whether Christ ever existed at all. According to Albert Schweitzer, who wrote the definitive summary of historical Jesus research, Bruno Bauer was the first to question whether Jesus existed. Bauer's rejection of Jesus' historicity was based solely on his opinion that certain sayings like "let the dead bury their own dead," in his opinion, "would not have been fitting for Jesus to speak."[14] Therefore he thought they were later made up by someone else.

It is worth noting no one questioned the historicity of Jesus until after the Enlightenment. Novel interpretations of Scripture were not based on new evidence, but an *a priori* assumption that precluded the supernatural, and none have garnered widespread acceptance.

Russell claimed no good person can believe in everlasting punishment because the idea is inhumane. Using the same flawed logic, some people deny the Holocaust because they cannot accept its inhumanity. The issue, however, is whether it happened, not how we feel about it. If we are less inclined to believe it because of the inhumanity of it, we are only deluding ourselves to make ourselves feel better.

In Budapest, Hungary, I visited the House of Terror museum. It is housed in the former headquarters of the Soviet State Protection Authority. In that building, from 1945 to 1956, Communist secret police beat, tortured, and executed political prisoners by the hundreds. It would be very unkind to put reports of "fears and terrors" like that in the ears of Hungarians back then *if they were not true.* Since all those ghastly horrors did in fact happen, however, it was actually quite responsible to warn people about this place. Likewise, Jesus' teaching about hell is inhumane *only if it is not true.* Russell's entire argument was based on an *a priori,* unproven assumption that hell is not real. Until Russell proved otherwise, he had no grounds to call Jesus unkind. It could, in fact, have been quite responsible of Jesus to warn people about going there, just like a responsible Hungarian parent would counsel a teenager to avoid tangling with the secret police.

[original argument on page 94]

The Emotional Factor

Russell's argument that people select their beliefs emotionally is a double-edged sword. It cuts as much against his own position as anyone else's. Russell lost his father, mother, sister, and grandfather all by age six. It would be natural for anyone who endured such loss to question God's goodness.

[original argument on page 95]

Has Religion Made Useful Contributions to Civilization?

Russell's suggestion that religion's only useful contributions are calendars and predictions of astronomical events demonstrates how deeply he was in denial. According to the American Hospital Association's 2013 annual report, 58 percent of community hospitals are not-for-profit, and the majority of these are religious, which means about 21 million people received medical care in faith-based hospitals last year in the US alone.[15] Catholic orphanages are found in all large American cities. Close to 300 orphanages provide a home to nearly 50,000 children; that is just one branch of Christianity in one country.[16] Just one Christian organization, the Salvation Army, provides beds for 23,752 homeless people, houses 19,800 people in addiction recovery programs, cares for 1934 refuges, and assists 1 million people in disaster recovery every year.[17] The way Russell ignored religion's humanitarian contributions reveals either complete ignorance or a willful intent to mislead. By opening an essay with such a misleading statement, Russell demonstrated his willingness to say anything, however untrue, to make his point. He revealed he had no sincere interest in honest answers.

[original argument on page 95]

Christianity and Sex

Regarding the effect of religion on sex, I remained a virgin into my late twenties because I wanted to follow God's plan for marriage. I admittedly did so with much frustration; I saw it as an act of devotion. Therefore, one of the first lifestyle changes I made after giving up on religion was freely engaging in sex. However, I soon found it even less fulfilling than abstinence. There was often a disconnect between what it meant to one partner versus the other, which led to numerous fights and hurt feelings. Even the enticing "perfect" no-strings-attached encounters eventually left me feeling emotionally empty.

It seemed to me that people like Russell who claim religion ruins sex have fully subscribed to pop culture instead of reality. Contrary to how marriage is portrayed on TV and in films, numerous scientific studies have shown married couples have both more sex and more varied sex than singles.[18] A University of Virginia study found not only is there more sex within marriage, but the quality is so much better that twice as many married as single women say they are "very happy."[19] Myths that are circulated as "common sense" about sexuality, like the common prescription for cohabitation before marriage, have been disproven by studies showing cohabiters who marry are 46 percent more likely to divorce than people who marry without living together first.[20]

Russell strongly advocated the joy of extramarital sex. This makes me wonder: If he found extramarital sex as fulfilling as he claimed, why did he get married four times?

?????

The problem of God being both good and omnipotent was one of Russell's best arguments. It caused me to put down his book and stop for reflection. At face value, he seemed to have a valid point: is God responsible for suffering if He possesses both attributes? While it initially sounds compelling, it is logically flawed on many levels. First, it completely fails to account for free will. Regarding his example of giving birth to a homicidal child, we do not hold any parent responsible for a child's actions unless there was some unusual scenario like abuse, where the child's will was overruled such that they were carrying out the parent's will instead of their own. Bertrand failed to reconcile omniscience with free will. *Knowing* of a future crime does not equal *causing* a future crime.

Second, *everyone* knows bringing a child into the world will mean pain. This is nothing unique to God. There is the pain of scraped knees, broken bones, or a broken heart from the breakup of our first "true love." Although we do not know the exact form that pain will take, we do know that pain is a certainty. Therefore, by Russell's definition, every parent is evil for bringing a child into a world despite the reality of pain.

Russell invited us to accompany him to the children's ward of a hospital and then ask ourselves how a good God would allow such suffering. He failed to consider how humans respond to suffering. Consider, for example, what happened after the tragic shootings of December 14, 2012 at Sandy Hook Elementary. Why is it whenever there is a tragedy like Sandy Hook, millions of parents forego working overtime to spend time with their children, take family vacations, or simply turn off the TV in favor of family time? The same opportunity was always available to them before. Why does it take a tragedy to change our behavior? Psychologist John Grohol says we forget "appreciation for life" in times of tranquility.[21] It seems human nature prevents us from appreciating the good we have without the existence of evil as a frame of reference.

We work long hours and take time with our children for granted until others lose theirs. Our behavior seems to suggest that we grasp our own blessings only in light of others' suffering. It is human nature that gratefulness is proportional to adversity. As adversity approaches zero, so does gratefulness.

How do we understand the blessing of a healthy baby when we

have never seen a sick one? In a world where every baby is born in perfect health, "healthy" becomes meaningless. In such a world, it is just another baby.

If Ferrari were to open a factory in Mexico that allowed them to sell Ferraris for $18,000 and they were as common as Toyota Camrys, would that not diminish the prestige of owning a Ferrari? More importantly, what would the value of a Ferrari be if it were just like every other car on the road?

? ? ? ?

Theodicy would be a problem if this world is all there is. However, the whole "problem" is tied to the corollary assumption that nothing follows this life. It is simply assumed that this world is the only thing that matters. Thus the possibility that evil could accomplish some future good is ruled out *ipso facto*.

Take the example of a baby chick struggling to be born. If you break the egg to make birth "easier" for him, you will kill him. He needs the struggle to get through the first stage of his life. The struggle is what gives him the strength to get by in the "real world" beyond the shell. If you break the chick out, he will be weak, fragile, and unfit for life. If you assume the shell is everything, then of course life inside the shell is a torturous existence indeed. On the other hand, if there is anything beyond the shell, the struggle is part and parcel of living on the other side. In short, theodicy is a problem only if it is assumed that evil cannot possibly be preparation for eternity.

The obvious objection is that God cannot be excused for evil on the assumption that there is an afterlife. Bear in mind, though, the very question of evil presumes God's existence. C.S. Lewis, the famous atheist turned Christian, said the problem of theodicy was one of the main things that led him to faith. He realized that asking why there was injustice in the universe assumed an absolute standard of justice as his point of reference. As he said in *Mere Christianity*,

> My argument against God was that the universe seemed
> so cruel and unjust. But how had I got this idea of just and

unjust? A man does not call a line crooked unless he has some idea of a straight line. What was I comparing this universe with when I called it unjust?[22]

In other words, when we ask why God could allow evil, the question *presumes* God's existence. The argument requires us to sit in God's lap in order to slap his face! For Lewis the atheist, the problem of why he thought there *was evil* in the world was an even bigger problem than why God would allow it. Without God, there is no natural or moral evil that requires a reckoning. Things are just the way they are. Without God, what is *is*. Our innate awareness that things *ought* to be different presumes a moral agent capable of making them that way.

In sum, the problem with evil is not "Why does God allow evil?" The real problem is "Why do I think *anything* is evil?" The moment we perceive something is evil (rather than simply recognizing it as the way things are), we have presumed a standard of good as our basis of comparison.

[original argument on page 96]

The Soul and Immortality

Russell's suggestion that early Christians shifted the focus of piety onto personal holiness rather than societal change is conceptually profound. Unfortunately, it is historically wrong. By the time Peter preached his second sermon, long before he sent out missionaries or took time to organize the church's leadership structure, the church was already pooling their resources so that "there were no needy persons among them" (Acts 4:34). Russell, who seems at times to be biblically literate, completely overlooked Paul and Barnabas' famine relief efforts in Jerusalem during the mid AD 40s (Romans 15:26). This is exactly the kind of meaningful social contribution he claimed did not exist in the early church. The church has always prioritized the care of the poor, elderly, and downtrodden. In fact, it took secular life insurance companies 1700 years to catch up with what the church was doing for widows and orphans since the first century.[23] Russell is simply completely ignorant of history.

The atheist argument that "Christians are so heavenly minded they are of no earthly good" is a tired one dating back to Russell.* While it sounds good conceptually, like Russell's inaccurate portrayal of historical evidence, it has no evidentiary basis.

[original argument on page 97]

The Doctrine of Free Will

Materialists struggle to explain free will. The contradiction between materialism and free will prevented me from embracing atheism. We intuitively sense that writing a poem and committing a murder are not equivalent actions, but if it is true all our actions are simply the product of our brain chemistry, there is no basis to label one "immoral" and the other "virtuous." I could not help but notice that although Russell acknowledged this problem, just like Nietzsche, he offered no solution.

Russell's claim that man has no more dignity than animals is the kind of candidly honest revelation from a great skeptic that pushed me back toward faith. When I listen, really pay attention, to what materialism means, I wonder how atheists glaze over these problems. In materialism, it simply will not do to ascribe more dignity to man than you would to a snake or even a rat. This does not seem to reconcile with reality. I cannot believe that poisoning my family is morally equivalent to laying out rat poison to kill the family of rats in my attic.

We inherently understand that if I behave like a lion and use physical violence to drive all other males from my street in order to have all the females to myself, I have failed morally. However, the same behavior by a lion is not a moral failure on the lion's part. We instinctively know that man is distinct from nature. Russell's denial of this betrays a fundamental flaw in his worldview.

Hume argued that a miraculous report like Jesus turning water into wine is more likely to be a mistake or a forgery than a transgression of a law of nature. He invoked billions of witnesses to the immutability of natural laws, those who have never seen water spontaneously change its chemical makeup. He then compared this to the wedding miracle,

---

* At least the popularization of it started with Russell. The argument itself dates back to Xunzi. It is so old that it predates Christianity.

but he *assumed* Jesus was human. He committed the logical fallacy of begging the question. If we remove the *a priori* assumption that Jesus was human and allow even the tiniest possibility that God was present at the wedding, then surely the God who created the laws of chemistry is capable of intervening in them whenever he wishes. Hume's entire argument is founded on an *a priori* assumption that there is no deity capable of intervening in nature.

Ultimately, Hume only advanced an argument against the *exceptional*, not the *supernatural*. For example, the argument applies equally to an exceptional event like the Big Bang. It applies irrespective of whether one believes the Big Bang was natural or supernatural. By Hume's logic, we should be more skeptical of the Big Bang than we are even of miracles, because no one in the history of humanity has witnessed a universe spring into existence from nothing. That makes it an improbability of the highest magnitude—even more improbable than miracles witnessed by thousands. Yet no one argues we should be more skeptical of the Big Bang due to all the "contrary witnesses" who have observed that universes do not spontaneously spring into existence. Thus, Hume's concept of contrary witnesses proves irrelevant. We judge any event by the evidence for it, miracles included.

? ? ? ? ?

In a godless world, according to Russell, there is no moral difference between someone who commits a crime and someone who has the flu. In Russell's atheism, this is rational morality. I find this anything but rational. Imagine that you work hard your whole life to save for your retirement. Then, just as you prepare to enjoy your golden years, someone forges checks against your savings and deprives you of everything you worked for. When the forger leaves you penniless and destitute, can you logically believe that he is morally equivalent to a man with the flu? I believe Russell is a lunatic to suggest that such crimes against humanity deserve no punishment. These are among the completely irrational arguments that prevented me from embracing atheism.

Sensible people believe that the forger should spend one day rotting in prison for every day you are forced out of retirement back to work due to his crime. The problem is, *if atheism were true*, Russell's position actually makes sense. In real life, it does not. For me, that is where atheism disconnects from reality. I needed a belief system that worked in the real world, not just in intellectual discussion at Starbucks. For Russell to say the forger bears no greater guilt than a man with the flu is a big red flag that his belief system does not correspond with reality.

[original argument on page 98]

The Idea of Righteousness

Russell said that "the herd is righteous *by definition.*" In atheism, he is correct. This is the problem with a godless ethical system. Germany's genocide of the Jews was righteous because the herd wanted it, and the herd, *by definition*, is right.

Atheists try to counter that the herd is all humanity; but, as we saw in the previous chapter, Nietzsche clearly did not think so. In fact, he said the herd actually needed enemies to take out its hostilities on. Otherwise, it would resort to internal violence.

To this, atheists simply say Nietzsche and Russell were wrong. But wrong according to whom? There is no absolute moral standard in atheism. To call anything wrong presupposes a theistic worldview.

[original argument on page 99]

Russell's Famous Reply to God

Russell's reaction to meeting God reminds me of Ebenezer Scrooge's reaction to meeting the ghost of Jacob Marley in Charles Dickens' *A Christmas Carol.* Standing face-to-face with Marley's ghost, Scrooge remains unconvinced of what he sees. The ghost asks, "Why do you doubt your senses?" Scrooge scoffs that "a little thing affects them. A slight disorder of the stomach makes them cheat. You may be an undigested bit of beef, a blot of mustard, a crumb of cheese, a fragment of an underdone potato. There's more of gravy than grave about you, whatever you are!"

While Dickens is fiction, we all know a real-life Scrooge—not someone stingy with their money, but someone so adamantly committed to materialism that even if someone returned from the dead they would be more inclined to ascribe what they saw to indigestion than the supernatural.

Consider the example of the deluded wife who simply cannot admit her husband is cheating on her, a sadly relevant illustration for many. Her husband works late, often on short notice. He comes home smelling of perfume but always has some excuse. She is surrounded by evidence that is obvious to everyone else around her, but the deluded bride does not wish to accept the truth. I can only guess how God would respond to Russell's question, but I suspect it would be something along the lines of, "My dear Russell, no evidence is good enough for the person who wills to not believe."

[original argument on page 100]

Russell on Dachau

I agree with Russell that, within atheism, one cannot prove concentration camps were wrong. I find his candid honesty commendable. Russell is absolutely right that atheism affords no mechanism to prove that the slaughter of 31,951 prisoners at Dachau was objectively, morally wrong. While Dachau was eventually enlarged to imprison Jews, it was originally for notable political prisoners, including writers, politicians, royalty, scientists, clergy, and Communists. As we saw with Nietzsche, not only is the dominant power justified in exacting suffering on its enemies, it *must* do violence to others to prevent it from doing violence to itself.[24] According to Nietzsche and Russell, this is logical atheism.

For my part, the genocide of tens of thousands in concentration camps is wrong *prima facie*; it is not just a feeling as it is to Russell. Thus I cannot deny that moral compass within me by embracing atheism.

[original argument on page 101]

What I Believe

The problem of mental causation goes back as far as Plato and was famously addressed by René Descartes.[25] In materialism, there is no mechanism beyond the brain capable of causing thoughts. As Russell rightly observed, in materialism, thoughts seem to have a "chemical origin." The example Russell cited is iodine deficiency's effect on mental capabilities.[26] This chemical problem raises our awareness of other chemical problems we may not have discovered yet. If the lack of iodine keeps one from being intelligent, could the lack of another chemical element keep one from believing in God? Perhaps Russell's brain simply lacked the God-chemical.

Russell brought up the chemical origin of thoughts in order to argue against immortality: Our thoughts are contingent upon chemical processes in our brain that cease when the brain dies. However, he failed to address the problem of how he could trust his own thoughts, *including his thoughts about atheism*, in a purely materialistic world.

?????

Similar to Dawkins, Russell explicitly stated, "I do not pretend to be able to prove that there is no God."[27] These honest admissions are why I found my journey into atheism so disappointing. I came to it asking, "Show me why there is no God," predisposed to accept any reasonable answer. However, the atheist arguments I read essentially amounted to "I cannot even begin to do that."

?????

Russell failed miserably to live by his own standard of judging an act by its consequences. Having had numerous affairs, he did not seem overly concerned about consequences. I venture his jilted wife or the husband of his mistress would not have found his actions as "loving" as Russell thought they were. Ergo, when Russell talked about weighing an act "by reference to its probable consequences," he seemed to be referring only to the consequences *for him*, not for others affected by his actions. While he talked nobly about love, the type he described seemed quite self-centered, and therefore not very loving at all.

[original argument on page 101]

Our Sexual Ethics

Russell often referred to human happiness as a standard for judging good or bad. Ironically, elevating the pursuit of happiness as the sole arbiter of truth often leaves us even less happy. For example, Russell, like many atheists, challenged the social taboo against divorce. He felt the ability to freely exit marriage would result in greater happiness. How has that worked out for us?

Since 1936, our culture has essentially adopted his stance. According to a 2010 Pew Research Center report on marriage, the vast majority of Americans (94 percent) say family is very important to them, but fewer than ever are experiencing family life.[28] Marriage rates are down from 72 percent in 1960 to 52 percent in 2008. People who said, "I can't make *this* marriage work" are finding they cannot make *any* marriage work. While divorce rates for first marriages are 50 percent, they rise to 67 percent for second marriages and 74 percent for third marriages. Russell's idea that people would be happier if they could exit their marriage more easily has proven false. While the majority of married people (84 percent) are very satisfied, only half of divorced people report being satisfied. In simple terms, the grass has not proved greener on the other side.

In a *Psychology Today* article that explored why second and third marriages fail at higher rates than first marriages, psychiatrist Mark Banschick observed, "There are some individuals in second and third marriages who consider divorce manageable and not necessarily a tragedy."[29] With the social stigma of divorce removed, people are finding it easier than ever to pursue happiness, just as Russell advocated. The problem is they are not finding it. Tearing down the predominantly religious social prohibition against divorce has not led to greater fulfillment. Instead it has resulted in 44 percent of young people feeling marriage has become obsolete.[30]

Russell's argument derailed on the suggestion that human happiness alone is a sufficient foundation for a sexual ethic. With all his divorces and affairs, it seems *in practice* he was just pursuing his own happiness, although *in words* he claimed his ethics were about the happiness of others. It seems to me he suggested an ethical system that he himself could not abide by. This ironically makes him guilty of the very charge he leveled against religion for suggesting an ethic "almost unattainable by modern life."[31]

My objection has nothing to do with whether his ethic is moral; it is just completely unrealistic. Robert Fulghum, author of the *New York Times* bestseller *All I Really Need to Know I Learned in Kindergarten*, seems to have coined the quote, "The grass is greenest where it is watered."[32] This seems especially true of relationships. We do not need the Bible to understand that what Russell suggested is merely a downward spiral of diminished returns. New sexual experiences are always exciting, but good sex alone does not make a good relationship, and passion inevitably diminishes to some degree as the newness wears off. I think the fallacy is evident in light of the fact that of all the irreligious couples I know, none are swingers. They do not practice monogamy because of any religious moral ideal but merely because it makes for a healthy, happy marriage.

Regarding Russell's claim that virginity is undesirable before marriage, while I respect his right to his opinion, studies have shown otherwise. Professor Dean Busby studied 2035 married people and determined that couples who waited until after marriage to have sex rated their sex lives better and reported their marriages were more stable and satisfying as a whole than couples who had not waited.[33] Finally, Russell's notion that wives are just "one client prostitutes" is simply disgusting at face value.

Russell's idea that adultery is wrong only because it creates the possibility of fathers raising someone else's child is laughably absurd. In essence, Russell was suggesting that adultery is not immoral if I wear a condom. Can any rational person take such statements seriously?

Russell's point that moralists obsessed with sex lay too much emphasis on it at the expense of other socially useful ethical considerations is well taken. I have met many Christians who do exactly that, classifying sexual sin of greater severity à la the Catholic concept of mortal versus venial sin. They thereby excuse themselves for numerous "smaller" social injustices because they are busy patting themselves on the back for not sleeping with their neighbor's wife. However, Russell's conclusion that this makes the Christian view of sex problematic does not logically follow. It simply means those Christians need to take a broader view of morality.

[original argument on page 102]

Can Religion Cure Our Troubles?

As we saw earlier, Russell subscribed to Nietzsche's view that right and wrong are illusionary. For Russell, the "basis in social utility" was what defined actions as right or wrong. Therefore, I am left scratching my head when Russell condemns people for promoting religion on the grounds that it is useful. After all, the test of usefulness, according to Russell, defines the value of a proposition.

Russell's suggestion that Christianity should not be promoted simply because it serves an end of social utility directly contradicts his position that the value of promoting *any* system of morality is its social utility. Apparently this applied to any system of morality except Christianity, which he held to an inconsistent standard. He was so blindly against Christianity that he was incapable of noticing when he was arguing against his own position.

[original argument on page 103]

Summary

Russell's purpose is immediately differentiable from Nietzsche's. While Nietzsche seemed to be writing reflections on the meaning of life post-Darwin, Russell was more focused on religion and what is wrong with it. His writing style was primarily logical but occasionally polemic.

Particularly polemic is a lengthy section in which he examined a hypothetical child that was stigmatized because, through no fault of his own, his parents were not married. He possibly inherited venereal disease because his parents did not use contraception according to church teaching. He was statistically more likely to be the victim of incest growing up in poverty. He did not get the best healthcare, and so on and so on. The problem with such polemic arguments is they ultimately prove nothing other than which writer is the better wordsmith. I could wax equally polemic about an orphan whose life was saved when he was taken in by a Catholic orphanage. Free healthcare and education from Christian hospitals and schools save the orphan much suffering. But in the end, neither of us has proven anything beyond the fact that skillfully woven words are able to elicit an emotional response.

There is little value in polemic writing, as virtually anything can be argued in this manner. A polemic attack can be waged against the "evils" of a democracy that allows one in four children to go to bed hungry every night[34] (as long as the benefit of people being rewarded for hard work and ingenuity is ignored). Or you could discuss the "good" of Communism, in which there is universal employment and healthcare (as long as you turn a blind eye to human rights abuses that habitually accompany systems with such totalitarian controls). Polemics are primarily emotional arguments that hardly ever take an honest, broad view but rather focus on anecdotal stories that make for a good emotional response. Christopher Hitchens relied heavily on polemic writing, Sam Harris does to a lesser degree, and Russell, much to his credit, takes that road only on occasion. I respect him highly for that.

One problem I do have with Russell is the way he contradicts himself. He said in a speech that there is no reason the universe could not be eternal, but then acknowledged in an essay that he knows the Second Law of Thermodynamics probably makes that impossible. He said he did not believe Jesus performed miracles, yet faulted Jesus' character for miraculously cursing a fig tree. He claimed there is no such thing as what we ought to desire, but then said in another essay it is important to teach teens they ought not to desire to have children before twenty. He said in a speech the problem with the church is people debasing themselves as miserable sinners, but later said the problem is they think too highly of themselves. All the flip-flopping left me wondering if Russell sincerely believed anything he said at all. It seems like he was simply willing to say anything to disprove Christianity. I suppose if you take both of the opposing sides on the same issue, odds are you will be right at least 50 percent of the time. However, this kind of argumentation destroys any claim Russell has of open-mindedness when he disingenuously argues for opposite sides on the same issue.

Reading Russell, I realized I could be an atheist in words only. Although I might say a thief is morally equal to a poet, in real life I would press charges against the one who breaks into my house. Moreover, it seems to me the vast majority of atheists live with a similar disconnect between their beliefs and their actions. When I stopped going to church, my circle of friends came to include a lot of unbelievers. Most of them believed certain actions were truly wrong—not just against societal norms. However, the more I came to understand atheism, the more I realized such a view of moral wrong was illogical in the context of atheism. Russell's view of human dignity is still another obstacle. He rightly observed that in Darwinism we cannot "make claims on behalf of man" which we could not also make for any other form of life on Earth, even a rat. I simply cannot believe man has no more dignity than rats. As I observed in my comments on Nietzsche, the issue is not just that these ideas seemed awful, but that they did not seem to correspond with reality.

Certain subjects resurface throughout *Why I Am Not a Christian.* Sex comes up as much as any issue, and Russell seemed to be fairly obsessed with it. He was a known philanderer, which raises the legitimate question of whether his sexuality was the effect or the cause of his atheism. He clearly understood that his lifestyle was incompatible with Christian ethics, and that presented a huge obstacle for him to accept Christianity. This cannot be discounted as possibly having an influence on how he interpreted evidence of God.

Ultimately I found Russell unconvincing because he seemed willing to force evidence to conform to his notions like a person committed to the notion he has not gained weight tries to fit into an old pair of pants. Nietzsche was indifferent to contrary arguments, often not even bothering with examples or evidence to sway those who think differently. Russell, on other hand, tries to make all the evidence fit his premise even when his argument is just grasping at straws. For example, he said he thought the universe is eternal and had no creator, but qualified this by saying that even if it did have an origin, that still would not require a creator. This is a "heads I win, tails you lose" argument. According to Russell, no matter what the facts turn out to be, they will confirm his position. He seems blindly committed to his foregone conclusions. Thus, he seems to be starting with the premise of atheism and making the facts fit his premise rather than advancing an open-minded and convincing argument.

Russell's Key Concepts

Key Concept	Evidence Offered
Communism is a religion.	He observes numerous parallels: both favored socialism, the Ogpu was like the Inquisition, and both belief systems are held firmly.
Darwinism destroys the argument from design for God.	*None offered*
Whether a religion is true is a separate issue from whether it is useful.	*None offered*
Faith is belief "contrary" to evidence.	*None offered*—he simply substitutes the definition of *fideism* for the definition of *faith.*
Religion is responsible for group hostilities.	*None offered*
The proposition that God made the universe raises the bigger question of "Who made God?"	*None offered*
An eternal universe adequately solves the problem of infinite regress and invalidates the cosmological argument.	*None offered*
If the universe did come into existence, it could have done so without a cause.	*None offered*

Key Concept	Evidence Offered
Argument of poor design	Ku Klux Klan and Fascists
Belief in God is wishful thinking.	*None offered*
We simply believe what we were taught as children.	*None offered*
Morality comes from our parents (or society), not from God.	*None offered*
Argument for remedying of injustice is not an argument for God.	If you open a crate of oranges and the top layer is bad, you do not assume the bottom layer must be good to redress the balance.
Belief in God is just a response to fear.	*None offered*
Questions whether Jesus even existed.	*None offered*
Questions whether Jesus' teachings were moral.	Disagrees with Jesus' treatment of animals and trees.
Teaching about hell is unkind.	*None offered*
People accept religion on emotional grounds.	*None offered*
Religion has made minimal useful contributions.	Gregorian calendar and Egyptian calendar
Christians do not follow Christ's teaching.	Inquisition and the Ku Klux Klan

Key Concept	Evidence Offered
Religion has ruined sex.	*None offered* (just some anecdotal stories)
God is responsible for pain and misery because, in his omniscience, he chose to create a universe that would have pain and misery.	Hypothetical example that he would be responsible for his child's actions if he chose to beget a child knowing it would be a homicidal maniac.
The problem of theodicy.	The children's ward at any hospital
Christianity focuses on personal piety at the expense of valuable social virtue.	Oppression under totalitarian Roman Empire forced early church to refocus on personal holiness over social good.
Jesus was antifamily.	He spoke harshly to his mother and said he would cause strife within families.
Man has free will, which makes him accountable for his actions.	*None offered*
Evolution means man has no greater dignity than any other animal.	*None offered*
Miracles are a violation of the laws of nature.	*None offered* (granted, he seems to reference Hume's arguments)
Forgery and contracting the plague are morally equivalent.	*None offered*
Religion has held back secular humanism from fixing mankind's problems.	*None offered*

Key Concept	Evidence Offered
When he dies he will challenge God, "Why did you not give me better evidence?"	Evidence not applicable
"Dachau is wrong" is not a fact.	He *felt* killing hundreds of thousands in concentration camps was wrong, but he did not believe he could *prove* it.
"Thinking seems to have a chemical origin."	*None offered* (He simply makes the analogy that tracks in brains are like roads; if he has scientific evidence, it is not stated.)
"I do not pretend to be able to prove that there is no God."	Evidence not applicable
All we need is love and scientific knowledge; there is no such thing as what we "ought" to desire.	A few anecdotal stories; he freely admits he cannot prove this is right.
Atheism results in greater sexual freedom.	Once we eliminate the concept of "sin," we can define sexual boundaries by more practical concerns like the desire to be certain of paternity.
We ought to teach women not to have children before 20.	Undesirable physiological and educational consequences
There is nothing wrong with extramarital affairs.	The problem is the social stigma attached to unfaithfulness, which makes a man jealous but only for his reputation, not for affection from his wife.

Key Concept	Evidence Offered
Virginity till marriage is actually a bad thing.	A person without previous sexual experience will not be able to distinguish between mere physical attraction and the congeniality necessary for a successful marriage.
Wives are "one client prostitutes."	Compares an idle wife to a gigolo.
There is a universal concept that some things are indecent.	Almost every society regards pornography and exhibitionism offensive.
Adultery came to be regarded as bad because of "the desire of males to be certain of paternity."	The siege of Troy was an example of social upheaval due to disrespect for the rights of husbands.
Christianity should not be promoted on the basis of being useful.	He says it should only be argued for on the basis it is true, not that it serves some social utility.

Replies and Rebuttals to Russell's Key Concepts

Arguments for Atheism/Against God	Rebuttal
Communism is a religion.	By this loose logic almost any organization from the PTA to the Rotary Club could be deemed a religious institution.
Darwinism destroys the argument from design for God.	Darwinism cannot explain either the design of the first living cell or the design of the universe that contains it.
Whether a religion is true is a separate issue from whether it is useful.	*Agreed*—when the New Atheists argue against the effects of religion, they are ultimately not saying anything about God.
Faith is belief "contrary" to evidence.	Confuses *fideism* with *faith*. The primary definition of *faith* is "trust." In the words of Inigo Montoya from *The Princess Bride*, "You keep using that word. I don't think it means what you think it means."
Religion is responsible for group hostilities.	History gives ample evidence group hostility is inevitable with or without religion; even when religion appears to be causal (i.e., Ireland), there are often underlying nonreligious causes.
The proposition that God made the universe raises the bigger question of "Who made God?"	Category mistake fallacy—the question itself is illogical, like asking, "What color is the number nine?"

Arguments for Atheism/Against God	Rebuttal
An eternal universe adequately solves the problem of infinite regress and invalidates the cosmological argument.	Refuted in his own day by Second Law of Thermodynamics; later decisively refuted by the Big Bang.
If the universe did come into existence, it could have done so without a cause.	This contradicts everything we know by observation; if you accept this, it is self-contradictory to say the resurrection is impossible on the basis that it contradicts current observation.
Argument of poor design	Poor design is still design; you cannot judge a design unless you know the purpose.
Belief in God is wishful thinking.	Even Nietzsche acknowledged that this is absurd.
We simply believe what we were taught as children.	Unlike Santa Claus and the Easter Bunny, people come to believe in God for the first time in adulthood; alternately, belief in God outlasts childhood beliefs in Santa Claus. Russell never questioned the atheism he was taught in his childhood.
Morality comes from our parents (or society), not from God.	Fails to explain how people coming from very different upbringings and/or cultures arrive at essentially the same morality.
Argument for remedying of injustice is not an argument for God.	*Agreed*—however, there is no argument against God here.

Arguments for Atheism/Against God	Rebuttal
Belief in God is just a response to fear.	Fails to explain why people keep coming to faith despite the fact that we no longer fear thunder, lightning, and hurricanes.
Jesus may not have existed at all.	This was not even suggested for over 1800 years and then only by people with an *a priori* commitment to materialism; it is a fringe view with minimal support among historians.
Jesus' teachings were immoral.	Both examples he cites come from miracles which Russell elsewhere argues are impossible; Jesus cannot be blamed for something Russell claims he never did.
Teaching about hell is unkind.	Fallacy of begging the question—it is only unkind if it is untrue, which the argument assumes without proof.
People accept religion on emotional grounds.	Fails to acknowledge his own emotional bias as someone who experienced so much death in his family by age six.
Religion has made minimal useful contributions.	A completely ignorant statement that willfully overlooks Christian orphanages, soup kitchens, homeless shelters, hospitals, addiction recovery programs, and schools.
Christians do not follow Christ's teaching.	*Agreed*—many do not; however, this is an argument against Christians, not against believing in Christ.

Arguments for Atheism/Against God	Rebuttal
Religion has ruined sex.	This claim is refuted by numerous studies showing married couples have more and better sex than singles.
God is responsible for pain and misery because, in his omniscience, he chose to create a universe that would have pain and misery.	Fails to consider free will's relationship to omniscience; inconsistent in not faulting all parents because we all know our kids will cause and experience hurt.
The problem of theodicy	By asking the question, we have already presumed the existence of a moral standard which the world falls short of.
Christianity focuses on personal piety at the expense of valuable social virtue.	Before launching mission trips or even getting internally organized, the church was already caring for the poor and needy.
Jesus was antifamily.	Not true—for his argument, Russell pulls two verses out of context and simply ignores numerous verses to the contrary; his argument is poorly grounded.
Man has free will, making him accountable for his actions.	Where does this come from in materialism? Our perception of moral accountability does not square with a materialist view of the brain.
Evolution means man has no greater dignity than any other animal.	*Agreed,* if materialism is true; however, most materialists cannot live life consistent with their own position.

Arguments for Atheism/Against God	Rebuttal
Miracles are a violation of the laws of nature.	Fallacy of begging the question—assumes there is no agent capable of intervening; if I catch a falling object I have not violated the law of gravity, merely intervened.
Forgery and contracting the plague are morally equivalent.	Try telling me that after you have been defrauded.
Religion has held back secular humanism from fixing mankind's problems.	Since Russell wrote this, atheism has had its chance in countries like the Soviet Union and China and failed miserably.
When he dies he will challenge God, "Why did you not give me better evidence?"	Like a bride who does not wish to believe her husband is unfaithful, there is no "better" evidence for someone who wills not to believe.
"Dachau is wrong" is not a fact.	If your worldview cannot explain why the genocide of millions in concentration camps is factually wrong, you need a better worldview.
"Thinking seems to have a chemical origin."	*Agreed*, which is why in materialism, any conclusion is suspect *including the conclusion there is no God.*
"I do not pretend to be able to prove that there is no God."	Fairly common knowledge but worth pointing out: an honest atheist does not pretend to know there is no God.
All we need is love and scientific knowledge; there is no such thing as what we "ought" to desire.	Loving to whom? Himself? Or the wives he cheated on? Not a real solution because it fails to address whom we ought to love.

Arguments for Atheism/Against God	Rebuttal
Atheism results in greater sexual freedom.	Or does the desire for sexual freedom result in atheism? It is questionable which of these is the cause and which is the effect.
We ought to teach women not to have children before 20.	*Agreed*—however, this contradicts his earlier claim that we should not allow others to define what we should desire.
There is nothing wrong with extramarital affairs.	"The grass is greenest where it is watered"—seeking fulfillment outside marriage perpetuates a downward spiral; it would be more rational to work on the ailing marriage.
Virginity till marriage is actually a bad thing.	His opinion against studies that have shown the contrary; besides, studies show they are happy, which is how he elsewhere defines what is good.
Wives are "one client prostitutes."	Just his personal opinion (and a rather depressing one at that)
There is a universal concept that some things are indecent.	*Agreed*—however, this seems to oppose his case that all morality is community convention.
Adultery came to be regarded as bad because of "the desire of male to be certain of paternity."	Is this suggesting an infertile woman could never be an adulteress? The position is logically absurd.
Christianity should not be promoted on the basis of being useful.	Social utility is the only basis for arguing for *any* ethical system in materialism.

7

Sam Harris—New Atheism

*"The End of Faith is one of those books that deserves
to replace the Gideon Bible in every
hotel room in the land."*[1]

RICHARD DAWKINS

In fairness, I must disclose that by the time I read *The End of Faith*, I had read a huge amount of atheist literature, watched numerous debates, and listened to countless podcasts. By this point I was repeatedly hearing the same arguments. There were only slight variations on the same general themes sometimes backed up by different illustrations. I was not expecting to find anything substantively new in *The End of Faith* and found only one surprise therein. Granted, Sam Harris' book is well written. But I had already heard, pondered, and researched the points he raises. Harris wrote very little that is not already stated by Dawkins, Hitchens, Dennett, and other atheists.

I made every effort to give the book the respect it deserves as the second-bestselling atheist book after Richard Dawkins' *The God Delusion*.[2] By 2007 it had sold more than a quarter of a million copies and spent 33 weeks on the *New York Times* bestseller list. Nine years after its release it was still Amazon's number-one Kindle book in the comparative religion category and number-two print book in the rationalism category.[3] The sheer volume of sales demonstrates that a significant number of people take Harris' argument seriously, so it deserves an honest hearing.

Harris' Biography

Sam Harris is as all-American as they come. He grew up in Los Angeles, the son of an actor and TV producer. His mother was a secular Jew and his father a Quaker, but Harris has repeatedly stated his upbringing was entirely secular. He is a devout student of martial arts and credits Ecstasy for opening up spirituality for him.[4] That is not to say that drug use makes one American, but it does make him relatable, especially compared to pastors who maintain a façade of perfection while everyone knows they are more human than they pretend. I believe Harris will be the new face of atheism because his youth, good looks, and charisma make him more appealing on a popular level. Although he is 48 at the time of this writing, Harris looks even younger, especially compared to Richard Dawkins (74) or Daniel Dennett (73). While these superfluous issues may not matter to intellectuals, in a society where the circulation of *People* magazine far exceeds those of *Scientific American* and *Christianity Today* combined, it is no wonder that Harris has joined the ranks of the most well-known atheists.

Harris is clearly the most open-minded to spiritual topics among the "four horsemen" of the New Atheist apocalypse. Harris left Stanford University after his second year as an English major to travel to Asia to study meditation with Hindu and Buddhist teachers.[5] He has stated that there is "nothing irrational about seeking the states of mind that lie at the core of many religions. Compassion, awe, devotion and feelings of oneness are surely among the most valuable experiences a person can have."[6] However, he is not open to monotheism and does not believe we will find such spiritual experience in "our current beliefs about God."[7] Harris returned to Stanford 11 years later to complete a BA in philosophy in 2000.

The September 11 terrorist attacks played no small role in Harris' life. Indeed, his book grew out of "a long essay...produced in those first weeks of collective grief and stupefaction" immediately after September 11, 2001.[8] That essay would become *The End of Faith*.[9] He then went on to complete a PhD in cognitive neuroscience at UCLA in 2009.

In my perception, there is a disparity between Sam Harris the speaker and Sam Harris the author. He is perhaps the most cordial, kind, and soft-spoken of the New Atheist debaters. I have never seen him lose his cool or act uncivilly in a debate. His writing, however, is a bit more radical. Harris has been outspoken about the need for *in*tolerance of religious views, stating it would be appropriate to mock someone who believes in Jesus' resurrection with the "ill-concealed laughter" we might reserve for someone claiming that Elvis is still alive.[10] Harris' controversial support for a nuclear first strike against Islamists[11] because "certain beliefs place their adherents beyond the reach of every peaceful means of persuasion...[so that] tolerant people may be justified in killing them"[12] has been criticized by journalists Chris Hedges and Madeleine Bunting for sounding "exactly like the kind of argument put forward by those who ran the Inquisition."[13]

Personal information about Harris is scant online or in print. His website has only a few sentences on the "About" page.[14] Since the same set of facts are available to both theists and atheists, it is always interesting to note how different life experiences potentially influence people's interpretation of facts, from Nietzsche's alleged homosexuality to Russell's philandering or Harris' atheistic upbringing. Any factors that might influence Harris are largely unknown.

Harris' Arguments

Reason in Exile

Harris opens the chapter with a vivid, emotional story of a young man on a bus wearing an overcoat packed with explosives, nails, and ball bearings which he uses to kill himself, innocent bus passengers, and bystanders. The objection Harris raises in the aftermath of this attack is that "the role that faith played in his actions is invariably discounted. His motives [according to religious people] must have been political, economic, or entirely personal." While he acknowledges that even "without faith, desperate people would still do terrible things,"[15] he wishes to shine the spotlight on his hypothetical bus bomber's religious motivations. Harris feels that because of people like the suicide bomber, "Words like 'God' and 'Allah' must go the way of 'Apollo' and 'Baal' or they will unmake our world."[16]

In this same section, Harris observes, "Certainty about the next life is simply incompatible with tolerance in this one."[17] If someone believes on the basis of religious authority that killing others is not only acceptable but may bring reward in the next life, then "religious faith perpetuates man's inhumanity to man."[18]

[response on page 151]

Reason in Exile: The Myth of "Moderation" in Religion

Before digging into the problems with religious "moderation," Harris observes how religious moderates retreat from scriptural literalism. Says Harris:

> The first thing to observe about the moderate's retreat from scriptural literalism is that it draws its inspiration not from scripture but from cultural developments that have rendered many of God's utterances difficult to accept as written.[19]

> ...the utility of ignoring (or "reinterpreting") certain articles of faith is now overwhelming.[20]

> Religious moderation is the product of secular knowledge and scriptural ignorance...By their light, religious moderation appears to be nothing more than an unwillingness to fully submit to God's law.[21]

Harris cites Deuteronomy 13:7-11 as an example of a passage being ignored or reinterpreted by religious moderates. In it we are told if a son, daughter, spouse, or intimate friend tried to seduce an Israelite from the worship of Yahweh, the Israelites were commanded, "You must stone him to death, since he has tried to divert you from Yahweh your God." Harris observes that today this would include stoning your son or daughter who returned from yoga class advocating the worship of Krishna. The problem with moderation, according to Harris, is that these passages are still in the Bible. Moderates may look to such a passage for only a "symbolic" reading. However, by not rejecting the Bible entirely as an antiquated Bronze Age book, moderates provide shelter for zealots who share the same Bible and take such passages literally.

After commending religious moderates for not taking the Bible literally, Harris identifies two problems still facing moderates. First, even though they do not engage in religious extremism themselves, they fail to disassociate themselves from such groups and thereby do "not permit anything very critical to be said about religious literalism."[22] Harris feels, for example, that the majority of peaceful Muslims prohibit society from attacking the militant and violent Muslims because the moderates consider the extremists part of their flock. Second, moderate religion, according to Harris, "offers no bulwark against religious extremism and religious violence."[23] In other words, they shelter religious extremists because they see them as members of an in-group.

[response on page 154]

Reason in Exile: The World Beyond Reason

Harris raises the mind-body problem—how can anyone who believes in materialism be certain of any thought since, in materialism, our thoughts are nothing more than products of our biology? In his own words, "nothing arises in consciousness that has not first been structured, edited, or amplified by the nervous system. While *this gives rise to a few philosophical problems* concerning the foundations of our knowledge, it also offers us a remarkable opportunity to deliberately transform the character of our experience."[24] Harris does not, however, offer any solutions to these "few philosophical problems."

While he does not elaborate on the subject in this book, in a later book entitled *Free Will*, Harris argues, "The concept of free will makes no sense and so those who believe they act freely and are responsible for those actions are being duped by their biology."[25]

[response on page 156]

The Nature of Belief

In chapter 2, Harris observes how willing we are to believe things that do not correspond with reality. We do this because choosing to believe things despite evidence makes us feel good. However, this does not make the belief valid. As he points out, "The fact that I would feel good if there were a God does not give me the slightest reason to believe one exists."[26] Harris concludes, "The truth is that religious faith is simply *unjustified* belief in matters of ultimate concern—specifically in propositions that promise some mechanism by which human life can be spared the ravages of time and death."[27]

[response on page 157]

In the Shadow of God

Harris opens chapter 3 with a two-page list of torture methods from the Inquisition. The gruesome tortures rival the *Saw* films. The methods "religious" people have come up with to torture other human beings is disturbing to say the least. The Catholic Church found justification for these atrocities, according to Harris, because "a literal reading of the Old Testament not only permits but requires heretics to be put to death."[28] Harris observes, "The problem with scripture, however, is that many of its possible interpretations (including most of the literal ones) can be used to justify atrocities in defense of the faith."[29]

[response on page 158]

In the Shadow of God: The Holocaust

Harris opens this section with a quote from Rudolf Hess: "We believe that the Fuhrer is obeying a higher call to fashion German history. There can be no criticism of this belief."[30] Harris points out the Nazis' dogmatic allegiance to "outlandish dogmas" like Heinrich Himmler's absurd belief that the Aryans had not evolved from monkeys and apes but had come down to earth from the heavens. Harris says such baseless beliefs paved the road to the atrocities of World War II.

Harris brings charge for "the overt complicity of the [Catholic] church in the attempted murder of an entire people."[31] He points to the Catholic Church's sinister willingness to open its genealogical records to the Nazis, which enabled them to trace the extent of people's Jewish ancestry.[32] He observes how throughout World War II the Catholic Church continued to excommunicate theologians and scholars and to censor books by the hundreds, "and yet not a single perpetrator of genocide—of whom there were countless examples—succeeded in furrowing Pope Pius XII's censorious brow."[33] In fact, Harris observes that not a single leader of the Third Reich—not even Hitler himself—was ever excommunicated from the Catholic Church.

[response on page 160]

The Problem with Islam

Chapter 4 opens with the frank admission that there are "unmistakable" differences between faiths. For example, Harris observes Jainism does not produce terrorists like Islam because there is nothing in Jain theology to inspire adherents to commit atrocities against unbelievers. After acknowledging that not all religions lead to violence, Harris spends the rest of this chapter building his case that Islam is one religion that certainly does. As he says, "Islam, more than any other religion human beings have devised has all the makings of a thoroughgoing cult of death."[34]

Harris freely admits that his opening chapter example of the Muslim suicide bomber "ignores the painful history of Israeli occupation," ignores "the collusion of Western powers with corrupt dictatorships," and "ignores the endemic poverty and lack of economic opportunity" that plague the Arab world. He says, however, it is justified to discount these factors since "the world is filled with poor, uneducated, and exploited people who do not commit acts of terrorism."[35]

Harris acknowledges several specific economic and educational factors: In 2002, the combined GDP of all Arab countries fell short of the GDP of Spain. Also, Spain translates more books into Spanish each year than the entire Muslim world has translated into Arabic since the ninth century.[36] Nevertheless, he says such statistics "should not lead us to believe that poverty and lack of education are the roots of the problem."[37]

He observes that Ahmed Omar Sheikh, who organized the kidnapping and murder of *Wall Street Journal* reporter Daniel Pearl, studied at the London School of Economics. Also, the leaders of Hamas are all college graduates, and some have master's degrees. According to Harris, "These facts suggest that even if every Muslim enjoyed a standard of living comparable to that of the average middle-class American, the West might still be in profound danger of colliding with Islam,"[38] and,

"There is no reason to believe that economic and political improvements in the Muslim world, in and of themselves, would remedy this."[39]

Harris feels that though we are at war with Islam, our political leaders will not admit it, because doing so does not serve their foreign policy objectives.

[response on page 163]

A Fringe Without a Center

Harris sees few doctrinal differences between fundamentalist Muslims and the mainstream. He says Muslims themselves do not refer to Muslims who take military action as "fundamentalists" or "extremists," but simply "Islamists." Says Harris, "Moderate Islam—really moderate, really critical of Muslim irrationality—scarcely seems to exist."[40]

He goes on to say that even those who appear "tolerant" should be suspect. Simply because they are in the minority does not mean they are peaceful. They may simply be "biding their time"[41] until they have sufficient numbers to act.

Harris cites disturbing statistics from the Pew Research Center, which asked Muslims, "Is it ever justified to target civilians in the defense of Islam?"[42] Evidently 73 percent of Muslims living in Lebanon responded yes. More than half of Muslims living in the Ivory Coast and almost half of Nigerian Muslims agreed. Even in the most westernized Islamic state, Turkey, 13 percent thought suicide bombing was justifiable. Harris wants to make the world aware of how many Muslims are willing to kill civilians in the defense of Islam.

[response on page 164]

Perfect Weapons

This is one of Harris' stronger points. He responds to the views of leftist philosophers like Noam Chomsky, who have suggested that terrorism against America is the consequence of our sins returning to roost. As an example, Chomsky cites the 1998 American cruise missile strike on the Al-Shifa pharmaceutical plant in Sudan, which the US mistakenly thought was being used by al-Qaeda to make chemical weapons.

Instead, we only succeeded in destroying 50 percent of Sudan's medicine supply. Our actions denied crucial medicine to tens of thousands of innocent Sudanese who, as a result, may have died of tuberculosis, malaria, and other terrible diseases.[43]

Harris, however, points out a critical difference in our intent versus the intent of Muslim terrorists. The US had no intention of denying vital pharmaceuticals to the Sudanese. We thought we were thwarting the production of chemical weapons of mass destruction. Eliminating an important source of medicine was merely the unfortunate result of poor military intelligence.

In stark contrast, Muslim extremist Kamel Bourgass, caught by London's Metropolitan Police Service in 2003, was preparing to unleash ricin poison in a planned attack against the London Underground (subway). London's *Daily Star* newspaper claimed that as many as 250,000 could have died.[44] Unlike Sudanese women and children who later died as an unintended effect of the pharmaceutical plant bombing, Bourgass specifically intended to target men, women, and children alike. It was his explicit *intention* to harm people. They were his desired victims, not collateral damage of some "legitimate" attack. As Harris says, "Where ethics are concerned, intentions are everything."[45]

Harris points out that "collateral damage" casualties like in Sudan are not the result of some irrational religious philosophy, but rather the unfortunate consequence of less-than-perfect military intelligence and imperfect weapons. If we had perfect military intelligence, America would never (again) blow up a wedding convoy of innocent civilians in Yemen.*[46] If we had the technology to prevent civilian casualties, we would use it. Al-Qaeda would show no such restraint if they had a cruise missile. To the contrary, they would strike with the intent to maximize casualties.

[response on page 167]

---

* The US killed 14 innocent people in a wedding convoy and wounded 22 others in a 2013 drone attack. But according to Harris "intentions are everything." The US didn't *intend* to kill innocent civilians on their wedding day, so their families couldn't possibly want revenge...right?

West of Eden

Harris suggests that allowing religious ideas to determine government policies presents a grave danger to everyone, even here in America. He points out how Ronald Reagan viewed the Middle East through the lens of biblical prophecy and included men like Jerry Falwell and Hal Lindsey in national security briefings. He observes how US foreign policy toward Israel has been shaped largely by the belief that the rebuilding of Solomon's temple will "usher in both the Second Coming of Christ and the final destruction of the Jews."[47] Harris further notes that the first international support for the Jewish return to Palestine, Britain's Balfour Declaration of 1917, was at least partially inspired by biblical prophecy. Says Harris, "These intrusions of eschatology into modern politics suggest that the dangers of religious faith can scarcely be overstated."[48]

[response on page 172]

A Science of Good and Evil

Harris is unique in maintaining that atheism affords a foundation for absolute morality. He disagrees that ethical truths are culturally contingent while scientific truths are not.[49] To Harris, we do not "get our sense that two plus two equals four from the pages of a textbook on mathematics,"[50] nor do we get our sense that cruelty is wrong from the pages of the Bible.

His later work, *The Moral Landscape*, is essentially a book-length explication of this chapter. The core of his position is that "questions of right and wrong are really questions about the happiness and suffering of sentient creatures."[51]

Of course, God cannot be the source of morals because, as Harris points out, "the God of Abraham is a ridiculous fellow—capricious, petulant, and cruel."[52] The human attributes exhibited by God in the Bible—jealousy, wrath, suspicion, and the lust to dominate—are not qualities upon which we can found ethics. Harris says the problem of theodicy (the challenge of vindicating an omnipotent and omniscient God in the face of evil) is insurmountable.

[response on page 176]

The Demon of Relativism

In this section, Harris brilliantly claims that some worldviews really are better than others. He points out how moral relativism is ultimately self-contradictory. He explains pragmatism, the view that the utility of a belief trumps all other concerns, then proceeds to explain how pragmatism lacks cognitive coherence. Finally he explains realism and says "for the realist, our statement about the world will be 'true' or 'false' not merely in virtue of how they function amid the welter of our other beliefs, or with reference to any culture-bound criteria, but because reality simply is a certain way, independent of our thoughts."[53] In other words, ethics, like physics, is a truth out there waiting to be discovered. Ethics is an external reality in the same way as is two plus two equals four. Whether we are right or wrong is a matter of whether we believe the answer is 4, not a question of what we have been taught to believe.

Harris then adds that consensus might be the arbiter of truth, but it cannot constitute it, meaning group consensus can help us arrive at truth but something is not true merely because the majority believe it. As Harris explains, "It is quite conceivable that everyone might agree and yet be wrong about the way the world is. It is also conceivable that a single person might be right in the face of unanimous opposition."[54]

[response on page 177]

Intuition, Ethics, Self-Interest, Happiness, and Other Topics

Harris argues intuition is a necessary component in delineating ethics. He says, "While this is true in matters of ethics, it is not less true in science. When we can break down our knowledge of a thing no further, the irreducible leap that remains is intuitively taken. Thus, the traditional opposition between reason and intuition is a false one."[55]

Intuition is Harris' explanation for his assertion that happiness and suffering are the foundation of ethics.[56] He says it is a "fact that we must rely on certain intuitions to answer ethical questions."[57] In the next paragraph he says that "for ethics to matter to us, the happiness and suffering of others must matter to us."[58] I do not think I am putting words in his mouth by saying he suggests that human flourishing is an absolute foundation for ethics that comes to us via pure, simple intuition.

Harris parts company with atheists like Richard Dawkins when he claims, "To say that something is 'natural,' or that it has conferred an adaptive advantage upon our species, is not to say that is it 'good' in the required sense of contributing to human happiness in the present."[59] He also says, "Appeals to genetics and natural selection can take us only so far, because nature has not adapted us to do anything more than breed."[60] If nature were the measure of good, the highest good would be men lining up at sperm banks to father thousands of children for whom they would bear no financial responsibility.

After stating that ethics comes from intuition and not nature, Harris lays out his definition of ethics: "To treat others ethically is to act out of concern for their happiness and suffering."[61] He then adds, "Love is more conducive to happiness, both our own and that of others, than hate." He contends that this is a discovered truth, like math, not a culturally derived principle. Using the example of literacy, he says, "Not learning how to read is not another *style* of literacy, and not learning to see others as ends in themselves is not another style of ethics. It is a *failure* of ethics."[62] From everything I have read, this absolute view of ethics is unique to Harris.

Harris then adds the caveat that "compassionate people can still be horribly unlucky."[63] Ergo, we cannot simply look at people's general happiness as a measure of whether this model works, though individuals can expect exercising love and compassion will increase their happiness in most cases.

[response on page 177]

A Response to Sam Harris

> *"As a bona fide pinko-liberal-feminist...Harris'*
> *presentation of religion as inherently repressive is just*
> *plain wrong...I too fear the dogma, meanness and*
> *narrow mindedness of the religious right, but I know*
> *from first-hand experience—learned at my mother's*
> *knee—that the left hand of God is also one of the*
> *greatest powers for social change on this planet."*[1]

ATHEIST MARGARET WERTHEIM
REVIEWING *THE END OF FAITH* FOR *THE HUFFINGTON POST*

Although Harris has publicly stated it is appropriate to mock people because of their beliefs,[2] he nevertheless usually refrains from doing so. I admire his demeanor. While I disagree with him on several points, hopefully I have responded with equal civility.

Reason in Exile

Harris tries to build a case that the Koran is the lone cause of terrorism based on one hypothetical Palestinian bus bomber who allegedly had no political, economic, or personal motivation. However, Harris completely ignores that 3.5 million Muslims living in America[3] read the same Koran yet, absent the political and economic factors present in the Middle East, they find nothing in the Koran that compels them to commit acts of terror. Moreover, more than three times as many Muslims live in the Asia-Pacific as live in the Middle East-North Africa (roughly a billion versus 317 million), yet we very rarely hear of Islamic acts of terrorism in the more politically stable and economically prosperous areas of Asia. Invariably, when the United States finds Osama bin Laden hiding in a terrorist cell in Pakistan, or extremists attack the US embassy in Benghazi, or a Muslim group kidnaps 200 girls from a school in Nigeria, these events almost always occur in unstable political regions with failed economies and other nonreligious contributing factors. In fact, if you make a map of the locations of more than 200 terrorist attacks in 2013[4] and place it on a map of the most politically unstable and economically depressed regions in the world, they overlap almost 100 percent. I have personally traveled extensively through Egypt, Israel, Jordan, Turkey, India, Morocco, and the Asia-Pacific. I have stayed in the home of a Turkish Muslim and we have hosted Moroccan Muslims in our Florida home. I have experienced firsthand the real impact of the political, economic, and personal forces in these areas that Harris cavalierly dismisses in his desire to pin terrorism exclusively upon religion.

When a depressed, failed secular American businessman puts a gun in his mouth and pulls the trigger, Harris understands that is not religious fanaticism. However, if that same man lives in the Middle East and reads the Koran, it must be religious fanaticism. Consider Tarek Bouazizi, whose suicide sparked the 2011 Arab Spring uprising in North Africa. Tarek's father died when he was three. Tarek had to drop out of school when he was ten to work to support his family in a city with 30 percent unemployment.[5] He was making roughly $140 a month selling produce on the street when police seized more than $200 worth of his goods, more than he earns in a month, even though he broke no law.[6]

Harris naively assumes that only Islam could explain Tarek's suicide. Furthermore, he suggests it could not be outrage over Tarek's tragic story of poverty and government corruption that caused the 2011 Arab Spring uprising, even though it broke out *the very next day*. One wonders how much clearer links must be before Harris will acknowledge them.

Harris' candid admission "without faith, desperate people would still do terrible things"[7] is worthy of book-length exposition. Adam Lanza is a prime example. On December 14, 2012, Lanza walked onto the campus of Sandy Hook Elementary School and fatally shot 20 children and 6 adult staff. Contrary to Harris' claim that religion is the root of all evil, being irreligious did nothing to thwart Lanza from becoming a killer. Lanza was deeply disturbed without religion. He did not speak till he was 3 and was diagnosed with Asperger's, Autism,[8] sensory-integration disorder, and obsessive-compulsive disorder. His father suspected that he was schizophrenic.[9] He changed his socks 20 times a day, and his mother did three loads of laundry a day.[10] He would go through an entire box of tissues daily because he refused to touch doorknobs. He had no known friends at school.[11]

Lanza expressed no religious motivation for his terrorism. He did terrible things without faith having a part. Had he quoted Scripture or made insane comments about sending children to heaven, this would only mean he was expressing his pre-existing mental illness in the vocabulary of his upbringing.

Religion did not make Adam Lanza a sociopath. However, if Lanza had quoted even one Bible verse, Harris may have opened his book with Lanza's story instead of the hypothetical bomber. For Harris, any mention of religious beliefs is sufficient to make one a religious terrorist. He is willing to discount any and all familial, political, economic, mental, and personal influences.

Research has demonstrated that about one percent of the global population is psychopathic.[12] With or without religion, these deranged people are ticking time bombs. When these people do go off, common sense suggests they will delineate their motivations in the vocabulary of their culture and upbringing. Their mental illness can be voiced either religiously ("I hate people in Allah's name") or irreligiously ("I hate people"). Ergo, when a psychopath like Min Yongjun from East Asia, where irreligious people are the majority, stabbed 23 children at Chenpeng Elementary the same day as Lanza's rampage, it would surprise me if he claimed any religious motivation. If a psychopath from the Middle East flew an airplane into the World Trade Center, it would surprise me if he did *not* cite religious motivation. People will express their mental illness in the terms of their culture. Stripping religion from culture solves nothing. As Harris admits, "without faith, desperate people would still do terrible things." They will merely articulate their motivation in secular terms. This raises the question: Why does Harris argue as if a world without faith would be free of terrible things?

It is naïve of Harris to suggest that eliminating religion will eliminate the problem. Adam Lanza did not need Islam to commit an atrocity. He did not shoot those children with hopes of being rewarded with celestial virgins. He had no skewed view of the afterlife to enable his actions. He was a mentally ill young man. The sad reality is sick people do sick things. Sometimes those sick people are also religious.

The irony of Harris' statement "certainty about the next life is simply incompatible with tolerance in this one" is that he fails to recognize how his own certainty about how life ends makes him intolerant of religious people.

[original argument on page 141]

Reason in Exile: The Myth of "Moderation" in Religion

Hearing Sam Harris lecture about scriptural ignorance is like hearing a lecture on medieval history from someone who only knows the Robin Hood fables. He does not seem to grasp why Christians call the Old Testament "old." After all, Judaism calls the same books the TaNaK, an acronym for the three sections: Torah ("Teaching"), Nevi'im ("Prophets"), and Ketuvim ("Writings"). Tanak carries none of the Christian title's implication of an outdated model. The reason Christians call it "old" has absolutely nothing to do with "ignoring" or "reinterpreting" certain passages for symbolic meanings, as Harris suggests.

When Harris suggests that not stoning your daughter for talking about Krishna after yoga class would represent "an unwillingness to fully submit to God's law," he demonstrates complete ignorance of the fact that those laws had an express expiration date many millennia ago. No Christian with the most rudimentary understanding of the Bible believes, as Harris suggests, that the Mosaic Law could or should be in effect today. The Old Testament clearly predicts its own expiration in Jeremiah 31:31-33:

> "Behold the days are coming," declares the LORD, "when I
> will make a *new covenant* with the house of Israel and Judah,
> not like the covenant I made with their fathers in the day I
> took them…out of the land of Egypt [i.e. the Mosaic Law
> Harris loves to quote]…this is the covenant I will make
> with the house of Israel after those days [their time in exile
> in Babylon 597-538 BC]", declares the LORD, "I will put
> my law within them, and *I will write it on their hearts* [i.e.,
> in contrast to the Mosaic Law, which was carved on stone
> tablets]."

This new law of conscience replacing the Mosaic Law is also echoed in Ezekiel 11 and 36. This is clearly not the "retreat from scriptural literalism" in light of cultural developments that Harris misrepresents it to be. Christians already understood 2000 years ago that the Mosaic Law had been replaced and was rendered obsolete by Jesus. As the writer of Hebrews said, the old system under the law of Moses was "but a shadow of the good things to come" (Hebrews 10:1). He then quoted Jeremiah 31 to remind his readers that the Mosaic Law always had an expiration date. Paul described the law as a tutor (Galatians 3:24). This is an apt analogy; once you understand the subject matter—in this case, morality—you no longer need the tutor. Paul expressed it most clearly in Romans 6:14: "You no longer live under the requirements of the law" (NLT).

No one besides Harris believes there is any requirement to stone your daughter for coming back from yoga class talking about Krishna. If Harris sincerely thinks so (and is not, as I suspect, just quote mining even though he knows better), he is demonstrating the very ignorance of Scripture for which he faults others. Perhaps some uninformed readers from his atheist fan base are stirred by Harris' writing. However, readers with even minimal biblical knowledge are left scratching their heads wondering when Harris will engage real biblical principles instead of distorted caricatures. Christians already agree that stoning your daughter because she became a Hare Krishna is absurd.

Harris' application of the Old Testament to an encounter with Hare Krishnas demonstrates his ignorance of the historical context of the ancient Near East and how dangerous the ancient "heretics" were.[13] Unlike peaceful people in orange robes passing out flowers at airports, the heretics in the Old Testament were the Canaanites and Ammonites, who sacrificed children to the god Moloch.[14] I suspect that if Harris' daughter came home extolling the virtues of a cult of human sacrifice, he would take it a lot more seriously than his simplistic Krishna analogy. It might even be enough to reverse his stand against the death penalty.[15] Surely, at the very least, a father with any sense of morality would demand cult members who killed innocent children and convinced his own daughter to do the same should be locked in prison.

Speaking of prison, this is another major contextual element Harris fails to consider. Israel had no prisons. The people were still a nomadic tribe wandering in the desert when Moses gave them these instructions. So what do you do with child killers when you have no means to incarcerate them? Let them go with a stern warning not to do it again? Execute them? Send them off into the surrounding desert alone? If so, you have effectively executed them. Here we begin to see how the context is far more complicated than Harris admits in his illustration. Not without cause do other atheists accuse Harris of "startling oversimplifications."[16]

Regarding Harris' comments that religious moderation is "no bulwark against religious extremism," this is another area which overlaps Dawkins, so I refer you to page 213, where I address this in response to Dawkins.

[original argument on page 142]

Reason in Exile: The World Beyond Reason

Harris mentions the mind-body problem only in passing. Although this is a major problem for materialists, Harris glazes over it with only a subordinate clause contained in a sentence about another topic. This unwillingness to address the biggest problems with his position is one of the reasons I found his book so unconvincing. I do not have enough blind faith to adopt Sam Harris' view when he refuses to engage the problems within that view.

[original argument on page 143]

The Nature of Belief

Harris raises the tired "wishful thinking" argument that goes back to German philosopher Ludwig Feuerbach. Feuerbach argued in 1841 that God was an invention dreamed up by human beings to provide metaphysical and spiritual consolation. This worn-out argument has been thoroughly refuted over the last 175 years. Even Nietzsche called it preposterous. First, wanting something does not equate with the lack of its existence. Human thirst actually points to a need for water. As C.S. Lewis observed, desires point toward the things that satisfy those desires:

> Creatures are not born with desires unless satisfaction for those desires exists. A baby feels hunger: well, there is such a thing as food. A duckling wants to swim: well, there is such a thing as water. Men feel sexual desire: well, there is such a thing as sex. If I find in myself a desire which no experience in this world can satisfy, the most probable explanation is that I was made for another world.[17]

I got married late in life, so there were many years I spent wishing for a wife. The fact that I wished to be married gives me no reason to doubt that I am married now or that I have a faithful spouse simply because I longed for one.

Second, the wishful thinking argument is like waking up in the middle of the night to find a burglar in your bedroom and solving the problem by pulling the pin on a hand grenade and dropping it in the middle of the room. It may address the problem of the burglar, but it creates a whole new set of problems for you! As Alister McGrath observed, atheism "can be seen as a response to the human desire for moral autonomy,"[18] so each group has its own set of wishes. For example, I shared in chapter 1 how, throughout his many years as an atheist, C.S. Lewis wished for freedom from God. Leveling the charge of wishful thinking is like bringing a grenade to a knife fight; it is equally devastating for both parties.

[original argument on page 143]

In the Shadow of God

I have no qualms acknowledging that Christianity has made its share of mistakes over its 2000-year history. No worldview, including atheism, can claim a perfect track record. I would expect any religious (or irreligious) group that has existed for two millennia to have committed its share of sins. But how does Christianity's history measure up against other benchmarks? For example, America is one-tenth the age of Christianity. What is America's track record during that time?

The article "Child Labor in U.S. History" on the University of Iowa webserver begins with:

> Forms of child labor, including indentured servitude and
> child slavery, have existed throughout American history.
> As industrialization moved workers from farms and home
> workshops into urban areas and factory work, children
> were often preferred, because factory owners viewed them
> as more manageable, cheaper, and less likely to strike.[19]

In addition to child labor, America shamefully practiced slavery until 1865. We also forcefully relocated as many as 100,000 Native Americans from their homes to reservations west of the Mississippi River,[20] and massacred 7193 Native Americans between 1511 and 1890.[21] US soldiers mass-murdered between 347 and 504 unarmed South Vietnamese civilians on March 16, 1968, including women, children, and babies. Some of the victims were mutilated, others were gang-raped.[22] Our country did not grant all women the right to vote until 1920,[23] and rampant racism was still fueling major riots as late as the 1960s.[24]

Is there any atheist who would argue that America is not a great country despite child labor, slavery, massacring her native citizens, racism, sexism, and war crimes? Any author who suggests someone can be proud to be American but must hang their head in shame to be Catholic is practicing extremely selective forgiveness. While Harris decries Catholic Europe, he fails to note that a country with separation of church and state in its Constitution has committed its own share of atrocities. Officially atheistic countries like the Soviet Union and China have fared worse.

While it is certainly true the Catholic Church has committed atrocities, it is incredibly naïve to suggest a world free of religion would have the perpetual glee of Disney World. The officially atheistic Soviet Union advocated the control, suppression, and elimination of religious beliefs.[25] The state destroyed churches, mosques, and temples,[26] and forced secularization on society through the school and media.[27] Christian victims of Soviet policies are estimated at 12-20 million,[28] In stark contrast, Garcia Carcel estimates that between 3000 and 5000 were executed in the Spanish Inquisition.[29] Henry Kamen estimates "about 2,000 executions in persona in the whole of Spain up to 1530."[30] During the first five years of Soviet power, on the other hand, the Bolsheviks executed 1200 Russian Orthodox priests and millions of their fellow citizens. Believers were subject to torture, prison camps, labor camps,[31] and sent to mental hospitals for punitive psychiatric treatment.[32] So much for the absence of religion improving the world!

New Atheists frequently bring up the case of Galileo, as if human rights abuses have never occurred in secular societies. Father Gheorghe Calciu-Dumitreasa was atheism's Galileo, but Galileo's house arrest was a picnic compared to how Father Calciu was treated by Romania's atheist government. He was jailed for 16 years simply because he "protested atheism, the collectivization of the means of production, and destruction of the intelligentsia."[33] When released, the government forbade him to study theology. He spoke out against the government's persecution of religion. In response, the government sealed the gates to the seminary. Those brave enough to want to hear more climbed over the seminary walls to hear him. He was subsequently jailed again, tortured, beaten, and not allowed to eat, drink, speak, or relieve himself without permission.

When he was finally released, he was confined to house arrest and, like Galileo, would probably have spent the remainder of his life there were it not for pressure from the Reagan administration. Even after fleeing to America, Father Calciu had not fully escaped the atheistic regime. In 1989, the FBI warned Calciu that atheist Nicolae Ceausescu, general secretary of the Romanian Communist Party, had dispatched assassins to kill Father Calciu. He lived in hiding in rural Pennsylvania before deciding to stop living in fear of Romania's atheist government, which had twice already attempted to poison him.

The tired old excuse for atheists' atrocities is that they were committed in the name of Communism, not atheism. The usual rationalization is that absence of a belief cannot provide positive motivation for oppression. Such statements are flagrant insults to people like Father Calciu, who were prisoned, tortured, and often killed expressly for opposing atheism.

[original argument on page 144]

In the Shadow of God: The Holocaust

Harris' implication that the Catholic Church acted as an accomplice to the Nazis is an outrageous distortion of history. In early 1933, Hitler told Herman Rauschning, "Matters [between the Nazis and the church] will never come to a head. They will recognize a firm will, and we need only show them once or twice who is the master. They will know which way the wind blows."[34] In January 1934, Hitler appointed the neo-pagan and notoriously anti-Catholic Alfred Rosenberg as the cultural and educational leader of the Reich.[35] Rosenberg outlined Hitler's envisioned future for religion in Germany with a 30-point program. Among the key points: The Reich was to control all churches; publication of the Bible was to cease; crucifixes, Bibles and saints were to be removed from altars; Bibles were to be replaced by *Mein Kampf* as God's "most sacred book"; and the Christian cross was to be removed from all churches.[36]

Hitler manifested his hatred of the church in overt actions. Of 2720 clergy imprisoned at Dachau, 95 percent were Catholic, including 400 German priests.[37] The Nazis phased out Catholic schools in Germany by 1939 and closed the Catholic press by 1941. Monasteries and convents were targeted and church property seized.[38] In Germany, thousands of clergy were arrested, often on trumped-up charges of currency smuggling or "immorality."[39] Outside of Germany, beyond the view of German citizens, Nazi persecution of the church was even more severe. At least 1811 Polish clergy died in Nazi concentration camps as Hitler tried to systematically dismantle the church.[40]

While Harris is correct that the Catholic Church never excommunicated Hitler, Harris' claim that it never denounced Hitler's actions is historical fantasy. Harris is remiss to not mention *Mit brennender Sorge* (German for "With Burning Anxiety"), issued by Pope Pius XI on March 10, 1937. It was read from the pulpit of every German Catholic church on March 21, 1937 on Palm Sunday, the busiest Sunday of the year. It condemned the elevation of one race above others,[41] condemned "the so-called myth of race and blood,"[42] denounced the Nazis as pagans, implicitly called Hitler "Satan," and called on Catholics not only to pray but take action to sever ties with the enemy. Although it is too lengthy to quote in full, here are just a few excerpts:

> We wished neither to be an accomplice to equivocation by an untimely silence.

> *Whoever exalts race*, or the people, or the State, or a particular form of State, or the depositories of power...*he is far from the true faith in God.*

> *None but superficial minds* could stumble into concepts of a national God, of a national religion; or attempt to lock within the frontiers of a single people, *within the narrow limits of a single race,* God, the Creator of the universe, King and Legislator of all nations.

> Your priests and Faithful, who have persisted in their Christian duty and in the defense of God's rights *in the teeth of an aggressive paganism.*

> [On the Nazi idea of an Aryan race:] Behold what manner of charity the Father hath bestowed on us, that we should be called and should be the sons of God" (1 John iii. 1). To discard this gratuitous and free elevation in the name of *a so-called German type amounts to repudiating openly a fundamental truth of Christianity.*

> It [the Gospel] admits no substitutes or arbitrary alternatives such as certain leaders pretend to draw from *the so-called myth of race and blood.*

[On Jews:] The use of this word ["Revelation" as used by the Nazis] for the "suggestions" of race and blood, for *the irradiations of a people's history*, is mere equivocation. False coins of this sort do not deserve Christian currency.

[On the need for action:]...the judgment which the Church and all her sons must pronounce on what was and what is sin. Secret and open measures of intimidation, the threat of economic and civic disabilities, bear on the loyalty of certain classes of Catholic functionaries, a pressure which violates every human right and dignity...*there is but one alternative left, that of heroism.* If the oppressor offers one the Judas bargain of apostasy he can only, at the cost of every worldly sacrifice, answer with Our Lord: "Begone, Satan!"

Whoever counters these erroneous developments with an uncompromising "No!" from the very outset, not only serves the purity of his faith in Christ, but also the welfare and the vitality of his own people.

Although Harris tries to rewrite history, there can be no doubt that the Nazis understood that the Catholic Church opposed them. Frank Coppa describes how the Nazis viewed the above encyclical as "a call to battle against the Reich" and how Hitler was furious and "vowed revenge against the church."[43] Nazi reprisal was swift and furious. The Gestapo raided every German Catholic church the next day to confiscate all the copies of *Mit brennender Sorge* they could find, and the presses that had printed the letter were closed.

According to Eamon Duffy, history professor at the University of Cambridge, the encyclical "dispelled at once all suspicion of a Fascist Pope...The last year of his [Pope Pius XI] life left no one any doubt of his total repudiation of the ring-wing tyrannies in Germany."[44] As Thomas Bokenkotter describes it:

When Hitler showed increasing belligerence toward the Church, Pius met the challenge with a decisiveness that astonished the world. His encyclical Mit brennender Sorge was the 'first great official public document to dare to confront and criticize Nazism' and 'one of the greatest such condemnations ever issued by the Vatican.'... It exposed the fallacy and denounced the Nazi myth of blood and soil; it decried its Neopaganism, its war of annihilation against the Church, and even described the Führer himself as a "mad prophet possessed of repulsive arrogance."[45]

Carlo Falconi echoes this sentiment: "the pontifical letter still remains the first great official public document to dare to confront and criticize Nazism, and the Pope's courage astonished the world."[46] The Church's opposition to Hitler is an undisputable historical fact. So undisputed, in fact, that I would encourage anyone to simply search online "Nazi persecution of the Catholic Church in Germany." This issue is a good example of how egregiously Harris misrepresents history.

Catholic opposition to Hitler cost thousands of clergy their lives. Thousands more spent years in concentration camps. The Church lost its schools, presses, and cathedrals. One wonders what more it could possibly have done to receive any credit from Harris.

[original argument on page 144]

The Problem with Islam

Harris' "Islam-alone" explanation of terrorism is powerless to explain how more than a billion educated Muslims living outside regions of poverty and exploitation find no motivation *in Islam alone* for terrorism.[47] Harris acknowledges but dismisses Fareed Zakaria—journalist, editor of *Time*, and CNN host—who points out that millions of Muslims living in the United States, Canada, and Europe "have found a way of being devout without being obscurantist, and pious without embracing fury."[48] I find Zakaria more convincing than Harris. It seems unlikely that Islam necessitates violence; have millions of peaceful Muslims missed that fact? Have only Harris and a few Muslim extremists stumbled upon the "true" meaning of Islam? To me this makes as much sense as saying that *Romeo & Juliet* has a really cheerful ending that most people have overlooked.

As we saw above in "Reason in Exile," if you plot the more than 200 terrorist acts in 2013, it looks like a map of regions of poverty, lack of education, and exploitation.[49] By Harris' own admission, "Turkey is an island of ambassadorial goodwill compared with the rest of Muslim world."[50] The fact seems lost on Harris that Turkey has the least poverty, best education, and least exploitation of all the countries he lists. No wonder they are full of goodwill! It is not because Turkey has a special edition of the Koran.

Dr. Giles Dorronsoro, an award-winning professor of political science in Paris, spent several months traveling in Afghanistan in the spring and summer of 2009.[51] Dr. Dorronsoro's experience makes him an authority on the Taliban in a way Harris could never be. This was Dorronsoro's observation after living among the Taliban:

> Most of the fighters do not join the Taliban for money. They join because the Afghan government is unjust, corrupt, or simply not there. They also join because the Americans have bombed their houses or shown disrespect for their values. For young people, joining the Taliban is a way to earn social status…Whatever his initial motivations in joining the Taliban, once a fighter has seen a friend or family member killed by foreign forces, he becomes fully committed to the cause…loyalty is often not a matter of individual choice; it's a matter of family honor to fight the people who've killed your father or your brother.[52]

[original argument on page 145]

A Fringe Without a Center

When Harris questions the sincerity of tolerant Muslims, it reminds me of Richard Dawkins questioning the sincerity of Pope John Paul II's affirmation of evolution. Dawkins' response was "that the pope was a hypocrite…he could not be genuine about science."[53] Dawkins simply refuses to believe that the Pope believes in evolution, despite what the Pope says.

Pause for a moment to let that sink in. No matter what religion says, no matter how religion acts, for the New Atheists, religion is always wrong. Why? Did the Pope deny evolution? No. Were moderate Muslims intolerant? Not at all. But the Pope is still wrong on the basis of what Richard Dawkins *thinks* the Pope is thinking. The moderate Muslim is judged by how Harris *thinks* he wants to act. Even when religious people believe the same thing and act the same way as atheists, religion is still judged guilty on charges of insincerity. No group could stand up to imaginary projections of their hypothetical worst thoughts, not even atheists.

I found the 2002 Pew Research study cited by Harris and a more recent 2005 update. The 2005 study found support for terrorism had declined by an average of 11 percent in the three years since 2002 (with the exception of Jordan):

Suicide Bombing Is Justified in Defense of Islam[54]

Country	2002	2005	Change
Jordan	43%	57%	+14%
Lebanon	73%	39%	-34%
Pakistan	33%	25%	-8%
Indonesia	27%	15%	-12%
Turkey	13%	14%	+1%
Morocco	40%	13%	-27%
Overall average:			-11%

Did atheism make considerable inroads during those three years to cause that change? Hardly. The major change was that an additional three years had passed since the 2001 United States' invasion of Afghanistan. We should remember the context of the poll Harris cites. It was taken within one year of a major US military incursion into a Muslim country. Support for terrorism actually dropped off rather quickly following that invasion.

Pakistan and Turkey were surveyed one year before and after the March 2003 invasion of Iraq. The results provide fascinating insight into the effect of US military action on support for terrorism. In Pakistan, prewar support for suicide bombings was 33 percent in 2002. One year after the invasion, it jumped to 41 percent, before declining to 25 percent two years after the invasion. A similar pattern occurred in Turkey.[55] Was there a special 1400th-anniversary Extra Violent edition of the Koran released in 2003 that supports Harris' assertion? Of course not. The US invaded two Muslim countries in two years. The timing of the spike in support for terrorism rationally correlates with US military actions. That makes more sense than quote-mining the Koran for an explanation.

It has been said, "People who live in glass houses should not throw stones." Before accepting Harris' suggestion that all of Islam should be eradicated because some of its members advocate attacking civilians, we should consider what that says of the US. We intentionally targeted Japanese civilians in Hiroshima and Nagasaki, Japan, in August 1945 with atomic bombs. Conservatively speaking, the US killed 225,000 Japanese civilians, including women, children, and the elderly.[56]

It is interesting how support among Americans changed so dramatically when we felt our country was under attack. According to a 1945 Gallup poll during the height of the war, an overwhelming 85 percent of Americans approved of dropping atomic bombs on Japanese civilians. Only 10 percent disapproved.[57] When that same poll was repeated in July 2005, only a bit over half of Americans (57 percent) approved, while 38 percent disapproved. Harris condemned Islam because 53 percent of Muslims approved of violence in a poll taken while US military forces were actively fighting in Afghanistan.[58] However, 57 percent of Americans still approve of targeting civilian populations in Japan 70 years after the war ended. There are more Americans who justify bombing civilian cities seven decades after all hostilities with Japan have ceased than there are Muslims who justify attacks on civilians while the US has ongoing military campaigns in Muslim countries. When the US was under attack, more Americans felt justified dropping atomic bombs on Japanese civilians (85 percent) than the worst-of-the-worst of terrorists cited by Harris (82 percent in Lebanon).[59]

Even more telling, a recent 2010 Gallup poll found that Muslims were significantly more likely than atheists to condemn targeting civilians. The poll asked, "Some people think that for the military to target and kill civilians is sometimes justified, while others think that kind of violence is never justified. Which is your opinion?" Seventy-eight percent of Muslims said it was never justified to target and kill civilians, while only 56 percent of atheists said killing civilians was never justified.[60]

Wait! Muslims are more reluctant to attack civilians than atheists? If that result has you scratching your head, pay close attention to the wording of the question. A different Gallop poll found the level of support for attacks on civilians changes dramatically if one word is changed in the question—the word *military*. When asked whether *military* attacks on civilians are justified, 49 percent of Americans agree it is sometimes justified. This is higher than any country in the world, *including all Muslim countries.* However, when the wording is changed to whether *individual* attacks on civilians are sometimes justified, the percentage of Americans who agree drops by more than half to 22 percent.[61] The takeaway is profound. Nations approve of the way *they* fight their battles. It would appear that a country's propensity to approve of individual terror attacks has more to do with the strength of its military than with what religious books its citizens read.

[original argument on page 146]

Perfect Weapons

There are so many errors in Harris' argument that it is hard to know where to begin. For starters, none less than fellow atheist Christopher Hitchens disagrees with Harris' characterization of the Al-Shifa pharmaceutical plant attack as merely good intentions polluted by faulty military intelligence. Describing the attack for *Salon News,* Hitchens said, "He [Clinton] acted with caprice and brutality and with a complete disregard for international law."[62] Hitchens went on to point out that the attack "coincidentally" occurred on the night the Monica

Lewinsky saga returned to the grand jury, conveniently deflecting media attention from the president's sex scandal. Harris is right that "intentions are everything." He is just unrealistic about how altruistic America's intentions are. [63]

While Harris raises a valid point when he asks his readers to consider what might happen if Muslim extremists got their hands on a nuclear weapon, he conveniently fails to address what might happen if atheist dictator Kim Jong-un did the same. In this case, no imagination is required. Kim Jong-un hired a computer animation team to turn his vision for America's future into a video that he posted on North Korea's official government website. [64] The video (available on YouTube) begins benignly with the image of a sleeping young North Korean man and an elevator music soundtrack of the pop anthem "We Are the World." It quickly transitions to the image of a rocket launch followed by images of missiles raining down on what appears to be New York City, setting fire to high-rise buildings in scenes reminiscent of the 9/11 attacks. Over images of billowing smoke, the Korean-language captions say, "It seems that the nest of wickedness is ablaze."

Kim Jong-un perfectly illustrates the flaw in Harris' logic. Obviously someone can be a threat to civilization even without believing "some rather incredible things about this universe—in particular, about what happens after death." [65] Jong-un has the same views about death as Harris, but is still bent on annihilation. He needs no dogma of celestial virgins to inspire him to violence. Neither did atheist Soviet leader Nikita Khrushchev when he issued his famous invective "We will bury you!" to Western ambassadors in Moscow. Khrushchev found nothing in atheism to deter his hatred of America.

Harris' position that belief in "incredible things...about what happens after death" causes atrocities could lead to a bestselling book only in a country where people believe *E!* and *People* magazine are "news" sources. For anyone who spends as much time keeping up with current events as they do the Kardashians, a myriad of examples that refute Harris' premise immediately come to mind. There is atheist Timothy McVeigh, mastermind of the Oklahoma City bombing, and atheist Jeffrey Dahmer, who committed crimes that would never cross Osama bin Laden's mind. Harris must be counting on a good deal of public ignorance of the "Who's Who" of atheism when he makes the absurd claim that people need incredible views regarding life after death to commit evil.

If the right Muslims had "perfect" weapons, the entire Gulf War and its 18,000 US coalition casualties may have been avoided. The 1991 Shiite uprising in Iraq, which even Harris admits "surely ranks among the most unethical and consequential foreign policy blunders" of America,[66] could have succeeded in deposing Saddam Hussein without spilling a drop of American blood if the rebels had had better weapons. At the height of their revolt, Hussein lost control over 14 of Iraq's 18 provinces.[67] Within the first two weeks of the revolt, most of Iraq's cities had fallen to rebel forces. The rebellion failed in large part because the rebels had few heavy weapons and surface-to-air missiles, which left them defenseless against Hussein's helicopter gunships.[68] Also, the wrong Muslims—Hussein's loyalist forces—had and used Sarin nerve gas and mustard gas.[69]

Iraqi Muslims took up arms not in jihad against America, but to depose an evil, brutal dictator. Hussein had attempted the genocide of the Kurds three years prior in 1988, killing men from the ages of 13 to 70, in part by using chemical weapons. It is estimated that up to 182,000 were killed during his Anfal Campaign.[70] The tragedy of the 1991 uprising was not that weapons were in *Muslim* hands. The problem was the weapons were in the *wrong* Muslim hands. If the right Muslims had had the weapons they needed, the entire Iraq War may have been avoided.

[original argument on page 146]

Does Terrorism Require Religion?

In closing my critique on Harris' chapter about Islam, I would like to examine his premise that terrorism requires religion. According to the Oxford English dictionary, the first known use of the word *terrorist* was to describe the *nonreligious* supporters of the Jacobins in the French Revolution, "who advocated repression and violence in pursuit of the principles of democracy and equality."[71] The word comes to us from the French *terroriste*. The first terrorists were members of a French *political* movement.

The second most deadly terrorist attack on American soil was the April 1995 Oklahoma City bombing that killed 168 people and injured more than 680.[72] Agnostic terrorist Timothy McVeigh needed no false belief in celestial virgins to inspire his politically motivated attack. Contrary to Harris' claim that someone needs incredible beliefs about the afterlife to commit acts of terror,[73] McVeigh doubted its existence, but reckoned that if there was an afterlife, then he would probably spend it in hell for his actions. In a letter he wrote to the *Buffalo News*, McVeigh stated he would "improvise, adapt and overcome if it turned out there was an afterlife," and "If I'm going to hell, I'm gonna have a lot of company."[74]

?????

Why were there no kamikaze attacks at Pearl Harbor? If you know the answer, you have a better understanding of the relationship between spiritual beliefs and suicide attacks than Harris does.

According to the US Naval War College, the Japanese did not invent the kamikaze tactic until they had sustained such heavy losses that they could no longer put together a large number of fleet carriers with well-trained aircrews.[75] Also, newer US planes like the F6F Hellcat and F4U Corsair were beginning to outnumber and outclass Japan's fighter planes, making traditional warfare increasingly difficult.[76] It was in desperation, not religious fervor, that Japanese vice admiral Takijiro Onishi declared to the 201st Flying Group headquarters, "I don't think there would be any other certain way to carry out the operation [to hold the Philippines], than to put a 250-kilogram bomb on a Zero and let it crash into a US carrier in order to disable her for a week." Commander Tamai initially rejected the proposal, but eventually decided "there was no choice but to carry out the suicide mission."[77]

The pilots who flew the missions expected no reward in the afterlife. They were motivated by extreme nationalism, believing their death would pay the debt they owed their country and show the love they had for family, friends, and the emperor.[78] This extreme nationalism was programmed into the Japanese mindset not by imams or priests, but by the nation's school system. The Imperial Rescript on Education, in place since 1890, required students to ritually recite an oath to offer themselves "courageously to the State" and to protect the Imperial family.[79]

This pattern of resorting to self-sacrifice only at the point of desperation was repeated in Germany. It is largely unknown that Germany had its own kamikazes, the Leonidas Squadron. Just like Commander Tamai, Hitler was initially against the idea of self-sacrifice and did not see the war as being dire enough for such extreme measures. However, he eventually agreed to allow Fieseler Fi 103R airplanes to be developed as piloted bombs.[80] The 2000-pound bombs were so heavy that the aircraft could only carry enough fuel to reach its intended target. The unit was formed too late to make a significant contribution to the war, but *Selbstopfereinsätze* ("self-sacrifice missions") were carried out by Leonidas pilots April 17-20, 1945 to take out bridges over the Oder River in a last-ditch effort to stop the Soviet advance in the Battle of Berlin.

The Japanese and Germans had radically different philosophies and worldviews. The common element was desperation leading to drastic measures, but not until after all other options had been exhausted.

What's Wrong with Atheism? Why Be So Hostile?

Lest I cause offense, the title of this section is a play on a section in one of Dawkins' books, titled "What's Wrong with Religion? Why Be So Hostile?" The problem with Harris' mentality that religion is the root of all evil is that, if he is wrong, it is more than just a difference of opinion. If religion is not the root cause of terrorism, then all the time, effort, and resources he convinces others to invest in attacking religion is wasted on something other than fixing the problem.

Therein lies the real danger with Harris' argument. If the root problem is political, economic, and/or social, and the evidence clearly points in those directions, then Harris is drawing attention away from the issues that could actually fix the problem. For example, if US foreign policy is a major contributing factor, as the Pew Research data demonstratively shows, the propagation of Harris' ideology in Washington would be cancer. If congressmen who currently heed the wisdom in Fair/Shepherd's *Studies in Conflict & Terrorism*[81] end up buying into Harris' alternative suggestion that even *more* economic isolation and military intervention is needed, they will engage in more of the very actions that research has shown to cause the problem. All available evidence seems to suggest that pursuing the wrong course of action will only make matters worse.

Who is wrong, Fair and Shepherd, or Harris? Even Harris' strongest supporters should be able to recognize he is, at the very least, partially wrong. How would the elimination of religion have made any difference in the Oklahoma City bombing? McVeigh had no religious motive, no assistance from any religious organization, and no skewed view of the afterlife. Religion had no causal relationship to the actions of terrorists like McVeigh and Adam Lanza. At best, Harris' model that religion is the source of terrorism is significantly incomplete.

The problem with Harris' argument is that it does not differentiate or even acknowledge different kinds of terrorism. There is a significant difference between the psyches of McVeigh and the 9/11 hijackers. While understanding the differences may not offer comfort to the loved ones of the victims, it is important if we are to have any hope of preventing such attacks in the future. If we merely lump them together under one category, blurring the distinctions as Harris does, then we risk failing to understand their motivations and thereby failing to recognize possible future deterrents.

Harris' suggestion that religion alone is the problem does nothing to thwart nonreligious terrorism and draws attention away from real, viable solutions to "religious" terrorism by focusing on nonroot causes.

West of Eden

Harris again resorts to begging the question when he talks about prophecy. He asserts it was dangerous for Ronald Reagan to consider foreign policy decisions through the lens of biblical prophecy. However, he offers no argument whatsoever against hundreds of clear cases of prophecy. Instead, he cherry-picks an argument using just one prophecy, the obscure and difficult Isaiah 7:14 passage. Based on this very tenuous case, he argues as if his premise was true. This is another example of him preaching to the atheist choir. Ignoring the best evidence is only convincing to those who are uninformed about this subject.

To decide whether Harris' premise that biblical prophecy has no place in politics is true, we must ask whether there is any evidence biblical prophecy has ever come true. The prophecies about Jesus are a falsifiable litmus test. There are hundreds besides the obscure example Harris bases his entire argument on. Were any prophecies about Jesus true?

Some skeptics have suggested that Christians twisted vague Old Testament passages to make them fit Jesus after the fact. However, even secular scholars have noted that first-century Jews clearly understood Old Testament texts predicted a Messiah and expected his imminent arrival. This observation comes from irreligious biblical scholars with no confirmation bias.

For example, Enlightenment philosopher Herman Reimarus, a Deist who denied the supernatural origin of Christianity, came to the conclusion that Jesus was a Messiah impersonator who accidentally got himself killed.[82] Charles Hennell, in *An Inquiry Concerning the Origin of Christianity*, claims that Jesus was only human, the son of a member of the Essene religious order, which used him as a pawn. They orchestrated the events that led to his crucifixion, after which they took him down from the cross, comatose yet not dead, and resuscitated him in order to claim Old Testament prophecy had been fulfilled. Most recently, former Catholic-priest-turned-skeptic Dominic Crossan has written extensively about how messianic prophecies affected Jesus' view of himself.[83] No evangelical, Crossan is a noted member of the Jesus Seminar group that challenges the authenticity of roughly three-fourths of the Gospel teachings traditionally attributed to Jesus.

Even secular scholars commonly agree that first-century Jews clearly understood certain Old Testament passages were prophecies of a coming Messiah. Whether Jesus tried to take that role on himself, was tricked into it by the Essenes, or the role was projected upon him by those around him, the core that all these *nonreligious* scholars agree on is that the Jews had a very clear picture of who the Messiah would be, based on Old Testament prophecy.

Looking at only 21 of the Old Testament prophecies, it is readily obvious that they are much too specific to be fulfilled by vagueness, self-fulfillment, or chance:

1. His family tree would be:
   Abraham—Genesis 12:2-3; 22:18
   Isaac—Genesis 21:12
   Jacob—Numbers 24:17
   Judah (one of the 12 tribes of Israel)—Genesis 49:10, Micah 5:2
   family of Jesse (one family out of that entire tribe)— Isaiah 1:10; 11:1
   house of David (one of Jesse's eight sons)—Jeremiah 23:5

2. He would be born in Bethlehem—Micah 5:2

3. He would be presented with gifts from kings—Psalm 72:10

4. His birth would be accompanied by a mass execution of children—Jeremiah 31:15

5. His ministry would begin in Galilee—Isaiah 9:1

6. He would perform miracles—Isaiah 35:5, 6

7. He would be betrayed by a friend—Psalm 41:9

8. Thirty pieces of silver would be the price for his betrayal— Zechariah 11:12

9. That same money would later be thrown onto the floor of the temple—Zechariah 11:13

10. He would be forsaken by his own disciples—Zechariah 13:7

11. He would be accused by false witnesses—Psalm 35:11

12. He would be struck and spit upon—Isaiah 50:6

13. His hands and feet would be pierced—Zechariah 12:10

14. He would be executed among thieves—Isaiah 53:12

15. He would be rejected by the Jewish people—Isaiah 53:3

16. People would gamble for his garments—Psalm 22:18

17. He would be offered gall and vinegar for thirst while being crucified—Psalm 69:21

18. None of his bones would be broken during his execution—Psalm 34:20

19. His side would be pierced—Zechariah 12:10

20. The land would be covered in darkness at noon at his death—Amos 8:9

21. He would be buried in a rich man's tomb—Isaiah 53:9

The above are just a few of more than 300 Old Testament prophecies about Jesus. The huge number of prophecies he fulfilled is a logical, rational explanation for why Christianity spread so rapidly. Jesus' disciples countered objections to the probability of the resurrection with the argument that it was miraculously foretold.

Starting with his first sermon, Peter claimed that the events which transpired fulfilled specific Old Testament prophecies. For example, he said, "What you see was predicted long ago by the prophet Joel" (Acts 2:16 NLT), "King David said this about [Jesus]" (Acts 2:25 NLT), and "This is how God fulfilled what he had foretold through all the prophets" (Acts 3:18 NIV). The prophecies are such common knowledge that Peter can safely assume that his audience's familiarity with them would lead them to recognize that Jesus fulfilled them.

I seriously investigated nonsupernatural explanations of Old Testament prophecy. However, none of them seem to stand up to careful scrutiny. The possibility that the prophecies were supernaturally directed is the most probable explanation barring an *a priori* assumption of materialism that rules out the supernatural. To simply reject them based on preconceived notions is hardly honest inquiry.

It goes without saying that if hundreds of prophecies had already been fulfilled, it was not, as Harris suggests, dangerous for Reagan to apply

them to foreign policy. There is good evidence that numerous prophecies have been fulfilled. Harris offers poor evidence to the contrary.

[original argument on page 148]

A Science of Good and Evil

Harris starts with the traditional atheist assertion that we can
observe morality in nature, noting that monkeys will undergo extraordinary privations to avoid causing harm to others. However, he refutes
himself later in the chapter by noting that some animals practice rape.[84]
His discussion of primates conveniently fails to mention gorillas vio-
lently driving off other males and practicing infanticide against children of other males. Of course, whenever atheists claim we should look
to nature for morality, invariably they carefully avoid images of gorillas
bashing in the skulls of other gorillas' babies.

Harris is making a moral truth claim allegedly supported by nature.
Specifically, he states that undergoing hardship for one's species is morally superior to other natural actions like forced copulation and infanticide. However, the claim that the former is good while the latter is
bad is obviously based on more than observation of nature. Harris fails
to address why he deems the behavior of monkeys morally superior to
that of gorillas. The underlying question still remains: Why is altruism (which incidentally happens to be found among monkeys) morally superior to rape (which incidentally happens to be found among
orangutans)? In the end, he is still appealing to a standard outside of
nature; the spurious field trip with monkeys adds nothing.

When Harris says we cannot build an ethic on the Old Testament,
he adds nothing meaningful to the dialogue. Any Christian who understands the Bible already knows that the Mosaic Law served a specific
purpose for a specific time and place. The vast majority of Christians
understand a religious theocracy applied only to ancient Israel. The
harsh penalties were a temporary bulwark against the even more brutal practices of the ancient Near East as we discussed in the section on
moderation in religion.

Harris' claim that the God of Abraham cannot be the source of ethics is loosely equivalent to claiming America cannot build a legal system
on martial law. No reasonable person claims martial law is superior to

constitutional law. However, despite its inferiority, martial law has been enacted seven times in American history.[85] When it had to be put into effect, it was not an endorsement of suspending human rights. Rather, it was simply an acknowledgment that it can be necessary under dire circumstances. No atheist would suggest that we should throw out the Constitution because it had to be suspended seven times. Yet Harris asks theists to throw out the entire Bible because conditions *once* warranted the Mosaic Law. His argument against the Mosaic Law makes sense only if you are willing to ignore the context of its implementation.

[original argument on page 148]

The Demon of Relativism

I agree 100 percent. Harris is in a very small minority of atheists who get this. Well put, Sam.

[original argument on page 149]

Intuition, Ethics, Self-Interest, Happiness, and Other Topics

When evaluating whether I was being open-minded to Harris' argument, I noticed that his model conflicted with those of atheist thinkers like Nietzsche and Russell. As we saw in chapter 3, Nietzsche believed the rational implication of Darwinism is that man is merely the highest form of beast. He reasoned that hunger and sexual lust are sufficient to explain human actions.[86] He felt that evil and tyranny do as much to strengthen men[87] as generosity.[88] You could say he advocated the slogan "No pain, no gain" long before Nike. He did not see all men as equals, but felt that subservience was the natural condition of the vast majority of humanity.[89] In fact, he felt it was *necessary* to have some enemies[90] to prevent us from carrying out our baser instincts upon our own herd.[91] Russell agreed with Nietzsche that evolution has made man merely an animal because he is merely a part of nature.[92] Nietzsche thought views like Harris' on the nature of mankind were fundamentally flawed. He would argue that Harris' view is naïve and destined to fail due to man's nature.

On the other hand, while Russell shared Nietzsche's view that evil is illusionary, he did advocate a view similar to Harris' that we should live a life "inspired by love." Unlike Harris, though, Russell was clear this moral proposition was not absolute, could not be proved "right," and was merely his personal opinion.[93] He did not, as Harris does, pretend it was anything more than a personal preference. Both Nietzsche and Russell believed the prevailing atheist idea that morality is nothing more than herd instinct.[94] The bottom line is that two atheists, exempt from confirmation bias, would challenge Harris' premise. It is not just Christians who notice that Harris' argument has major flaws.

I agree with Russell. Harris' suggestion of seeking the maximum of human flourishing is just Harris' personal opinion, not the absolute that he strenuously claims it is. I do not find his opinion completely meritless (as Nietzsche would), but I do find Harris' definition of love inadequate. Harris' aphorism "love is more conducive to happiness, both to our own and that of others, than hate"[95] sounds great. However, Harris ultimately presents a false dichotomy between love and hate. As Dr. Leo Buscaglia, author of bestsellers like *Loving Each Other* and *Born for Love*, points out, "I feel very strongly that the opposite of love is not hate—it's apathy. It's not giving a damn."[96]

Harris presents a false dilemma when he claims that love is better than hate. No one is seriously advocating building an ethical system on hate, except perhaps a handful of Star Trek sci-fi junkies obsessed with Klingons. The Muslim extremist who spends his day assembling improvised explosive devices in a clandestine Iraqi warehouse still tucks his daughter in at night and reads her a bedtime story. Even Nietzsche, who wrote about man's animal instincts, never advocated actively trying to harm people. He merely accepted suffering as part of life and was thus ambivalent to it. What Harris needs to address is the problem of love verses *apathy*. In saying love is better than hate, he says nothing that is not common knowledge.

Harris acknowledges "love entails the loss, at least to some degree, of our utter self-absorption."[97] Given that love is sacrifice, even by Harris' own admission, the vital question Harris leaves unanswered is, Who do I have a *duty* to love?

Loving parents will work a second job, if necessary, to make sure their child does not go to bed hungry. But what is their obligation to a starving child in Africa? Those parents do not *hate* the poor, starving

African child; they may genuinely love all children. However, when it comes to *demonstrating* love, do they have a moral obligation to work overtime to send a donation to World Vision or the Red Cross? Harris says, "The happiness and suffering of others must matter to us."[98] However, there is a wide chasm between intellectually acknowledging that suffering matters and defining what our duty is to take action to end it. His aphorism is unable to bridge the chasm between intellect and action.

Here we find atheism advancing more "Starbucks ethics"—ideas that work better in an intellectual discussion over coffee than in the real world, where tangible improvements for the happiness of one group often come at the expense of another. For example, the United States accounts for only 5 percent of the world's population,[99] yet has roughly one-third of the planet's wealth.[100] According to BBC news, the average wage in the United States (and the United Kingdom) is $37,000 a year, or $154 per work day. Meanwhile, more than one-third of the world's population lives on less than $2 a day.[101] Clearly, redistributing wealth would have a tremendous impact on global happiness and suffering. It is easier to claim that, however, than to make the case that we should.

What would maximize overall human well-being is quite easy to visualize. To claim I have a moral *duty* to implement such a plan is a whole other thing. Saying an act *would* maximize human flourishing is completely different than the claim that I *should* therefore do it, especially if acting on it requires personal sacrifice. Harris claims that sacrificial giving will lead to personal satisfaction, but he cannot claim that people who disagree with him are "wrong" by any objective standard.

Harris' model simply cannot bridge the chasm between *would* and *should*. The chasm exists where Harris quietly and subtly shifts from a deontological argument to a utilitarian one. Harris says, "Whatever a person's current level of happiness is, his condition will be generally improved by his becoming yet more loving and compassionate."[102] That is a strictly utilitarian argument. He is claiming that since the *outcome* of love and compassion is happiness, people should be loving and compassionate. This is an argument backward from the end result. It is the very opposite of an absolute.

By Harris' own admission, people may not achieve elevated happiness by caring about human flourishing. Some people are horribly unfortunate. For anyone who does not increase happiness by decreasing selfishness, Harris has no basis to claim they have a moral duty to continue acting selflessly in the absence of reward. This is the point where his ethics prove to be utilitarian, and not the absolutes he claims.

[original argument on page 149]

Summary

What makes Harris unique among the New Atheists is his frequent references to his own spirituality. Says Harris, "There is clearly a sacred dimension to our existence, and coming to terms with it could well be the highest purpose of human life."[103] He goes on, "We cannot live by reason alone," and "It is time we realized that we need not be unreasonable to suffuse our lives with love, compassion, ecstasy, and awe; *nor must we renounce all forms of spirituality or mysticism to be on good terms with reason.*"[104] I find it fascinating and perplexing that he could be so open to spiritual experiences yet so closed to Christianity.

The main issue I have with Harris' writing is that, like Dawkins, he comes across as preaching to the atheist choir to sell books rather than engaging in a sincere dialogue. For example, when Harris asserts that we should not stone our daughter for coming home from yoga class speaking of Hare Krishna, his vivid imagery likely stirs up his atheist fan base. However, the overwhelming majority of Christians who already agree with him are still waiting to hear a meaningful point. I do not expect my book to convince many atheists to reconsider their worldview, but I believe, at the very least, I have done a decent job of explaining why this kind of atheist writing carries no traction with believers or even agnostics.

Harris is constantly on the offensive, but his attacks miss their mark. One example is his assertion that moderate religion is worse than no religion at all. I find it incredibly naïve for him to even suggest that a white, atheist professor living in a comfortable California suburb is in a better position to influence a Muslim extremist living in a cave outside Kandahar than his own flesh-and-blood relatives. Surely family members who see no sanction for violence in the Koran are a better voice to calm the extremists. While there is no tangible evidence that Harris' criticism of Islam has produced any positive change in the Middle East, it has created at least enough additional hostility that Harris now travels with bodyguards. [105] Not that we should ever back down to bullying, but Harris' extreme response of eliminating religion entirely has only engendered more hostility.

Speaking of hostility, I sternly take Harris to task for advocating killing people due to their beliefs. I find the suggestion of executing people solely based on their *thoughts* on par with the actions of the Catholic Inquisitors of whom he is so critical. In Harris' own words, "To my knowledge, the man [Ayman al-Zawahiri] hasn't killed anyone personally." However, Harris advocates dropping a bomb on him because "he is likely to get a lot of innocent people killed *because of what he and his followers believe* about jihad, martyrdom, the ascendancy of Islam, etc."[106] Harris is willing to hand out the death penalty for a thought crime. Think about it. Despite having committed no crime, Harris deems the man worthy of death because of what he *thinks*.

Personally, I find the US justified in bombing Ayman al-Zawahiri as a pre-emptive measure if credible evidence demonstrated that he was planning to attack and kill US citizens. However, the justification is based on the man's actions and only when capture is impossible. The exact same justification warrants shooting the Polish scientist planning to detonate a car bomb outside Poland's parliament when he is en route to his planned terrorist attack. [107] The justification for capturing or killing him is not that he was a scientist, but that he planned to harm people.

In order to hard-sell us on how evil Islam is, Harris is far too forgiving of US atrocities. That is according to fellow atheist Christopher Hitchens. Harris' justification for eliminating religion is so broad that it would not even allow America to exist. He hypocritically demands religion must pay for the crimes for which he acquits America or even the Soviet Union.

I do not merely find Harris' assessment of terrorism wrong, I believe it is downright dangerous, like someone talking a patient out of chemotherapy by persuading them instead to take herbs or acupuncture in lieu of lifesaving treatment. If Harris merely suggested the Koran had a role in facilitating terror *in addition* to the political, economic, and social causes, it would be an argument meriting consideration. Instead, his radical and overly simplistic "religion is the root of all evil" proposition draws attention away from real causes at a time when Americans cannot afford such diversion.

Moving from the war on terror to consider the bigger picture of war in general, Harris' assertion that religion is "the most prolific source of violence in our history" and the primary cause of war simply cannot be reconciled with reality.[108] Philip and Axelrod's *Encyclopedia of Wars* weighs in at over 4500 pages and chronicles 1763 wars waged over the course of human history. To say it is a thorough summary of warfare would be an understatement. Of those wars, the authors categorize 123 as being religious in nature.[109] Reading Harris, you would never get the impression that only 6.9 percent of wars are religious. If you subtract out those waged in the name of Islam, the percentage is cut by more than half to 3.2 percent.[110] This is no statistical cherry-picking. In his exhaustive *The Encyclopedia of War*, editor Gordon Martel concludes that 6 percent of the wars listed in the encyclopedia can be labeled religious wars.[111] The truth is that all faiths combined—minus Islam—have caused less than 4 percent of all humanity's wars and violent conflicts.

That is yet another example of why I found Harris unconvincing. Again and again his allegations that religion causes violence completely unravel upon closer investigation. There simply is nothing convincing in Harris' arguments to anyone who is not already blindly committed to atheism and willing to accept his untenable claims without any fact-checking.

Harris is unique in that he claims to have an intuitive, absolute ethic without God based upon the precept "To treat others ethically is to act out of concern for their happiness and suffering."[112] Further analysis, however, reveals this is "Starbucks ethics" because there is a world of difference between intellectual assent to it over coffee and real-world implementation. Despite claiming to not be a pragmatist, Harris offers a strictly utilitarian justification for his proposed moral system—those who follow it will experience "generally improved" conditions.[113] Such justification by the end result is contrary to an absolute ethic by definition. Also, for people who do not experience his promised improved conditions, Harris has no basis for why they *should* or *ought* to remain committed to the model that is not increasing their happiness. Thus it becomes clear there is nothing absolute about Harris' system after all.

I admit that there are many Christians who unquestioningly accept dogmatism solely on the authority of pastors or priests. Reading the New Atheists, however, opened my eyes to how much dogmatism there is in atheism. Granted it was easy to find a few humanists like David Boulton who call out Harris for "oversimplification, exaggerations and elusions,"[114] but the fact that so many people—skeptics included—bought Harris' book *The End of Faith* shows how ready even skeptics are to accept atheist dogmatism without serious consideration of evidence.

For example, the way Harris handles history like World War II and the Kashmir conflict is enough to make historian William Durant roll over in his grave. Only someone with a strong confirmation bias toward atheism could accept these gross distortions of history as evidence for atheism. I believe I have adequately documented how anyone with an open mind and a willingness to fact-check would find Harris' arguments unconvincing.

While there is a lot of overlap between the New Atheists, it is reasonable to say Harris primarily builds his arguments upon (distorting) history and the (alleged) negative effects of religion. For an atheist argument that focuses more on science, we turn to the chapters on Dawkins.

Harris' Key Concepts

Key Concepts	Source	Evidence Offered
People commit acts of terror in the name of religion.	Russell	A hypothetical example of a young man blowing up a bus.
"Certainty about the next life is simply incompatible with tolerance in this one."	Harris	"Religious faith perpetuates man's inhumanity to man."
"Extraordinary claims require extraordinary evidence."	Russell	A less inconceivable report, like a forest fire, could be believed on the reputation of a respectable news anchor who stands much to lose by lying.
Communism is a religion.	Russell	Lysenko's faulty biology was embraced over Mendelian genetics by fiat of the Soviet government, which shielded Lysenko from criticism.
Religious moderates retreat from scriptural literalism.	Harris	We do not stone our daughter who comes back from yoga class talking about Krishna.
Religious moderation "offers no bulwark against religion extremism and religious violence."	Harris	*None offered*
Religious claims upon the territory of Kashmir have led to more than one million pointless deaths.	Harris	*None offered* (He spends a few pages describing atrocities but fails to establish how religion was causal.)

Key Concepts	Source	Evidence Offered
Naturalism has real philosophical problems with how materialists can trust any of their thoughts.	Harris	*None offered*—he glazes past the subject in half a sentence.
Beliefs must have correspondence with reality.	Harris	"The house is full of termites" and "Muhammad ascended to heaven on a winged horse" are not equivalent beliefs.
Belief in God is just wishful thinking.	Feuerbach	A wife who chooses to believe her husband is faithful despite evidence to the contrary because it makes her feel good.
When extraordinary beliefs are rare we call them "delusional." When they are common we call them "religious."	Harris	Compare the belief that God will reward a man with 72 virgins if he kills a score of Jewish teenagers with the beliefs of someone who thinks creatures from Alpha Centauri are speaking through his hair dryer.
The Bible can be used to justify atrocities like the Inquisition.	Harris	Verses in Deuteronomy command Israel to kill heretics.
The Catholic Church has committed atrocities.	Harris	The Inquisition, witch trials, persecution of Jews
The Catholic Church was complicit with Hitler's genocide.	Harris	The Catholic Church opened its genealogical records to the Nazis and never excommunicated Hitler.

Key Concepts	Source	Evidence Offered
Isaiah never prophesied Jesus' virgin birth.	Harris	The Hebrew word *alma* means "young woman," not "virgin."
Religion, not external factors, is the cause of terrorism.	Harris	"The world is filled with poor, uneducated, and exploited people who do not commit acts of terrorism."
A disturbing number of Muslims think violence against civilian targets is justified.	Harris	Pew Center study of 12 predominantly Muslim countries found 53 percent, on average, agreed violence is justified against civilians.
The difference between civilians killed by Muslims versus Americans is due to imperfect weapons.	Harris	Intentionally killing a child to affect its parents is "terrorism," but accidentally killing a child while trying to kill a child murderer is "collateral damage."
Biblical eschatology intruding into modern politics is dangerous.	Harris	Britain's Balfour Declaration of 1917. US policy toward Israel.
Crime comes from bad genes or bad parents.	Russell	*None offered*
Belief in God results in irrational laws about sex, drugs, and stem-cell research.	Russell/Harris	Laws against oral sex, marijuana use, and stem-cell research
The problem of theodicy is insurmountable.	Russell	God acts capricious, petulant, and cruel in the Bible.

Key Concepts	Source	Evidence Offered
Religion creates moral communities that are indifferent to the suffering of other communities.	Harris	*None offered*—he gives Nazi troops' indifference to Jews as an example of community indifference but gives no examples where religion is involved.
To say something is "natural" does not mean it is "good."	Harris	"Nature has not adapted us to do anything more than breed."
Ethics are absolute, not cultural.	Harris	Ethics is like literacy. Not learning how to read is not another style of literacy. It is a failure of literacy.
"To treat others ethically is to act out of concern for their happiness and suffering."	Harris	"Honor killings" are not really honorable at all; they are a failure of love and therefore a failure of ethics.
"Millions of Muslims around the world" would like to see us living under the Taliban.	Harris	*None offered*
"I do not consider myself a Buddhist."	Harris	His article "Killing the Buddha" wherein he (allegedly) criticizes Buddhism.

Replies and Rebuttals to Harris' Key Concepts

Arguments for Atheism/Against God	Rebuttal
People commit acts of terror in the name of religion.	Cherry-picking fallacy (a.k.a. fallacy of incomplete evidence). Fails to adequately consider political, economic, and personal motivations, as well as mental illness. If just being religious is the sole cause, why has the Pope never blown himself up?
"Certainty about the next life is simply incompatible with tolerance in this one."	*Agreed*—if Harris were not so certain that the annihilation of body and mind await us in the "next life," he would not be so intolerant of religion in this one.
"Extraordinary claims require extraordinary evidence."	Based on an *a priori* belief that materialism explains everything, which is *ipso facto* an article of faith itself, since it is not based on empirical observation.
Communism is a religion (based on the Soviet government selectively choosing which scientists they supported and censured).	Non-sequitur logical fallacy. The US government poured $500 million tax dollars into now-defunct Solyndra while simultaneously denying grants for other research firms. By Harris' standards, this makes our government a religion.
Religious moderates retreat from scriptural literalism.	The Mosaic Law Harris cites always had a finite expiration date (Jeremiah 31). There is no "retreat"; Harris simply does not understand why the Old Testament is called "old."

Arguments for Atheism/Against God	Rebuttal
Religious moderation "offers no bulwark against religion extremism and religious violence."	Incredibly naïve to suggest a white, Western atheist is better equipped to influence an Arab Muslim in Kandahar than his own family who believes the same Koran yet doesn't use it to justify violence.
Religious claims upon the territory of Kashmir have led to more than one million pointless deaths.	The real source of the conflict was the oppression of the majority by a minority. Such behavior is sufficient to cause violence even without religion.
Naturalism has real philosophical problems with how materialists can trust any of their thoughts.	Agreed—furthermore, I note Harris does not even attempt to offer a solution to this serious problem within materialism.
Beliefs must have correspondence with reality.	Agreed—however, Harris commits the logical fallacy of begging the question, arguing as if belief in God does not correspond with reality without ever first establishing that God does not exist.
Belief in God is just wishful thinking.	Wanting something does not mean the object does not exist (i.e., thirst does not disprove water). Atheists have the same problem (i.e. wishing for moral autonomy).
When extraordinary beliefs are rare we call them "delusional." When they are common we call them "religious."	General public beliefs mirrors atheists' beliefs on other issues they deem probable (alien life) and improbable (Elvis lives). Since people seem to be rational about everything else, perhaps they are not as irrational about religion as the New Atheists think.

Arguments for Atheism/Against God	Rebuttal
The Bible can be used to justify atrocities like the Inquisition.	A tree can be used to make a Stradivarius violin or a battering ram to attack a castle. How people use (or misuse) it does not make the tree good (or evil).
The Catholic Church has committed atrocities.	Agreed, but so has America, even with separation of church and state. Also, atheist countries like the Soviet Union and China have committed atrocities that make the Catholic Church look like…well…saints.
The Catholic Church was complicit with Hitler's genocide.	Historically false. Even if Harris was accurate, handing an armed robber your wallet does not make you "complicit" with the crime.
Isaiah never prophesied Jesus' virgin birth.	Alma can mean "virgin." It is used to describe virgins elsewhere in the Old Testament, and the context of Isaiah favors the same interpretation there.
Religion, not external factors, is the cause of terrorism.	Comparing a world map of poverty and exploitation with a map of terrorist attacks shows near-100 percent geographic correlation. Also, Harris drastically oversimplifies reasons why other poor groups remain peaceful.
A disturbing number of Muslims think violence against civilian targets is justified.	An even larger percentage of Americans (57 percent vs. 53 percent) believe dropping atomic bombs on civilians in Hiroshima and Nagasaki was justified even 7 decades after the war, while 85 percent justified it during the war.
The difference between civilians killed by Muslims versus Americans is due to imperfect weapons.	If atheist dictator Kim Jong-un had better weapons, a lot more people would die. Even other atheists acknowledge that many US atrocities cannot be dismissed due to imperfect weapons technology.

Arguments for Atheism/Against God	Rebuttal
Biblical eschatology intruding into modern politics is dangerous.	Begging the question fallacy—the assertion is true *if* biblical eschatology is wrong. However, Harris never seriously attempts to prove this. Also, Jesus appears to have fulfilled a significant number of prophecies.
Crime comes from bad genes or bad parents.	If true, you could not say murder was any worse than forgery when both are merely the result of genes and/or parenting.
Belief in God results in irrational laws about sex, drugs, and stem-cell research.	Begging the question fallacy—Harris assumes God does not exist, so neither should those laws. Yet he never proves his premise that God does not exist. Also, the Bible actually never prohibits oral sex or drug use.
The problem of theodicy is insurmountable.	*Agreed*—it is insurmountable *for atheism*. In asking what is wrong with the world, we have already presumed the existence of a moral standard that the world falls short of.
Religion creates moral communities that are indifferent to the suffering of other communities.	Christianity teaches the equality of numerous diverse moral communities in Christ (Galatians 3:28; Colossians 3:11). World Vision is one of numerous faith groups providing aid to people without regard to race, gender, or religion.

Arguments for Atheism/Against God	Rebuttal
To say something is "natural" does not mean it is "good." "Nature has not adapted us to do anything more than breed."	*Agreed*—it is a very simple concept which seems lost on Richard Dawkins.
Ethics are absolute, not cultural.	*Agreed*—why is Harris the only atheist who seems to get this?
"To treat others ethically is to act out of concern for their happiness and suffering."	*Agreed*, but intellectual assent is quite different from physical action. Acting on this entails sacrifice, and Harris fails to define why we *ought* to make such sacrifices.
"Millions of Muslims around the world" would like to see us living under the Taliban.	Actually, according to *The London Times*, the true number appears closer to 36,000. Makes you wonder what else Harris misportrays.
"I do not consider myself a Buddhist."	Harris can consider himself whatever he wants, but the ideology he espouses is indistinguishable from Buddhism.

9

Sam Harris and Buddhism

*"One could surely argue that the Buddhist
tradition, taken as a whole, represents the
richest source of contemplative wisdom
that any civilization has produced."*[1]

SAM HARRIS, *KILLING THE BUDDHA*

*"There is more to understanding the human condition
than science and secular culture generally admit."*[2]

SAM HARRIS, *WAKING UP*

In the final chapter of *The End of Faith*, Harris discusses the quest for happiness and takes a surprising turn as he suggests how we can find it. He questions whether health, wealth, and meaningful relationships can bring happiness. He observes how Indian yogis who have renounced all material things and familial attachments seem to have achieved happiness, and he loosely defines "spirituality" as the search for happiness.

Harris' Views on Consciousness

Harris points out that almost all scientists now reject Descrates' declaration that there are two substances in the universe: matter and spirit. However, Harris parts company with scientists who are physicalists—those who believe consciousness is wholly dependent on the working of our brain and ceases on its death. In his own words:

The truth is that we simply do not know what happens

after death. While there is much to be said against a naïve
conception of a soul that is independent of the brain, the
place of consciousness in the natural world is very much an
open question. The idea that the brain produces consciousness is little more than an article of faith among scientists.[3]

It goes without saying that Harris' openness to the idea of a conscious,
nonmaterial existence after death puts him in a very small minority of
atheists.

Having defined spirituality as the search for happiness, Harris adds
that "investigating the nature of consciousness...is simply another
name for spiritual practice"[4] and says spiritual practices like fasting,
chanting, sensory deprivation, prayer, meditation, and the use of psy-
chotropic plants are merely "our attempts to explore and modify the
deliverance of consciousness."[5]

In a section defending that the essence of "I" is separate from the
body but also related to it, Harris suggests that our feeling of separation
from the universe is the ultimate source of pain. In his words, "Almost
every problem we have can be ascribed to the fact that human beings
are utterly beguiled by their feelings of separateness [from the uni-
verse]."[6] He says that "a spirituality that undermined such dualism [or
separateness from the universe]...could not help but improve our situation."[7] The implication is that our situation would be improved if we
recognized our oneness with the universe.

At this point, Harris qualifies his argument because he recognizes
it "will strike certain readers as a confusing eruption of speculative philosophy."[8] He counters objections by pointing out that he is drawing
upon the wisdom of Eastern philosophy. He admits the ideas might
be confusing to some readers due to "the illusion of self...many of us
in the West are conceptually unequipped to understand."[9] He blames
our reluctance to accept mysticism on "the Christian, Jewish and Muslim emphasis on faith itself."[10] This, he claims, is a mistake because the
great philosopher mystics of the East like Buddha, Shankara, Padmasambhava, and others "have no equivalents in the West."[11] As proof,
he quotes a passage by Padmasambhava at length and claims its supe-
riority to other religious teaching, stating, "I invite the reader to find

anything even remotely like this in the Bible or the Koran."[12] The challenge sounds suspiciously like the Muslim claim that the Koran is a "miracle" of Mohammad as evidenced by its sheer beauty (which can only be appreciated in the original Arabic text). Although the passage he cites speaks of "clarity," "emptiness," and "pure observing...without anyone being there who is the observer," Harris insists the passage "is a rigorously *empirical* document, not a statement of metaphysics."[13]

In a section titled "Meditation," Harris continues explaining the illusion of self. He claims meditation "refers to any means whereby our sense of 'self'—of subject/object dualism in perception and cognition—can be made to vanish."[14] He explains that mediation is not the cessation of thinking but a breaking of our identification with our thoughts. Says Harris, "Break the spell of thought, and the duality of subject and object will vanish—as will the fundamental difference between conventional states of happiness and suffering."[15]

For a scientist who emphasizes the empiricism of ideas, it is surprising Harris says, "Your consciousness, while still inscrutable in scientific terms, is an utter simplicity as a matter of experience."[16] He says the more negative social emotions we harbor, the more difficult will be our experience of the "selflessness of consciousness." If we can let go of self, however, "the more the feeling of self-hood is relaxed, the less those states that are predicated upon it will arise—states like fear and anger."[17] Although this cannot be scientifically explained, Harris says it is empirical in the sense that mystics can communicate about it afterward "just as athletes can communicate effectively about the pleasures of sport."[18]

Harris continues to insist that all this is rational (while maintaining religion is not) because it is a different way of perceiving reality. As he says, "The roiling mystery of the world can be analyzed with concepts (this is science), or it can be experienced free of concepts (this is mysticism)."[19] In fact, he claims mysticism is both the beginning of a rational approach to our deepest concerns and the end of faith.

A Response to Harris' Views on Consciousness

Of all the surprise endings I have ever read, the shocking revelation that Sam Harris—one of the "four horsemen" of the atheist apocalypse—is actually a Buddhist hiding in an atheist's clothes was the biggest one of all. Of course, Harris himself denies it. On his website SamHarris.org he states, "While I consider Buddhism to be almost unique among the world's religions as a repository of contemplative wisdom, I do not consider myself a Buddhist."

Harris protests the allegations that he is a Buddhist by claiming his criticism of Buddhism has been published in his article "Killing the Buddha." But the article is not at all critical of Buddhism. It speaks of Buddhism uncovering "genuine truths about the mind and the phenomenal world—truths like emptiness, selflessness, and impermanence."[20] Harris seems to include himself amongst students of Buddha when he says, "As students of the Buddha, we should dispense with Buddhism."[21] The only thing Harris criticizes is the claim that these truths are *exclusive* to Buddhism. The editors of the *Shambhala Sun* Buddhist magazine point out Harris' "criticism" amounts to the claim that Buddhist "practices would benefit more people *if they were not presented as a religion*."[22] In other words, Harris apparently thinks the tenets of Buddhism are true. He simply does not view them as religious truths.

Harris' denial of being a Buddhist makes as much sense to me as someone denying he is a socialist while affirming he believes the government should own all businesses and control production. If you believe all the tenets of socialism, you are a socialist. It is the content of your beliefs that matter, not how you rebrand them.

To me, if someone believes all the tenets of Buddhism, he is a Buddhist. Ultimately, the reader must decide for himself whether to believe Harris' advocacy of Buddhist ideology or his verbal denial of Buddhism. You must judge either his words or his actions, because they are self-contradictory.

Eckhart Tolle immediately comes to mind for his own denials of being Buddhist. This author of multiple *New York Times* bestsellers was listed by the Watkins Review as the most spiritually influential person in the world. Watkins ranked him even more influential than the Dalai Lama.[23] In his book *The Power of Now,* Tolle claims to be a "teacher who is not aligned with any particular religion or tradition."[24] However, he quotes Buddhist sayings,[25] conversations with a Buddhist monk,[26] and

Buddhist texts. [27] What Tolle refers to as "the Now" is virtually indistinguishable from the Buddhist doctrine of nirvana.

Harris similarly offers a "debranded" Buddhism with a bit more intellectual flare. Whether Harris is a bona fide atheist comes into question when we compare his claims side-by-side with Tolle's writing. Whether Tolle actually is or is not a closet Buddhist is open to interpretation. That Tolle is not an atheist is undeniable.

Here is a fun game: See if you can tell which of the following statements came from the atheist, and which came from the Buddhist/ spiritualist:

> Meditation is less a matter of suppressing thoughts than of breaking our identification with them.

> There are many ways to create a gap in the incessant stream of thought. This is what meditation is all about.

> Break the spell of thought, and the duality of subject and object will vanish.

> In being, subject and object merge into one.

> Personal transformation, or indeed liberation from the illusion of the self, seems to have been thought too much to ask.

> Free from the illusion that you are nothing more than your physical body and your mind. This "illusion of the self"...is the core error.

> The place of consciousness in the natural world is very much an open question.

> Consciousness seems to be subject to a process of development, but this is due to our limited perception.

Most readers will not be able to tell which statements came from the (supposed) atheist and which from the (Buddhist) spiritualist author. What if I told you every other statement came from Harris? I bet you still could not determine which ones came from who. Although Harris repudiates Buddhism, you have to wonder when Harris' philosophy cannot be distinguished from Buddhist teaching.

More than any other atheist, Harris demonstrates the viability of spiritual beliefs. He says mysticism can be objective because the experiences can be dialogued about "just as athletes can communicate effectively about the pleasures of sport."[28] However, if communicating about experiencing oneness with the universe through meditation makes it *objective* because the practitioners communicated similar experiences, then wouldn't millions of Christians who have had similar experiences while praying to a personal God constitute objective "proof" of that reality?

Most importantly, one of the "four horsemen" of the atheist apocalypse candidly admits "the truth is that we simply do not know what happens after death" and "the idea that brains produce consciousness is little more than *an article of faith* among scientists at present, and there are reasons to believe the methods of science will be insufficient to either prove or disprove it."[29] This would seem to indicate the subject is less settled than hardcore atheists like Richard Dawkins or Peter Boghossian would admit. Harris ironically opens the door to spiritual beliefs, including continued conscious existence after death. He even concedes that the "roiling mysteries" of the world can be experienced through mysticism as well as science.[30]

Of course, Dawkins and Boghossian would merely say Harris is wrong. They would claim the annihilation of consciousness after death is a foregone conclusion. However, this does not negate the fact that a very critical, evolution-believing, PhD-credentialed, atheist scientist who agrees with them on almost every other belief about the universe is open to conscious existence after death and spiritually transcendent experiences. Moreover, he arrived at the beliefs not on the basis of even a scrap of scripture. It would seem spiritual beliefs cannot be as inherently irrational as the hardcore New Atheists allege when an atheist scientist of Harris' notoriety believes at least some of them are true. If Harris is right, then the conversation at least starts with the foundation that spiritual truths are possible and we merely need to differentiate between true and false spiritual experiences.

10

Richard Dawkins—New Atheism

"Richard Dawkins is known throughout the world as one of the greatest writers about science living today or perhaps who has ever lived."[1]

LAWRENCE KRAUSS,
THEORETICAL PHYSICIST AND COSMOLOGIST

It was a warm, muggy night in Orlando, Florida the evening I hosted the first meeting of the spiritual topics book club. I hoped to engage people of diverse spiritual beliefs, including those lacking beliefs, in open-minded discussion. Members of the Florida Atheists, Critical Thinkers & Skeptics (F.A.C.T.S.) saw the discussion on Meetup.com and reposted it for their roughly 700 members. The turnout exceeded the seating capacity of the small vegan coffeehouse, so we ended up on chairs outside. Some people had to stand because there were not enough seats.

The sizeable turnout precluded taking the time for everyone to introduce themselves and share their backgrounds. There were three people there whom I knew were Christians. Beyond that, I did not know the beliefs of the majority of the people present. After we got about 20 minutes into the discussion, I thought I had figured out who the Christians and atheists were by observing who spoke for or against Dawkins' book.

I was dead wrong. One fellow, perhaps thinking that Christians were monopolizing the conversation, asked all the atheists to raise their hands. I was shocked when everyone but the three Christians raised their hands. Everyone else there, including several people who had spoken critically of Dawkins' book, was an atheist!

I have had numerous individual discussions with atheist friends. However, that night was my first exposure to an atheist discussion group. I was surprised by the diversity of opinions expressed. Before that night, I had been critical of myself for finding Dawkins' book unconvincing. I questioned my open-mindedness toward atheism when I kept finding Dawkins' arguments illogical and his illustrations poor. After all, I was reading the Grand Poobah of atheism. Surely his writing would be convincing, right? The fact that atheists saw problems in Dawkins' book convinced me that his poor arguments were at fault, not my open-mindedness. Ironically, it was a group of atheists that helped me make up my mind about Dawkins.

The God Delusion was the first book I read about atheism. That worked both for and against it. To its detriment, my expectations may have been too high. I expected arguments for atheism. Instead, Dawkins predominantly attacks other people's beliefs. I was surprised and disappointed to find that only one chapter in the entire book actually advances arguments for not believing in God. The other chapters consist of rebuttals to theists' arguments, discussions about morality, and discussions about the impact of religion on society.

In its favor, I read *The God Delusion* during the height of my doubt. It had the best chance of winning me over completely. But I believe my experience with the book club demonstrates that even open-minded people can disagree with Dawkins. Criticism of his book has come from atheist academics like Michael Ruse, professor of philosophy at Florida State University, who said, "Richard Dawkins in *The God Delusion* would fail any introductory philosophy or religion course. Proudly he criticizes that whereof he knows nothing... *The God Delusion* makes me embarrassed to be atheist."[2] *Prospect Magazine*, which earlier had declared Dawkins one of the top three intellectuals in the world, said *The God Delusion* "is incurious, dogmatic, rambling and self-contradictory."[3] Dawkins is such an icon of atheism that people tend to draw battle lines around him. However, it is acceptable for even atheists to disagree with him.

As I already mentioned, I am grateful to Dawkins for corresponding with me during the writing of this book and proud to say that he described my summary of his book as "admirably fair and thorough."[4] It was important to me to address each author's best arguments and not to create straw men. He requested changes to only one section, which, of course, I was obliged to include. If you feel that I have misrepresented Dawkins' position, I challenge you to spot the section he deemed misleading. I dare say you will not find it until I point it out.

Dawkins' Biography

Richard Dawkins is arguably the best-known atheist author, speaker, and advocate, having been voted most prominent world thinker in *Prospect Magazine*'s 2013 global poll.[5] Often referred to as one of the "four horsemen of atheism,"[6] Dawkins is popularly regarded as the scientist of atheism, while Sam Harris is the scholar, Daniel Dennett is the philosopher, and the late Christopher Hitchens was the rebel.

Dawkins is a 73-year-old British biologist who first taught zoology at the University of California, Berkeley, but has spent the majority of his academic career at the University of Oxford. He has appeared on numerous TV and radio shows, debated several theists, and produced a dozen or so documentary films about science and religion. Emblematic of his popular global association with atheism, Dawkins even appeared in Ned Flanders' dream of hell in an episode of *The Simpsons*.

Dawkins was raised Anglican[7] but became an atheist during his teenage years. While he attributes his conversion to Darwinism,[8] it is worth noting that he was not a scientist by any conventional definition when he became an atheist. He brought atheism to his zoology studies at Balliol College, Oxford, rather than vice versa.

Dawkins has written nine books on science and belief. Over time, his work has shown a shift from the scientific focus of *The Selfish Gene* (1976) to *The God Delusion* (2006), which is primarily about supporting atheism with scientific illustrations. Dawkins would probably see that distinction as arbitrary because he appears to think his disbelief is inextricably linked to science. Dawkins acknowledges his shift to proselytizing for atheism: "my earlier books...did not set out to convert anyone...this book...does!"[9]

Dawkins, like most of the New Atheists, thinks religion is not merely another competing worldview but is actually dangerous. He has said that the "trend toward theocratic thinking in the United States is a danger not only for America but for the entire world."[10] He encourages atheists to self-identify, and founded the Out Campaign to encourage atheists worldwide to be more proud and public about their beliefs.[11] He was an advocate and heavy financial underwriter of the Atheist Bus Campaign in 2008, which placed ads on city buses reading "There's probably no god. Now stop worrying and enjoy your life."

I am not speaking critically of Dawkins' atheist activism efforts, which constitute constitutionally protected speech. I do observe, however, that Dawkins, ironically, has been very publicly outspoken about atheism even though a common complaint from nonbelievers is that religious people are too intrusive about their beliefs.

Dawkins' Arguments

As would be expected from an evolutionary biologist, Dawkins presents scientific arguments for the idea that God is a delusion. He posits that natural selection and Darwinian evolution are sufficient to explain life on Earth. However, he does not stop there. He also sees an evolutionary explanation for the origins of religion and morality.

Dawkins' first chapter provides a lengthy definition of God as a "supernatural creator that is 'appropriate for us to worship.'"[12] He acknowledges deism but does not object to a deist God that "has no specific interest in human affairs."[13] He wants to make it clear exactly what kind of God he is arguing against: a personal God who answers prayers and forgives sins, not some distant God or a mere metaphor for order in the universe. His naturalism is based on the belief that there is "one kind of stuff in the universe [that] is physical, out of this stuff come minds, beauty, emotions, moral values—in short the full gamut of phenomena that gives richness to human life."[14]

The God Hypothesis: If He Exists, He Must Be Evolved

Chapter 2, "The God Hypothesis," presents the core of Dawkins' argument. He sums up his position in this way: "[A]ny creative intelligence, of sufficient complexity to design anything, comes into existence only as the end product of an extended process of gradual evolution."[15] His initial support is a single sentence: "Creative intelligences, being evolved, necessarily arrived late in the universe, and therefore cannot be responsible for designing it."[16] He later gives a fuller argument in chapter 4, "Why There Almost Certainly Is No God."

NOMA and the Explanatory Capability of Science

Dawkins takes scientists like Alister McGrath, Stephen Jay Gould, and T.H. Huxley to task for declaring that "the God question could not be settled on the basis of the scientific method."[17] In particular, he criticizes Gould for introducing the concept of NOMA (non-overlapping magisteria), the idea that science and theology are separate, non-overlapping disciplines, an idea Dawkins flatly rejects. As Gould described it, "science gets the age of rocks, and religion the rock of ages; science studies how the heavens go, religion how to go to heaven."[18] Dawkins' position is that science can and does address the existence of God, that the question is "strictly scientific" by nature. Dawkins takes the position that science and atheism are equivalent. He is "baffled" that any scientist could believe in "resurrection, forgiveness of sins and all."[19/20] He finds such beliefs irreconcilable with science.

[response on page 218]

The Great Prayer Experiment

Dawkins discusses studies on the efficacy of prayer. He notes that Darwin's cousin Francis Galton was the first to "analyze scientifically whether praying for people is efficacious"[21] in 1827 when he observed that members of the British royal family lived shorter lives than other classes of people, despite the fact that prayers were offered for the royal family every Sunday in the Church of England.

Dawkins describes in greater detail the 2006 "Study of the

Therapeutic Effect of Intercessory Prayer," STEP for short. STEP divided 1802 patients recovering from coronary artery bypass surgery into three groups. Groups 1 and 2 were told that they might receive prayers, but only Group 1 actually did. Group 3 was informed that they would receive prayers and subsequently did. There was no statistically significant difference in the recoveries of those in Groups 1 and 2—52 and 51 percent respectively suffered major complications and mortality. However, those in Group 3, who were receiving prayers, actually fared slightly worse. They experienced a 59 percent mortality rate, perhaps due either to psychological guilt over not recovering despite everyone praying for them, or just a statistical anomaly. Dawkins points to this as "clear-cut" evidence that prayer has no effect, citing that "there was no difference between patients who were prayed for and those who were not."[22]

Actually, I must retract that last sentence since it is not fair to his position. As you'll recall, I opened the chapter with a challenge to spot where I had misrepresented Dawkins. That last quote was it. I again express my thanks to Mr. Dawkins for reading an earlier draft of this book and clarifying his position on prayer. He asked me to clarify that "failure to show that prayer has an effect is *not* the same as showing that it has no effect. I suggest delete [sic] the entire sentence in bold above [the last sentence of the previous paragraph]."[23]

His point is well taken. Claiming that the effectiveness of prayer has not yet been demonstrated is not the same as claiming that it could never be effective. He was merely pointing out that *if* prayer does have a positive effect, it has not yet been demonstrated. Fair enough. While I appreciate his suggestion to just remove the error altogether, I deemed it better to own up to it. I feel it demonstrates that if I have erred in other summaries, those errors are likely to be equally minor, and never due to intentional or malicious misrepresentation.

[response on page 220]

Evidence for God's Existence

Regarding evidence for God's existence, Dawkins says, "If he existed and chose to reveal it, God himself could clinch the argument, noisily and unequivocally, in his favour."[24] On the next page, he shares

Bertrand Russell's parable of the celestial teapot. The parable is so iconic to atheists that the image of the teapot floating in space is found on the banner of the atheist forum of the popular message board Reddit. For those unfamiliar with it, Russell's parable compares the premise of God to the premise of a Chinese teapot revolving around the sun in an elliptical orbit somewhere between the Earth and Mars. It is too small to be detected by our most powerful telescopes, yet those who believe in its presence consider it an "intolerable presumption on the part of human reason to doubt it."[25] To Dawkins, God is one of "an infinite number of things whose existence is conceivable and cannot be disproved."[26] It is no easier to disprove God than to disprove Russell's celestial teapot. Thus, to Dawkins, it is unreasonable for theists to fault atheists for being unable to disprove the unprovable.

[response on page 222]

One God Further

One final thought-provoking argument Dawkins raises in chapter 2 is, "When asked whether I am an atheist, [I] point out that the questioner is also an atheist when considering Zeus, Apollo, Amon Ra, Mithras, Baal, Thor, Wotan, the Golden Calf, and the Flying Spaghetti Monster. I just go one god further."[27] In an interview, Dawkins points out that Incas, Mayans, and American Indians each had their own creation mythologies.[28] Dawkins objects to the fact that we disbelieve Inca or Mayan mythology, yet we adopt the Hebrew creation story without question because we were born into a culture that taught it from childhood. We need to realize, says Dawkins, that Christianity is just one of hundreds of myths and not give it special pleading simply because we were born under its influence. I am not certain who deserves credit for originating this idea, but it is frequently invoked by atheists because it is a powerful point.

There is a strong logical flow to Dawkins' first four chapters, which I appreciate:

- Chapter 1: eliminate the kind of God you're not talking about (order in the universe, pantheism, etc.)

- Chapter 2: define the God you are talking about
- Chapter 3: debunk arguments for that God
- Chapter 4: provide positive arguments against that God

[response on page 224]

Debunking Arguments for God's Existence: Aquinas' Proofs

This brings us to chapter 3, "Arguments for God's Existence," in which Dawkins courageously devotes 32 pages to laying out theists' arguments relatively fairly. He starts with Thomas Aquinas' *Quinque viæ* or five proofs for God: the unmoved mover, the uncaused cause, the cosmological argument, the argument from degree, and the teleological argument. Dawkins addresses in depth two of the most enduring of these, the cosmological argument and the teleological argument.

The cosmological argument is that the existence of the cosmos itself is evidence for God because "there must have been a time when no physical things existed. But, since physical things exist now, there must have been something non-physical to bring them into existence."[29] Dawkins observes "there is absolutely no reason to endow that terminator [the first cause] with any of the properties normally ascribed to God: omnipotence, omniscience, goodness, creativity of design, to say nothing of such human attributes as listening to prayers, forgiving sins and reading innermost thoughts."[30] According to Dawkins, asking "Who banged the Big Bang?" is not proof of God.

The teleological argument, which Dawkins calls the "Argument from Design" (Aquinas himself used the word *design*), is the basis of William Paley's argument that a watch implies the existence of a watchmaker. Dawkins feels that Darwin has blown Aquinas' and Paley's argument out of the water. Says Dawkins, "Thanks to Darwin, it is no longer true to say that nothing that we know looks designed unless it is designed. Evolution by natural selection produces an excellent simulacrum of design."[31] Against Aquinas' claim that an arrow streaking toward its target points to an archer, Dawkins counters that a tiny insect can move like a heat-seeking missile toward a heat source due to goal-seeking behavior, despite the fact that it is not designed.

[response on page 225]

Debunking Arguments for God's Existence: The Argument from Scripture

In order to undermine Scripture as an argument for God's existence, Dawkins points out that the Gospels were written long after Jesus' death, and that there are many competing accounts like the Gospels of Thomas, Peter, Nicodemus, Philip, Bartholomew, and Mary Magdalene, which were excluded from the official canon. Dawkins claims that there is little historical evidence that Jesus claimed divine status, and that "it is even possible to mount a serious, though not widely supported historical case that Jesus never lived at all, as has been done by professor G.A. Wells of the University of London."[32]

[response on page 227]

The Worship of Gaps

Dawkins attacks "God of the gaps" arguments, which state, "If an apparent gap is found, it is *assumed* that God, by default, must fill it."[33] Dawkins points out that such arguments are futile because science constantly fills those gaps, leaving ever-diminishing space for God. Seeing God in the gaps amounts to arguing that the things we do not know are positive arguments for the God we think we do know. The logical problem is that ignorance is not an argument. Currently unexplainable phenomena like biogenesis or the Big Bang could have naturalistic explanations, just like evolution explains the diversity of life.

Within the section on gaps, Dawkins brings up the argument of poor design. However, this is an old argument that we already discussed in our look at Russell.

[response on page 231]

The Anthropic Principle

Anthropos is the Greek word translated "human." The anthropic principle is the philosophical consideration of why the universe appears inherently "human friendly." Dawkins quotes theoretical physicist Freeman Dyson's observation that "[the universe] must have known we were coming."[34] More precisely, the argument is that the universe must be compatible with conscious life by virtue of the fact that conscious life is there to observe it. If it were not conducive to life, who would be asking the question? In its purest form, the anthropic principle is a philosophical argument similar to "If a tree falls in the forest and no one is there to hear it, does it make a sound?"

Dawkins quickly moves past the philosophical issues to the scientific ones, like the fact that there can be no life without liquid water. Therefore, life-supporting planets must fall in "a so-called Goldilocks zone—not too hot and not too cold, but just right—for planets with liquid water."[35] He observes how Earth seems to have been "singled out for the evolution of life."[36] Not only is our orbit within the Goldilocks zone, we also have Jupiter serving as a massive gravitational vacuum cleaner intercepting asteroids that threaten Earth, a single large moon that stabilizes our axis of rotation, and a nonbinary sun that is not locked in mutual orbit with a companion star.

He acknowledges the problem that even if a planet is in the Goldilocks zone, the appearance of life is still "a highly improbable occurrence"[37] and "natural selection cannot proceed without it."[38] Furthermore, he raises the problem that the origin of the eukaryotic cell (complex cells with a nucleus, mitochondria, and other features not present in bacteria) was "an even more momentous, difficult and statistically improbable step than the origin of life."[39] I found this particularly interesting: It makes chance interactions explaining life even more statistically improbable, yet I never heard that argument from a theist. It is ironic to get a good argument for theism from an atheist.

Dawkins then moves from these planetary and biological issues to issues of physics and cosmology, where he finds still more things that must fall in a very small Goldilocks zone to support life. He uses the example of the strong force, one of six constants identified by Martin Rees, which Dawkins says are "finely tuned in the sense that, if [they] were slightly different, the universe would be comprehensively different and presumably unfriendly to life."[40]

Dawkins explains what he means by "finely tuned": If the strong force were 0.006 instead of 0.007, the universe would be lifeless, containing nothing but hydrogen. If it were 0.008, all the hydrogen would have fused together to make heavier elements, leaving no hydrogen to support life. Thus the strong force had to be exactly what it is for life to exist.

In all this, Dawkins reveals the overwhelming statistical improbability of life existing by chance, but he is still convinced chance is the best answer. To address why we should not doubt chance in the face of its statistical improbability, he borrows philosopher John Leslie's analogy of a man facing death by firing squad. If, against all odds, all ten men of the firing squad miss, the surprised survivor might be tempted to speculate causes like bribery or drunkenness rather than to just cheerfully say, "Well, obviously they all missed, or I wouldn't be here thinking about it."[41]

To Dawkins, finding life in the universe despite the odds "recalls the proverbial needle in a haystack"[42] with the added qualification that "any beings capable of looking must necessarily be sitting on one of those prodigiously rare needles before they even start the search."[43] In other words, it may be difficult for the human outside the haystack to find the needle, but for the ant sitting on the needle the search is complete before it has begun.

Regarding theistic alternatives to natural explanations, Dawkins says "the theistic riddle of improbability is an evasion of stupendous proportions."[44] As he explains, "design certainly does not work as an explanation for life, because design is ultimately not cumulative."[45] For Dawkins, natural selection has incredible explanatory power. It can account for and explain things that are "complex almost beyond telling: more complex than anything we can imagine."[46] However, natural selection has no explanation for God or need of Him; therefore, Dawkins finds God extremely improbable.

[response on page 232]

Does Our Moral Sense Have a Darwinian Origin?

The moral argument is usually one of the "big three" arguments offered for God alongside the cosmological and teleological arguments. It is usually (mis)portrayed either as the argument that God is the best explanation for observed moral norms or that God is necessary for moral order to exist in the universe. Since this argument is common, it is not surprising that Dawkins seeks an alternative explanation for morality.

He cites a study by Israeli zoologist Amotz Zahavi on Arabian babblers, little brown birds who live in social groups, breed cooperatively, give warning cries that allow the entire community equal opportunity to escape predators, and even donate food to each other. These altruistic actions allow the babblers better chances of survival.

Dawkins extrapolates from Zahavi's study "four good Darwinian reasons for individuals to be altruistic, generous or 'moral' towards each other."[47]

> First there is the special case of genetic kinship.
>
> Second, there is reciprocation: the repayment of favours given, and the giving of favours in "anticipation" of payback...
>
> Third, the Darwinian benefit of requiring a reputation for generosity and kindness and
>
> Fourth...additional benefit of conspicuous generosity as a way of buying unfakeably authentic advertising.[48]

Dawkins attempts to demonstrate that, even without belief in God, altruism might emerge in the natural world as the result of evolutionary forces.

[response on page 236]

A Case Study in the Roots of Morality

Next, Dawkins cites Harvard biologist Marc Hauser's research on moral and ethical dilemmas. In Hauser's hypothetical dilemmas, a runaway trolley endangers people and an imaginary person, Denise, must make choices regarding the value of human lives. The dilemma imagines Denise standing at a juncture box. She has two choices: If she does nothing, the runaway trolley will kill five innocent people standing on the track. If she flips the switch, it will divert the trolley onto another track and kill only one innocent person. Given this scenario, 90 percent of people in Hauser's study said it was morally permissible to divert the trolley.

However, when the scenario involved shoving an overweight bystander off a bridge to block the trolley and save five people standing on the track, people struggled to articulate why the same tradeoff was no longer morally acceptable.*

Dawkins observes, "The main conclusion of Hauser and Singer's study was that there is no statistically significant difference between atheists and religious believers in making these judgments. This seems compatible with the view, which I and many others hold, that we do not need God in order to be good—or evil."[49]

[response on page 237]

Cargo Cults

Dawkins' account of the "cargo cults" that sprang up in the aftermath of World War II on Melanesian islands used by the US military as supply and staging depots is one of my favorite sections of his book. It is fascinating to read of the conditions under which new religions still continue to arise today. The primitive islanders were awestruck by massive silver birds (airplanes) that descended from the sky carrying not only humans but all kinds of wondrous cargo. It seemed whenever the white people needed an item, another giant silver bird would descend from the heavens with more cargo gifts.

One of these cults has survived to this day on Vanuatu, where the local adherents believe the messianic "King of America," John Frum, will return to the islands one day in a great cataclysmic event. Dawkins notes that although the cult goes back to only the 1940s, it is unclear whether anyone named John Frum actually existed.

Dawkins says the cargo cults suggest four lessons about the origin of religions in general:

First is the amazing speed with which a cult can spring up.

Second is the speed with which the origination process covers its tracks...

The third lesson springs from the independent emergence of similar cults on different islands...

---

* By flipping the switch, Denise was only choosing the lesser of two inevitable tragedies. The bystander was in no danger prior to being shoved off the bridge. Therefore, shoving the bystander is murdering one person to save five.

Fourth, the cargo cults are similar, not just to each other but to older religions.[50]

Dawkins points to the cargo cults as examples of how easily new religions can start and how religion can spring up even in the absence of any supernatural activity.

[response on page 240]

What About Hitler and Stalin?

Hitler and Stalin's actions are so frequently explained in terms of atheism that Dawkins wrote a section about each man's beliefs. Before delving into the specifics of their beliefs, he questions the value of such discussion, saying, "Even if we accept that Hitler and Stalin shared atheism in common...so what?...We are not in the business of counting evil heads and compiling two rival roll calls of iniquity."[51]

Dawkins questions the relevance of such comparisons by saying, "What matters is not whether Hitler and Stalin were atheists, but whether atheism systematically *influences* people to do bad things."[52] He distinguishes between crimes committed in the name of atheism and crimes committed by people who just happen to be atheists. For example, he says, "Individual atheists may do evil things but they don't do evil things in the name of atheism. Stalin and Hitler did extremely evil things, in the name of, respectively, dogmatic and doctrinaire Marxism, and an insane and unscientific eugenics theory tinged with sub-Wagnerian ravings."[53]

Unlike Christopher Hitchens, who denied Stalin was an atheist, Dawkins admirably avoids this revisionist error. He admits, "There seems no doubt that, as a matter of fact, Stalin was an atheist...Perhaps because of his training for the priesthood, the mature Stalin was scathing about the Russian Orthodox Church, and about Christianity and religion in general."[54]

Furthermore, unlike Hitchens, who continuously quote mines Hitler in order to portray him as a devout Catholic,[55] Dawkins has enough integrity to acknowledge that Hitler was two-faced about his beliefs. Dawkins acknowledges that Hitler seemed to espouse both religion and atheism at various times. He observes that Hitler never formally renounced Catholicism and told General Gerhard Engel, "I shall remain a Catholic forever." [56] However, he admits that such statements have to be balanced with the virulently anti-Christian views Hitler expressed in his *Table Talk,* such as:

> The heaviest blow that ever struck humanity was the coming of Christianity...

> The reason why the ancient world was so pure, light and serene was that it knew nothing of the two great scourges: the pox and Christianity.

> When all is said, we have no reason to wish that the Italians and Spaniards should free themselves from the drug of Christianity. Let's be the only people who are immunized against the disease. [57]

Dawkins entertains the possibility that by 1941 Hitler had either gone through a "deconversion or disillusionment with Christianity" or that he was simply "an opportunistic liar." [58] Dawkins acknowledges, "It could be argued that, despite his own words and those of his associates, Hitler was not really religious but just cynically exploiting the religiosity of his audience. He may have agreed with Napoleon, who said, 'Religion is excellent stuff for keeping common people quiet'" [59]

Dawkins can afford to be generous in acknowledging that Hitler may have been an atheist because, for Dawkins, ultimately it does not matter. That is because he sees Hitler's atheism as a separate issue from whether he acted "in the name of atheism." [60] As Dawkins points out, "Why would anyone go to war for the sake of an absence of belief?" [61]

[response on page 241]

What's Wrong with Religion? Why Be So Hostile?

In chapter 8, Dawkins tackles the question, "Does [religion] really do so much harm that we should actively fight against it?" [62] His answer is a resounding "Yes!" He cites three areas in which he considers religion is harmful: the subversion of science, homosexual rights, and abortion.

Regarding religion's impact on science, Dawkins says, "I am hostile to fundamentalist religion because it actively debauches the scientific enterprise. It teaches us not to change our minds, and not to want to know exciting things that are available to be known. It subverts the science and saps the intellect."[63] He cites American geologist Kurt Wise as an example. Wise studied geology at the University of Chicago before earning advanced degrees in geology and paleontology from Harvard, where he studied under famous American atheist and evolutionary paleontologist Stephen Jay Gould. According to Dawkins, one day Wise went through a Bible with a pair of scissors, cutting out every verse that contradicted science. There was so little left of the Bible that he had to choose between it and evolution. Wise chose to believe the Bible, forgoing a promising career in paleontology to direct the Center for Origins Research at Bryan College, a small Christian college in Dayton, Tennessee. After telling Wise's story, Dawkins blames religion for the oppression of homosexuals and the fight against abortion rights.

[response on page 244]

A Response to Richard Dawkins

*"The difference between life and non-life, it became
apparent to me, was ontological and not chemical. The
best confirmation of this radical gulf is Richard Dawkins'
comical effort to argue in* The God Delusion *that the
origin of life can be attributed to a 'lucky chance.' If that's
the best argument you have, then the game is over."* [1]

ANTONY FLEW,
FAMOUS ATHEIST TURNED DEIST

*"What Dawkins does too often is to concentrate his
attack on fundamentalists. But there are many believers
who are just not fundamentalists. Dawkins in a way is
almost a fundamentalist himself, of another kind."* [2]

PROFESSOR PETER HIGGS,
IRRELIGIOUS THEORETICAL PHYSICIST
AND NOBEL PRIZE LAUREATE

Before I read Dawkins, he seemed an imposing figure. What response
could someone with a theological background possibly afford
an eminent scientist? However, I quickly found that while Dawkins is
highly qualified in some of the subject areas he addresses, such as irreducible complexity, he ventures into numerous areas outside of his expertise,
including philosophy, sociology, biblical exegesis, ethics, history, and

cosmology. Only 14 pages of his book *The God Delusion* are directly related to his field of biology; 36 are semirelated to biology by offering "a Darwinian explanation"[3] of history, sociology, and ethics; and the remaining 370 pages—representing the vast majority of the book—are out of his field. I came to the book expecting a cadre of strong, objective scientific facts, but instead found a lot of subjective philosophical arguments. In summary, I find Dawkins unconvincing because he presents a false dichotomy between believing in evolution and believing in God while completely ignoring numerous bona fide alternatives.

For example, Dawkins completely ignores the "both-and" option held by scientists like Francis Collins, who believes in *both* evolution *and* God. Collins shares Dawkins' view of evolution yet sees nothing about evolution that conflicts with belief in God. In fact, in *The Language of God,* published the same year as Dawkins' book, Collins argues for belief in God on scientific grounds. Clearly there are credible theistic interpretations of the data offered by winners of the National Medal of Science[4] and the Presidential Medal of Freedom,[5] yet Dawkins simply ignores the possibility of any other options.

Nor does Dawkins even mention a fourth option, raised two years before his book was published. Frank Turek and Norman Geisler's book *I Don't Have Enough Faith to Be an Atheist* argues for the Big Bang and evolution, but suggests limits to their explanatory power.

Dawkins' book would have been fairly convincing if it had been the only one I ever read about God and, in particular, about creation, life, and origins, because his rhetorical skills are excellent. Unfortunately, I had read enough to know there were other rational, credible views that Dawkins simply ignored in his vastly oversimplified dichotomy of "You either believe in evolution or you believe in God."

Who Made God?

The very core of Dawkins' argument that "any creative intelligence, of sufficient complexity to design anything, comes into existence only as the end product of an extended process of gradual evolution"[6] is a straw man caricature of Christian theology and the vast majority of theists' beliefs. Christians also do not believe in a God that "comes into existence." The Christian worldview is of an eternal, immaterial God that *ipso facto* is not subject to evolution by his very nature. Dawkins never addresses that view at all. Instead, he talks about the effect of evolution on God, which makes as much sense as talking to a geologist about the effect of evolution on rocks.

Atheists should have no trouble with the concept of eternal things. For centuries, atheism's default claim about the origin of the universe was that it was eternal and, therefore, did not require a creator. Bertrand Russell argued this as late as March 1927, before further scientific understanding of cosmology rendered the position untenable.[7] Having argued for centuries for an eternal universe, atheists have suddenly developed an aversion to the concept of something eternal. On the heels of contending for centuries that an eternal universe requires no explanation, they now demand an explanation for who made an *eternal* God. The whole argument is so disingenuous it hardly requires a response.

Granted, Dawkins' argument is very effective against a small minority of beliefs about God, like the Mormon belief that God is a highly evolved being who *achieved* godlikeness. Such views raise a separate set of questions: Where did these beings come from? Why did they leave no material evidence of their existence? How do supernatural powers evolve in material beings? However, these have no relevance whatsoever to a permanent, eternal God. Either Dawkins cannot comprehend an eternal being, or he would rather substitute a substantially different surrogate that is easier to attack.

Consider an analogy. Suppose a documentary filmmaker receives a contract to produce a program about ghosts for the Science Channel. Not wanting to come across as credulous, he assembles a panel of skeptics to pose the question about what type of evidence they would deem reliable. Imagine the topics the panel might entertain. There might be discussion about the value and limitations of multispectral imaging or spectrometer readings or procedures for skeptical review of photographs or audio recordings to check for tampering. Imagine the absurdity of a skeptical panelist saying, "I would find the existence of ghosts more compelling if you could demonstrate they started out

as single-cell ghosts that gradually evolved into more complex ghosts."
After a rousing laugh, the filmmaker would say, "I'm not sure you
understand what a ghost is." Biological arguments have no relevance
to spiritual beings that do not produce offspring.

Dawkins' argument falls flat because the kind of God he argues
against is one Christians do not believe in. In Dawkins' own words,
"The whole argument turns on the familiar question, 'Who made
God?'"[8] However, Dawkins' whole argument turns on a category mistake, an ontological error in which "a property is ascribed to a thing
that could not possibly have that property."[9] It would be like asking,
"Is this a Christian banana?" There is no answer because bananas do not
possess the property of belief. In Dawkins' case, he asks who made an
unmade being. There is no answer because the question itself is inter-
nally incoherent.

NOMA and the Explanatory Capability of Science

Regarding Dawkins' rejection of NOMA (non-overlapping magisteria), I immediately noticed that his quarrel is not with theologians but
with agnostic scientists. T.H. Huxley, whom he takes to task for "declaring that the God question could not be settled on the basis of the scientific method,"[10] is none other than "Darwin's Bulldog," known for his
advocacy of Charles Darwin's theory of evolution. Huxley was not a
credulous believer but an eminent scientist: In 1894 he was the young-
est to earn the Royal Medal,[11] the most prestigious British science award.

Similarly, Stephen Jay Gould, who also argued science could not
disprove God, was an evolutionary biologist who taught at Harvard
University, worked at the American Museum of Natural History in
New York, and was named a "living legend" by the US Library of Congress.[12] Eminent agnostic scientists have already done all the work of
refuting Dawkins' argument for the theist. If the evidence is insufficient to convince atheist scientists, why on earth does Dawkins expect
theists to find it convincing?

Dawkins is advocating scientism. This is "the view that the charac-
teristic inductive methods of the natural sciences are the only source of
genuine factual knowledge and, in particular, that they alone can yield

true knowledge about man and society."[13] It is evident that he believes natural science explains everything because he claims that, as a scientist, his explanations trump historians in regard to the resurrection, trump sociologists in explaining religion, and trump philosophers in explaining ethics.

The problem with scientism is that it is self-refuting because the proposition that science is the only source of factual knowledge is itself not a scientific statement; it is a philosophical one. No scientist has ever looked in a microscope or telescope and found a sign stating, "Science explains everything." The very suggestion that all truth is empirically verifiable is an insult to the fields of anthropology, economics, political science, psychology, sociology, and, yes, theology. Great arguments can be advanced for democracy, free enterprise, ethics, and justice, none of which can be verified or disproved by lab experiments.

A good example of Dawkins' view of the exaggerated efficacy of science is his argument that the question whether Jesus came alive three days after he was crucified has a "strictly scientific" answer. Dawkins overstates the reach of science's ability to prove or disprove historical events. The absurdity of this position is evident if we step outside the realm of religion and ask what scientific experiment we can do in a laboratory today that conclusively proves or disproves George Washington crossed the Delaware River on the night of December 25, 1776. What can we burn over the low flame of a Bunsen burner or mix in a beaker that disproves a historical event?

Granted, the resurrection is a special case because it professes that someone rose from the dead. I fully understand the argument: Because we can presently provide conclusive proof people do not rise from the dead due to natural causes, it also did not happen in the past. However, yet again, this is a straw man. Christians do not believe that Jesus rose from the dead by natural causes. The claim is not that the disciples gave Jesus some herbal medicine or potion that restored dead tissues and organs to a living state. The claim is that God *super*naturally raised Jesus from the dead because of the special circumstance of who Jesus was and the significance of his death. In order to argue from a strictly scientific basis that this historical event never occurred,

Dawkins would have to first prove there is no God capable of intervening in history. Once it is conclusively demonstrated there is no God who could have intervened in Jesus' situation, then yes, Jesus absolutely would have been subject to the same natural laws we observe in the laboratory today.

The problem is, as Dawkins admits, we cannot scientifically prove there is no God. As long as it is possible God exists, regardless of how remote the chance, science alone cannot definitively eliminate the possibility of the resurrection. For that we must turn to history and eyewitness testimony. We must also consider historical issues like how Christianity survived the death of its leader without an empty tomb. We must consider issues like why the disciples, who did not believe in an individual but a corporate resurrection, suddenly came to believe this one man had risen from the dead. Whatever answer we arrive at, it is a strictly historical answer.

[original argument on page 203]

The Great Prayer Experiment

I would not advance the efficacy of prayer as an argument for God, but since Dawkins allegedly debunks the power of prayer, his poor argument deserves rebuttal. Labeling the Galton study "scientific" reveals the insincerity of his inquiry into prayer's efficacy. Galton's "scientific" analysis, as Dawkins generously labels it, was partly satire and was significantly flawed in that the prayers he considered only asked God for long life *for the queen*, not the entire royal family. However, Galton looked at the result of prayer on the entire royal family, including those who were never prayed for.[14] It seems like simple common sense that the question of whether a prayer has been answered must start with whether that outcome was prayed for in the first place.* Ironically,

---

* I asked the Vicar General for the London College of Bishops, Reverend Prebendary Nick Mercer, whether there had been any change to the prayers for the royals that I may have missed in my research that would support Galton's findings. He was unaware of "any prayer directly asking for long life for all the Royal family." This was so incredibly easy to confirm, it makes me wonder if Dawkins did any serious research at all (private email correspondence with the Vicar, April 15, 2014).

Queen Elizabeth II, who is the current recipient of that prayer, seems to be doing all the better for it as she nears 90 years old.

Then Dawkins turns to the slightly more scientific STEP study, which he describes in some detail but still manages to leave out key facts. For example, the people praying were given nothing but a first name and no personal information about the person for whom they were praying. They were not allowed to forge a personal connection with these complete strangers. Neither was anyone in the study required to identify him or herself as "born again" or to show any "manifestations of an active Christian life,"[15] like daily devotional prayer or regular church attendance. These are the kind of criteria the Bible says are required for effective prayers (James 5:16). The whole experiment was constructed specifically to test God, which is exactly the kind of prayer Jesus said God would not answer (Matthew 4:7). The experiment shows nothing except that God does not respond to tests, which is exactly what he promised.

The most disingenuous thing about Dawkins' section on prayer, however, is its deliberate omission of any reference to numerous studies that show prayer's effectiveness. He does not mention the fact that the *American Heart Journal* published five other studies about prayer between 1988 and 2006. Two showed a positive correlation with prayer, three showed none at all, and only the STEP study showed negative correlation.[16] It took me all of 30 seconds to find these studies with a Google search, along with the 1997 O'Laoire study showing positive results of prayer on anxiety and depression and the 1998 Sicher study showing positive results for patients with advanced AIDS. Dawkins' defenders will simply claim he focuses on STEP due to its large sample size. However, a study published in the *Annals of Internal Medicine* that studied 2774 patients—roughly 1000 more than the STEP study—found 13 trials "showed statistically beneficial treatment results."[17]

One wonders how an experienced writer like Dawkins could be unaware of competing studies. That he would focus on the one study that supports his point and completely omit any mention of studies that contradict it strikes me as cherry-picking evidence to support a foregone conclusion.

[original argument on page 203]

Evidence for God's Existence

I share Dawkins' frustration that God does not clinch the argument of his existence "unequivocally in his favour."[18] Any honest believer will admit to wrestling with periods of doubt when God seems distant, fails to act when we think he should, or, even worse, acts contrary to our expectations. When you feel like you are drowning in life, there is comfort in knowing your Father is right there with you. In such times, we wish God would make his presence more emphatically known. Even if we feel like children struggling to learn how to swim, and our Father allows us to flail and falter in the pool to show us we really can swim, there is still comfort knowing he is there to grab us so we do not drown.

Not only are there the times when we wonder if God is there; sometimes we feel as if he is actively working against us. That is how I felt during my years in Christian ministry. Rather than gold, it seemed that everything I touched turned to rust, as if God had set himself against me.

Speaking from experience, when you feel like God is against you, evidence of his existence is the last thing you want. Much better to believe you are going through a series of unfortunate circumstances with a light at the end of the tunnel than the hopelessness of knowing you are fighting against the creator of the universe. You do not have to believe in the historical accuracy of Exodus to be able to imagine yourself in Pharaoh's shoes. If you do not want to free your Hebrew slave workforce, do you really want unequivocal evidence that their God is real? Imagine Pharaoh's growing despondence as the undeniable evidence of the plagues unfurled and he realized he was up against a deity he could not possibly oppose. God clinching the argument "unequivocally in his favour" was not equally welcomed by Pharaoh and Moses.

Dawkins, like Pharaoh, disdains the idea of God's involvement. Dawkins opens chapter 2 with this:

> The God of the Old Testament is arguably the most
> unpleasant character in all fiction: jealous and proud of
> it; a petty, unjust, unforgiving control-freak; a vindictive,
> bloodthirsty ethnic cleanser; a misogynistic, homophobic,
> racist, infanticidal, genocidal, filicidal, pestilential, megalo-
> maniacal, sadomasochistic, capriciously malevolent bully.[19]

It is quite clear Dawkins finds God abhorrent. To him, God is much worse than the Greek gods, who clearly had questionable moral character but were largely indifferent to humanity. The God of Abraham, according to Dawkins, is "cruel, vindictive, capricious, and unjust."[20]

Dawkins not only does not believe in God, he finds God's nature odious. If Dawkins found "fossil rabbits in the Precambrian,"[21] which he claims would be irrefutable evidence of God, that would change his mind about the *existence* of God but not about the *character* of God. That would be like having your eyes opened to a God who seems intent on drowning you rather than helping teach you how to swim. It would be most depressing indeed to become firmly convinced of a God you detest, whom you could squander your whole life hopelessly opposing, only to face eternal damnation in the end.

I am not the first person to observe that providing unequivocal proof would not be very...well...godly of God. C.S. Lewis felt providing indisputable evidence was contrary to God's very nature. Lewis wrote:

> The Irresistible and the Indisputable are the two weapons
> which the very nature of God's scheme forbids Him to use.
> Merely to over-ride a human will (as His felt presence in
> any but the faintest and most mitigated degree would cer-
> tainly do) would be for Him useless. He cannot ravish. He
> can only woo.[22]

What is the "scheme" Lewis' refers to? Søren Kierkegaard explained it best. He told the parable of a great king wielding absolute power over his realm. This king saw the most beautiful of women among his subjects. He wanted to approach her and see if she might possibly love him. But, as the king, he could never approach her and know for sure whether her love was genuine, for his power was too great. Even if she despised him, she would surely feign love for him from fear of what he might do if she rejected him. After wrestling with this dilemma, the king realized he could only experience her love from free will if he approached her in the form of an equal—as another servant. So he gave up his authority and took on the garments of a peasant and went to her as one of her own. That, according to Kierkegaard (and Christian theology), is the story of the incarnation.

Dawkins says, "Bertrand Russell was asked what he would say if he died and found himself confronted by God, demanding to know why Russell had not believed in him. 'Not enough evidence, God, not enough evidence,' was Russell's (I almost said immortal) reply."[23] My question to Russell, Dawkins, or anyone who feels this way would be if God did exist, do you think he would be more interested in—people *serving* him, or people *loving* him?

Sure, I wish God would demonstrate himself more unequivocally, but I do not find his lack of action the problem that Dawkins does because I understand that that kind of demonstration of power would create a relationship of servility between God and billions of humans. It makes sense to me that a loving God would not force himself on people in that manner.

[original argument on page 204]

One God Further

Dawkins argues for going "one god further" and adding disbelief in God to all the other gods we already don't believe in—from Zeus to Ra to Baal to Thor. Yet the logical fallacy is easy to spot—just because two accounts have numerous similarities does not mean that if one account is false, any similar account must also necessarily be false. For example, there are a many similarities between *Star Trek* and NASA— men bravely launching into space, facing new and challenging frontiers in futuristic spacecraft, collecting samples, and running scientific experiments. However, just because *Star Trek* is fiction does not mean that NASA's shuttle program is not real. Every account stands or falls on its own evidence and merit. The argument of "guilt by similarity" is clearly fallacious.

For example, consider the small minority who believe the Apollo 11 moon landing was staged by the US government. Those who want to make that case need evidence, be it a Hollywood set where bogus film footage was shot, or proof that the reentry-scarred lunar capsule on display at Cape Canaveral, Florida, is a forgery, or proof that disputes the authenticity of the lunar rock samples. Simply postulating, "It didn't happen because it sounds an awful lot like *Star Trek*" is misguided and has no rational value.

[original argument on page 205]

Debunking Arguments for God's Existence: Aquina's Proofs

Moving to Dawkins' "refutations" of the arguments for God's existence, I agree with him that you cannot point to the Big Bang as evidence of a God who answers prayers, forgives sin, or reads thoughts. You certainly cannot validate one particular religion from an explosion. Even a child who makes his first baking soda volcano understands the absurdity of asking whether that was a Christian, Muslim, or Hindu eruption. You simply cannot arrive at the God of Abraham from the Big Bang.

Where I disagree with Dawkins is that you cannot arrive at "*any* of the properties normally ascribed to God"[24] from the cosmological argument. Einstein's general theory of relativity postulated that time, space, and matter are codependent. You cannot have one without the other. Consider our very understanding of time. A day is one complete revolution of a physical collection of matter—the Earth. A month is the orbit of another lump of matter, the moon. A year is a revolution in space of both of those lumps of matter around the matter of the sun. Take away the matter of the Earth, moon, and sun, and what becomes of a day, month, and year? Time becomes meaningless without matter and space. If we can wrap our head around the idea of nothing, we see the absurdity of asking how long nothing has been there—been there in relationship to what?

When we consider conditions before the Big Bang, we see a condition of timeless, immaterial spacelessness. We know this because we understand that time, space, and matter all exploded into existence at the Big Bang. Dawkins himself acknowledges this when he says, "The standard model of our universe says that time itself began in the Big Bang, along with space."[25] The spontaneous and simultaneous creation of time, space, and matter is a scientific model based on the red shift of light, the radiation afterglow, and temperature ripples in that background radiation. The theory is based entirely on observations from instruments like the COBE satellite and has nothing to do with the book of Genesis. Our observations of the cosmos' origins point to a cause that was timeless and immaterial because, whatever the cause, it preceded time and matter. Is that cause the God of Genesis? We cannot prove that. Does it have properties that are normally ascribed to God though? Yes, it clearly does!

Dawkins summarizes Aquinas' argument from design as "Things in the world, *especially living things,* look as though they have been designed."[26] This is a distortion of Aquinas' argument, which was actually about "natural bodies" that "lack intelligence." He did not reference living things at all. Dawkins ignores that and only addresses living organisms in his response. If for argument's sake we charitably just assume Dawkins is right about the illusion of design in living organisms, he still has a long way to go to refute Aquinas' argument. The teleological argument encompasses much more than living organisms. It refers first and foremost to the design of the universe, which makes evolution possible in the first place. There is mind-blowing fine-tuning and balance in the rate of universe's expansion. For instance, the difference of one millionth-millionth would have either made the Big Bang collapse back on itself or allowed no galaxies to have formed.[27] The precise balance of the centrifugal force of planetary movement balancing the gravitational force of the sun prevents us from crashing into the sun or being flung off into space. Finally, the rotation speed of the Earth strikes a balance between extreme temperature fluctuations and fierce atmospheric wind velocities, and even the 23-degree tilt of its axis is necessary for life to ever even begin. All this design had to be in place before evolution could start.

Astrophysicist Hugh Ross has identified more than 100 very narrowly defined constants that are necessary for life.[28] These are all properties of the cosmos that must be in place before the first single cell can form and evolution can begin. This is why I find Dawkins' arguments unsatisfying—he solves only one small part of the equation, then sits back and folds his hands as if he has answered the entire dilemma. In reality, he has not addressed the lion's share of the problem. There is a whole lot more that looks designed than just biological life forms. After repeatedly speaking outside his field of expertise on numerous other points, on this point Dawkins holds back. He fails to address design outside of biology at all. He merely speaks of Darwinism "raising our consciousness" of the power of science to explain the appearance of design in the cosmos. In reality, however, he is claiming much more when he suggests that his field trumps the work of astrophysicists like Ross and others.

By Dawkins' own admission, "It is important not to mistake the reach of Natural Selection"[29] yet he does exactly that. When he talks about Darwinism "raising our consciousness" of design in the universe, he is dramatically overstating the ability of biological processes to explain nonbiological matter like stars, planets, and space. Hence he must use a very ambiguous phrase like "raising our consciousness." If he were to flat-out state that Darwinism explains all order in the universe, the fallacy would be all too obvious, so he merely implies it.

[*original argument on page 206*]

Debunking Arguments for God's Existence: The Argument from Scripture

Dawkins' evaluation of the argument from Scripture would be devastating if it were true. But the only issue he describes fairly accurately is that there are numerous "gospels" that were excluded from the canon. They were excluded because the early church deemed them inaccurate portrayals of the person, teaching, and life of Jesus, not because they were "implausible," as Dawkins suggests.[30] The very fact apocryphal gospels were rejected demonstrates the early church's commitment to accurately conveying the life and teaching of Jesus.

Among the reasons the Gospels were not immediately written down is because so few people were literate, yet Dawkins entirely ignores this. Written books are not the best way to spread your message if only about ten percent of the population is literate and books have to be hand-copied.[31] In their setting, Hebrew boys memorized the Pentateuch (the first five books of the Old Testament) in its entirety. In my Bible, that is a whopping 184 pages of information! A society with a developed process of oral tradition capable of accurately handing down hundreds of pages of information for future generations could surely faithfully preserve Jesus' teaching for one generation before it was written down around AD 70.[32] This is a rather liberal estimate of how much time went by before the material was written. The majority of scholars believe there was an earlier source they call "Q" (for the German word *quelle*, meaning "source"), a common source for Matthew and Luke of material which was missing from the Gospel of Mark. If scholars are right about the date of this source (as early as AD 40), we have a complete written account of Jesus' life, teaching, death, and resurrection within only a few years of the events taking place.[33]

Dawkins' claim that the Gospels were "all written long after the death of Jesus"[34] is based on bad information and blatantly wrong. Although at one time the Tubingen School advanced this view, it has long since been thoroughly debunked. Among the long list of problems with the "late Gospels" view—besides the glaring fault that it was originally advanced on philosophical presupposition rather than evidence[35]—is that the apostolic fathers who wrote from AD 90 to 160 quoted the New Testament extensively. It is impossible to quote a book that has not yet been written.

Dawkins' assertion that there is minimal historical evidence Jesus claimed any sort of divine status is uninformed at best, deliberately misleading at worst. In his book *The Christ Files: How Historians Know What They Know About Jesus*, historian John Dickson assembled a list of things we know about Jesus without a single verse of Scripture. Citing reports about Jesus from Greco-Roman texts like Celsus, Lucian of Samosata, Suetonius, Tacitus, Pliny the Younger, Mara Bar Serapion, and Thallos, as well as ancient Jewish history like the Talmud and Josephus, Dickson comes up with the following list of what we confidently know solely from extrabiblical sources. I have italicized the historical items Dawkins has distorted.

- The name "Jesus"
- The place and time frame of his public ministry (Palestine during Pontius Pilate's governorship, AD 26–36)
- The name of his mother (Mary)
- The ambiguous nature of his birth
- The name of one of his brothers (James)
- His fame as a teacher
- *His fame as a miracle-worker/sorcerer*
- *The attribution to him of the title "Messiah/Christ"*
- *His "kingly" status in the eyes of some*
- The time and manner of his execution (crucifixion during the Passover festival)
- The involvement of both the Roman and Jewish leadership in his death
- The coincidence of an eclipse at the time of his crucifixion
- The report of Jesus' appearance to his followers after his death (if the second reconstruction of Josephus' comments is accepted)
- The flourishing of a movement that worshipped Jesus after his death[36]

All this comes from nonbiblical sources, some of which were actively opposed to the spread of Christianity. Then, of course, we have the testimonies of Jesus' disciples, sealed with their lives. Even if we take the most critical approach and reject the entire Bible's credibility, Dawkins' claim is still demonstrably absurd based on extrabiblical records alone.

Speaking of absurd claims, Dawkins asserts that "it is even possible to mount a serious, though not widely supported historical case that Jesus never lived at all, as has been done by, among others, Professor G.A. Wells of the University of London."[37] I had read several books on the historicity of Jesus without ever coming across Professor Wells' name, so I did some research. I was shocked to discover Dawkins' sole source for questioning whether Jesus ever lived was not even a historian but a professor of the German language! This is as preposterous as me writing a book making sweeping claims about evolution and citing as my sole authority a music professor at Berkeley.

These are the kinds of omissions and misdirections that make Dawkins self-refuting. His supporters may rush to point out that he qualifies his claims with "though not widely supported,"[38] but that is the only time he acknowledges that he draws almost exclusively from the controversial fringe of historical scholarship. By analogy, you can find fringe articles and books claiming 9/11 was a conspiracy planned and executed by the US government. However, when you read the bulk of credible research on the matter, like *The 9/11 Commission Report*, those myths are exposed as the crackpot theories they really are. Similarly, there is no denying you can find fringe historians who question whether Jesus actually lived, but they are clearly out of sync with the majority of historical scholarship on the issue.

How do scholars like Wells get around clear historical records like the *Terminoium Flavianum* (the testimony of Flavius Josephus), wherein Josephus described the condemnation and crucifixion of Jesus? They simply ignore the evidence! Robert Price "leapfrogs" over it and dismissively says, "My guess is that Eusebius fabricated it."[39] Professor John Dominic Crossan, who is certainly no evangelical Christian, rightly takes him to task, saying this "is not an acceptable scholarly comment as far as I am concerned."[40]

Likewise, I do not find Dawkins' willingness to reimagine the historical record very scholarly either. According to historian John Dickson:

> While historians cannot say Jesus *actually* healed the sick, they can, and generally do, say that Jesus did things which those around him believed to be miraculous. Whether or not you and I concur with this belief depends not on historical considerations but on philosophical assumptions (such as what we regard as *possible* in the universe).[41]

[original argument on page 207]

The Worship of Gaps

Dawkins arguing against God of gaps arguments is ironic and irrelevant because most Christians do not believe in this line of argumentation either. Sure, you can find some Christians who believe it, just like you can find some atheists who are Republicans, but it is not a mainstream Christian view, nor did the argument even originate with Christians. The earliest known reference to this idea goes back to nineteenth-century evangelist Henry Drummond from his lectures "The Ascent of Man." In them, he speaks out *against* Christians maintaining that things science cannot yet explain are "gaps which they will fill up with God."[42] Even Dawkins notes that Christian pastor and theologian Dietrich Bonhoeffer condemned the logic. Contrary to looking for God in the gaps, Bonhoeffer says, "We are to find God in what we know, not in what we don't know."[43]

I could not help but notice that Dawkins never cites a single Christian who actually believes in arguing for God by the gaps. I have not read or heard such arguments from William Lane Craig, Lee Strobel, Josh McDowell, Ravi Zacharias, or any other major contemporary apologist. While I suppose it is possible Dawkins has heard such statements from obscure fundamentalists, they are not a part of mainstream Christianity. The argument for God is based on the evidence of science and history, *not* the gaps in the evidence. Dawkins' whole argument is a red herring because he challenges a position that is not generally held by theists.

[original argument on page 207]

The Anthropic Principle

When it comes to Dawkins' argument that chance is a sufficient explanation of the universe despite the 1 in 10^{138} probability of it originating by chance, no one debunks his poor logic better than fellow atheist Bertrand Russell because Russell has no alternative agenda.[44] Unlike Dawkins, Russell understood the relationship of probability to the explanation of events by chance versus by design. Said Russell:

> There is, as we all know, a law that if you throw dice you will get double sixes only about once in thirty-six times, and we do not regard that as evidence that the fall of the dice is regulated by design; on the contrary, if the double sixes came every time we should think that there was a design.[45]

Russell understood that when a pair of dice comes up double sixes every roll, they must be designed, even though the odds against this occurring by chance are only 1 in 36 per roll.[46] Dawkins, on the other hand, examines the staggering odds against a life-sustaining universe forming by chance yet still concludes there is no design. This is despite the fact the odds are equal to a pair of dice coming up sixes every time for 69 consecutive rolls. Anyone who finds Dawkins' explanation satisfactory should try imagining himself in Las Vegas explaining to the skeptical pit boss how he rolled double sixes for the fortieth or fiftieth consecutive roll purely by chance. When we take Dawkins' illustrations outside the arena of religion, the absurdity of his suggestions becomes readily apparent.

When Dawkins discusses the precision of tuning in the universe, he cites the strong force as 0.006 and claims that a variance of just 0.001 would prevent life. I was watching the Winter Olympics when I read that. I observed the winner of the bobsled event was determined by less than one-tenth of one second. Therefore, it does not seem like a stretch to believe that the value of a force could fall within one-one thousandth of where it needs to be for life to "win." However, Dawkins never mentions the fact that we are talking about a force 6×10^{39} greater than gravity.[47] The precision of the tuning is simply not conveyed by Dawkins' inadequate description of the strong force. A better example would have been that shared by UCLA physicist Jeffrey Zweerink, who stated, "If the gravitational force were altered by 0.00000000000000000000 000000000000000001 percent, our sun would not exist, and, there-fore, neither would we."[48] That brings us a bit closer to understanding the statistical improbability of life by chance.

Not only does Dawkins fail to convey the precision of the tuning, he obscures how many constants are finely tuned. Dawkins cites a book titled *Just Six Numbers*. Granted, this happens to be the book's title, but it gives the impression that just six constants are necessary for life. As Frank Turek points out in *I Don't Have Enough Faith to Be an Atheist*, "there are more than 100 very narrowly defined constants that strongly point to an intelligent Designer."[49]

When we look at the number of finely tuned constants and the precision of that fine tuning, we see the fallacy in Dawkins' needle-in-a-haystack analogy. Dawkins misstates the problem as *finding* the needle in a haystack, when the actual issue is the improbability of the needle *being* there at all. The power of the cosmological argument is not the problem of finding a life-sustaining planet. We are on one. The problem is the statistical improbability of there *being* a life-sustaining planet anywhere in the universe, including under our feet, on the basis of chance alone.

Astrophysicist Hugh Ross calculated the probability that the 122 constants required for life would exist *for any planet* in the universe by chance (i.e., without divine design). He based his calculation on the existence of 10^{22} planets in the universe, which is on the generous side of Dawkins' own estimate.[50] The possibility that luck accounts for a life-sustaining universe is one chance in 10^{138}![51] To help you wrap your brain around the improbability of that, there are only 10^{70} atoms in the entire universe.[52]

This is not merely some Christian apologist's figure. Irreligious sci-entists who have come to the same conclusion also support Ross' calcu-lations. Stephen Hawking calculates the odds against life on the basis of just one constant, the rate of the universe's expansion one second after the Big Bang, as one in a hundred thousand million-million.[53] Paul Davies concludes the odds against life existing are "one followed by at least a thousand billion billion zeroes."[54]

I would critique Dawkins' dismissal of design in the anthropic principle by using his own illustration of the firing squad, though the analogy needs to be modified for accuracy (no pun intended). The analogy of all ten members of a firing squad accidentally missing their victim may appear reasonable in light of the examples of fine tuning Dawkins provides, but his example does not adequately convey either the magnitude of the tuning precision nor the number of variables finally tuned in the universe.

Now that we have examined the real odds, let us bring the argument back before the firing squad. Dawkins' example of ten firing squad shooters all missing does not even come remotely close to the actual probability of 1 in 10^{138} that our poor victim avoids his fate by luck. We can still capture a realistic illustration if we adjust it to reflect the data. Instead of facing a ten-member firing squad, the condemned man is put on the 50-yard line of the New Orleans Superdome and the dome is filled to its capacity of 76,468 people, each of whom is equipped with a high-powered rifle. Each rifle is capable of hitting a man even from the nosebleed section, and is equipped with the best available scopes for optimal aiming. Now we are starting to approximate the very best-case scenario that our poor victim will make it through his ordeal by luck. But we have not adequately illustrated Hawking's "optimistic" odds of "one in a hundred thousand million-million." To more accurately match either Hawking's or Ross' odds, we would need to replace every other shooter with a highly trained Marine sniper, hand out a couple of grenades to the guys on the sideline, and distribute a few bazookas throughout the bleachers. Now we finally have a statistically accurate illustration. Ready, aim, fire!

If our victim beats the odds, he could take Dawkins' view, "Well, obviously they all missed,"[55] but if he is unwilling to even entertain the possibility that someone designed his escape from death by loading the guns with blanks or bribing the shooters to fire over his head or manipulating the execution in some other manner, then I believe our survivor is a victim of his own delusion.

?????

On a new topic, Dawkins finds God extremely improbable because natural selection cannot explain him. He goes on to say that a design hypothesis of the universe does not work "because design is ultimately not cumulative."[56] Dawkins cannot understand God because he is committed to his *a priori* assumption that the material world is all that exists. This comes out when he makes statements like "design is not cumulative." No theist ever claimed it was. Dawkins is reinterpreting the design position in light of his own presuppositions. I referenced this problem earlier in my observation that Dawkins only argues against the view of an evolved God. He never interacts with or even mentions the concept of an eternal God. Dawkins assumes materialism, then demands that someone demonstrate God to him *within that framework*. Of course, it is impossible to prove anything that lies outside of a framework artificially constrained by presupposition.

For example, suppose a developer created true artificial intelligence within a computer. Suppose that immaterial software had genuine self-awareness and a real ability to use its own logic and reason to think freely apart from its programming. That software could examine and identify itself as a nonmaterial being existing within a nonbiological world of semiconductors and circuit boards. If that software were to try to define its programmer according to its own existence, it would always fail. As long the software projects its own limitations of nonmaterial, nonbiological existence onto a material, biological programmer, it will never grasp the nature of the programmer. The programmer can never be explained in terms of the software's world because the programmer is of a different essence than the program. Circuit boards and semiconductors simply cannot explain the programmer. As long as the program demands all explanations conform to its own nonmaterial, nonbiological existence, it cannot explain the programmer whose existence lies outside that framework.

All I have done is flip Dawkins' argument to show the absurdity of it. Just like an immaterial program existing in a nonbiological world cannot understand its material programmer while simultaneously demanding the answer conform to its own immaterial existence, a material, biological scientist cannot understand an immaterial, nonbiological God while demanding his explanation conform to the scientist's own material, biological existence.

This reminds me of the plot of *The Hitchhiker's Guide to the Galaxy* and the computer Deep Thought, built to explain the ultimate meaning of life. When the answer comes back "42," it is incomprehensible because no one knows what question has been answered. The problem becomes exacerbated when they realize they can either know the question or the answer, never both. Similarly, Dawkins can demand a material explanation to the question of God or he can understand the immaterial God, but he will never have both.

[original argument on page 207]

Does Our Moral Sense Have a Darwinian Origin?

Perhaps the best rebuttal to Dawkins' observation regarding moral patterns in animals is how fellow atheists Friedrich Nietzsche and Sam Harris argued against looking for moral patterns in nature. See pages 53 (Living by Nature) and 150 for how even an atheist can see the problem with Dawkins' model without any apologetic bent.

The Achilles' heel of Dawkins' Darwinian argument for morality is that it makes *moral* synonymous with *survival*. Anything that aids survival is deemed good, while anything that harms it is deemed bad. The problem is any action that aids survival, no matter how offensive or undesirable it may appear on its own, meets the definition of *moral* so long as it can be shown to aid survival.

The problem with Dawkins' example of Arabian babblers is that it is circular. He takes an action he already understands to be good— altruism—then looks to nature for an example that validates his foregone conclusion. Why is it good? Because it works in nature. Why does it work in nature? Because it is good.

The question is why point to Arabian babblers and not to frigate birds? Frigate birds, sometimes called pirate birds, are anything but altruistic.[57] Instead of hunting their own food, they will attack another bird that has already caught a fish. The victim, laden by the burden of his catch, must drop the fish to defend himself, at which point the frigate bird steals the meal. They even steal from their own species! They also are not respectful of another frigate bird's sexual partner. Rather, they will inflate their red gular throat pouches and exhibit intimidating behavior to drive off another frigate bird's partner if they are able. This behavior works so well for them that they are listed as a "least concern" for extinction[58] and are found in both hemispheres worldwide.[59]

Dawkins' argument from nature is a dead end because it can be used to justify stealing just as easily as sharing food. He has done nothing to address why stealing is bad and sharing is good. He takes something he knows to be true based on Europe's remnant Judeo-Christian ethic, then claims he has found independent Darwinian support for that belief in nature when he is really just cherry-picking an example that fit his foregone conclusion.

Another problem with moral arguments from nature is that we intuitively understand there is a fundamental difference between actions taken by humans and the same actions taken by animals. A male gorilla may forcefully copulate with any female he desires, but we would not say the gorilla is a rapist. A female mantis will kill and eat her partner after coitus, but we do not say the insect is a murderer. A bear may not respect a beekeeper's private property, but we do not say the bear is a burglar when it breaks into the keeper's beehives. Imagine the laughter if the beekeeper were to tell the police he wanted to press charges against a bear for burglary. The suggestion that animal morality can be equated to human morality may be a funny joke to the police officers, but Dawkins does not get the punch line.

[original argument on page 209]

A Case Study in the Roots of Morality

The consensus between atheists and religious believers on what actions are moral in Hauser's trolley study does not surprise me at all. I would, in fact, expect some level of consensus if we are all children of God. The theist position is that we all have a sense of right and wrong—including those who deny this—because we are created in God's image. Hauser's findings were perfectly consistent with a theist's worldview.

I note Hauser's study entailed only life-and-death scenarios. He did not touch on issues like rape, lust, lying, envy, gluttony, anger, greed, or pride. If Dawkins had cited a study that found consensus among believers and atheists in non-life-and-death scenarios, that would have been interesting. However, his argument that "I do not need God because I know not to murder people" is not compelling at all. I would hope he could at least recognize murder as wrong even without believing in God.

I have honestly never heard an atheist response to the moral argument that addressed the actual moral argument. Instead, atheists always respond to a straw man. The moral argument is not "Can atheists follow social norms?" Nor is it "We need God to follow social norms." Rather, it is the argument that God is required to have an absolute standard by which to define morality apart from the prevailing social norm of the times.

The famous atheist Sigmund Freud wrote, "Ethics are a kind of highway code for traffic among mankind."[60] If morality is nothing more than arbitrary rules we agree to follow to make society function smoothly, then asking, "Can atheists act morally?" is no different than asking, "Can atheists drive on the right side of the road?" Of course they can! However, that is not a question about acting morally. It is only a question of mimicry: "*Can* you act like your neighbor?" is not a moral question. "*Should* you act like your neighbor?" is.

I reject the notion that morality is nothing more than the current social norms we agree to follow. I do not think you believe it either. For example, is it wrong to rape a woman? If you said no, please stop reading and get a book on ethics instead, since you have some serious problems. For the rest of you who understand that rape is wrong, you may find it a bit disturbing that Professor Mary P. Koss of the University of Arizona found in a 1988 study that one in four men believed rape was acceptable if the woman asked a man out and he paid for the date.[61] There are a surprising number of perverts out there, but I assume you stand behind your position that rape is wrong even if one in four men disagrees with you.

That study is several years old though. Let's assume a new study based on good data were to return the result that now three in four people believe rape is socially acceptable. Once you get past the shock that a majority of the populace cannot see anything wrong with rape—knowing that you are now in the minority—will you change your position to align with social norms? Or do you still believe something is wrong even if you are the only person who seems to "get it"?

Every atheist I have ever met believes in utilitarian ethics. At least a few of them are actually consistent with it. For example, one atheist told me that if there were a reversal of the current tide in favor of homosexuality and society overwhelming rejected it, then she too would agree that it is wrong. However, the vast majority of atheists seem to really believe in deontological ethics* even though they verbally espouse utilitarian ethics.

For example, I had this conversation with an atheist at the Drunken Monkey Coffee Bar in Orlando during a book club discussing Christopher Hitchens' book *God is Not Great*...

> **Me:** Suppose the Messerschmitt 262 had been introduced early enough in the war to give Germany air superiority. As a result, Hitler went on to win World War II and succeeded in either converting or killing anyone who disagreed with his plan of genocide. If there were universal consensus that the genocide of the Jews was a good thing, would it still have been wrong?
>
> **Atheist:** Well, luckily we don't have to worry about that because the right side won.
>
> **Me:** What do you mean the "right" side won?
>
> **Atheist:** The Allies knew Hitler was wrong so they stood up to him and we won.
>
> **Me:** But you can't believe morality is utilitarian and say the "right" side won. All you can say is "The side that won

---

* The Greek word *deon* means "obligation" or "duty," so a deontological ethic places incumbent obligations or duties onto man. Utilitarian ethics, by contrast, is the idea that whatever maximizes utility (i.e., works best for the majority) is the best course of action.

is the side that won." If Hitler had won and his viewpoint
was propagated everywhere, wouldn't that make him right?

Atheist: No, because he was a genocidal dictator.

Me: So you're saying genocide is wrong regardless of what
the majority believes about it?

Atheist: <silence>

It all boils down to the simple question, "Can you imagine any
scenario when society would be wrong?" If Hitler had won the war
and the world embraced genocide, would we be wrong? Was America wrong to not allow gay marriage for its first 200 years? If the South
had won and America had continued to allow slavery, would we be
wrong? In utilitarian ethics, society can never be wrong because *society*
is the standard. If you can look at any period of history and say society got it wrong, you are holding to a deontological view of morality
that requires an absolute standard, which theists call God. That is the
real moral argument.

[original argument on page 210]

Cargo Cults

In *The God Delusion*, sometimes it seems like Dawkins is attacking religion with a boomerang. If you just keep reading, his arguments
often come back around and whack him in the head. For example, in
chapter 3, he claims that the apostles could not have been eyewitnesses
to Christ's life because "It is...possible to mount a serious, though not
widely supported, historical case that Jesus never lived at all"[62] and
"Nobody knows who the four evangelists were, but they almost certainly never met Jesus personally."[63] However, when he gets to the
section on the cargo cults, the core ingredient for a new religion is eyewitnesses to something which appeared supernatural to the religion's
first adherents. In the case of Christianity, it was the resurrection. In the
case of the cargo cults, it was "sufficiently advanced technology [which
seemed] indistinguishable from magic."[64] Granted, there was nothing supernatural in the Pacific Islands' case, but the events certainly

appeared supernatural to tribal people who had never seen such technology. However, disparity in technology cannot account for what happened in first-century Israel.

Dawkins has already gone on record as arguing that nothing supernatural happened in first century AD (after all, how could Jesus rise from the dead if he did not even exist?) and that eyewitnesses certainly did not start Christianity. But when he gives an example in chapter 5 of how he thinks religions start, the core element is that eyewitnesses reacted to something which at least appeared supernatural. Dawkins' example in chapter 3 returns like a boomerang to contradict his claims in chapter 5.

One is left scratching his head wondering whether or not Dawkins believes the appearance of supernatural events is required for the formation of a religion. He argues against it in chapter 3 but for it in chapter 5. Did he simply forget he had already argued against eyewitnesses and seemingly supernatural events two chapters earlier? Or is he so blindly committed to his position that he does not realize when he is citing examples that are contradictory?

This shows blatant "Heads I win, tails you lose" logic. To Dawkins, ultimately it does not matter whether there were eyewitnesses of an event that appeared supernatural because his position is not based on evidence. Rather, he is bending what evidence there is to fit his preconceived notion.

[original argument on page 211]

What About Hitler and Stalin?

Dawkins says, "We are not in the business of counting evil heads and compiling two rival roll calls of iniquity."[65] But what then is the list on the first page of his book if not just such a roll call?

> Imagine no suicide bombers, no 9/11, no 7/7, no Crusade, no witch-hunts, no Gunpowder Plot, no Indian partition, no Israeli/Palestinian wars, no Serb/Croat/Muslim massacres, no persecution of Jews as "Christ-killers," no Northern Ireland "troubles," no "honour killings"…Imagine no

Taliban to blow up ancient statues, no public beheadings of blasphemers, no flogging of female skin for the crime of showing an inch of it.[66]

Clearly the "we" he refers to excludes himself. What he really means is, "It's okay for me to assemble a roll call of religious iniquity, but you can't assemble such a roll call." No need to belabor the point; the hypocrisy speaks for itself.

I found an interesting phenomenon unfolding as I kept reading books on atheism and watching and listening to debates: Atheists often refute each other. For example, Christopher Hitchens was adamant that Hitler was a devout Catholic,[67] yet fellow atheist Dawkins disagrees. Dawkins is honest enough to at least acknowledge the possibility that Hitler was "an opportunistic liar."[68] This is sufficient rebuttal to Hitchens, since no one can assert Dawkins is subject to religious bias.

Ultimately, does it really matter whether Hitler was an atheist? I would say no were it not for the arguments atheists themselves raise, like when Dawkins opens his book with the challenge, "Imagine, with John Lennon, a world with no religion..."[69] That is not a question of whether religion is true or false, but a utilitarian argument that, regardless of whether religion is true or false, the world is simply better off in practice without religion. As atheist Douglas Murray points out, such a claim begs the question whether that irreligious world would be the utopian portrait Dawkins paints. If I am to take Dawkins' challenge seriously, then Hitler matters along with Stalin, Chairman Mao, Pol Pot, and Kim Jong-il. Why should I *imagine* a hypothetical world with no religion when these men give us numerous *actual* examples? We can look at North Korea, which is committed to atheism, and ask whether we would be better off living there. The country detains 50,000 to 70,000 of its own citizens in prison camps for their religious beliefs. In these camps, inmates are compelled to eat rodents and lizards to survive, and mothers are forced to drown their own babies.[70] Or we can choose North Korea's religiously diverse neighbor South Korea with its booming economy, quality education, and scientific progress. Of the two Koreas, the one with no religion is a nightmare.

Hitler defies the easy answer that he was raised Catholic but abandoned his faith. Around the middle of World War II, he was still making contradictory remarks affirming his Catholicism while simultaneously criticizing religion.

I see only two options that make sense of the contradictions. One, he sincerely believed both in a bipolar fashion. However, I question whether someone with psychiatric illness could have been so successful. The second option is that he believed one position and lied about the other. Bear in mind that before Hitler was a general, he was a politician. If there is one thing we know about politicians, many are excellent liars. I agree with Dawkins that Hitler was an opportunist liar.

The question then becomes, "Which position did Hitler lie about?" While we cannot know his mind for certain, it seems clear he stood to gain more if he were an atheist lying about being Catholic than vice versa. Europe was still largely religious and the Catholic Church, which still wielded tremendous influence, had not excommunicated Hitler. By convincing Pope Pius XII that he had not abandoned his Catholic upbringing, the Fuhrer avoided a direct standoff with the Pope. How much effect would a papal edict calling on Catholic German soldiers to lay down their arms actually have? Perhaps not enough to change the war, yet a skilled politician like Hitler would be smart enough not to find out.

On the flip side, if he was still Catholic, what benefit could he possibly hope to gain by lying about being an atheist? There was nothing advantageous about making such claims if he did not mean them. Hitler's contradictory statements make the most sense if he were an atheist lying about his Catholic faith for political gain.

Dawkins says, "Why would anyone go to war for the sake of an absence of belief?"[71] He suggests that a lack of belief is not sufficient to motivate action. However, the first sentence on the website of the American Atheists organization is "American Atheists *fights* to..."[72] This demonstrates that the absence of belief is sufficient motive to fight for all kinds of things. While the American Atheists may not have started a war, they did start a legal battle to have the Ten Commandments monument removed from the Starke, Florida, courthouse;[73]

fought to have prayer removed from schools; fought to have the phrase "In God We Trust" removed from US currency; and even fought to keep Bibles off the space shuttles.[74] They are currently fighting to keep the World Trade Center cross out of the 9/11 Memorial Museum.[75] Their current president, David Silverman, has gone on record as saying, "The Christian right should be threatened by us."[76] It is patently absurd to make the claim that people do not start fights on the basis of "an absence of belief." Perhaps Dawkins' question is better answered with a question—"Why would anyone spend a quarter of a million dollars to put antireligion billboards on city buses for the sake of an absence of belief?"[77]

[original argument on page 212]

What's Wrong with Religion? Why Be So Hostile?

There is nothing new about the New Atheists' claims about God. The *Internet Encyclopedia of Philosophy* says, "It is difficult to identify anything philosophically unprecedented in their positions and arguments."[78] What is new is their "outrage about the effects of religious beliefs on the global scene"[79] and their insistence that religion is harmful and should be eliminated.

Dawkins' claim that religion "subverts science" is patently out of touch with history and reality. Catholic Friar Gregor Mendel pioneered the field of genetics.[80] Roman Catholic priest Georges Lamaitre proposed the Big Bang theory two years before Edwin Hubble.[81] Father Angelo Secchi was the father of astrophysics. From his scientific work at the Vatican Observatory, he was the first to map the surface of Mars[82] and the first to look at stars through a prism in order to deduce their composition from their spectral lines.[83] NASA even named a component of the STEREO spacecrafts' sun-mapping mission SECCHI (Sun Earth Connection Coronal and Heliospheric Investigation) in his honor.[84] American scientist, botanist, and inventor George Washington Carver, famous for escaping slavery in Missouri to become one of the earliest prominent black scientists, said his "faith in Jesus was the only mechanism by which he could effectively pursue and perform the art of science."[85] And astronomer Enoch Fitch Burr once observed that "an undevout astronomer is mad."[86]

The Catholic Church promoted and financially underwrote scientific research before any government did. For example, Catholic funding for astronomy research built the observatory that allowed the creation of the Gregorian calendar, promulgated in 1582 by Pope Gregory XIII. This is the same calendar that Dawkins looks at every day as he claims that religion subverts science. A Google search of "Christian thinkers in science" produced 55 scientists in the twentieth century alone who are winners of the Nobel Prize, the National Medal of Science, the Royal Medal, the Copley Medal, the Davy Medal, the Perkin Medal, and the Gold Medal of the Royal Astronomical Society. They were inventors, researchers, and presidents of the Royal Society and the World Academy of Art and Science. These religious scientists discovered nuclear fission, founded Quantum mechanics, created the MRI, developed rockets and space exploration, discovered radioactivity, and discovered the chemical element argon among other scientific contributions.[87] One wonders how Dawkins is unaware that Christian paleontologist Charles Walcott discovered the Burgess Shale, one of the world's most celebrated fossil fields,[88] a huge contribution to the study of evolution.[89] This just scratches the surface of the immense number of scientists in this last century who were also Christians.

In an interview with *The Guardian*, famed theoretical physicist and Nobel Prize Laureate Peter Higgs finds Dawkins' insistence that science and religion are incompatible "embarrassing." Higgs attributes his own lack of religious beliefs to "a matter of my family background," not to science, and sees no "fundamental difficulty about reconciling the two [science and faith]."[90]

Judging by Dawkins' incredibly misleading representation of the Kurt Wise story, it seems to me that he willingly distorts the truth. During a discussion of Wise's studies at Harvard under Stephen Jay Gould, Dawkins tells the captivating story of Wise cutting out Bible passages he felt contradicted science. This implies a conflict between Wise's childhood religious notions and Harvard's scientific curriculum. What

Dawkins conspicuously fails to mention is that the Bible-cutting incident occurred during Wise's sophomore year of high school! Dawkins' chronology is misleading at best. Wise did not abandon his Harvard paleontology education as result of his cut-up Bible. He pursued higher scientific education years after that anecdote. Evidently when Dawkins wants to make a point, he does not let pesky details like facts stand in his way. Such distortions free readers from the delusion that Dawkins' views are evidence-based.

Dawkins inaccurately portrays Wise as believing he had to choose between science and the Bible, which was not the case at all. What Wise actually believes is that *"although there are scientific reasons for accepting a young earth*, I am a young age creationist because that is my understanding of the Scripture."[91] Wise did not choose between scientific evidence and faith, as Dawkins suggests. Rather, Wise believes there is scientific evidence for his young earth view, but he is simply being intellectually honest by acknowledging that the scientific evidence is not the primary source of his view.*

Regarding homosexual rights and abortion, I am amazed at Dawkins' egomaniacal position. It amounts to "I do not believe in God; therefore, you must defend your position *as if* he does not exist." His unjustifiable overestimation of his own position's validity is based on an assumed premise of God's nonexistence, which he freely admits he cannot prove. He demands others formulate their ethics without reference to God despite the fact authors have written book-length expositions exposing how Dawkins has failed to support that position.[92] While I respect Dawkins' right to not believe in God, it is only reasonable to expect a reciprocal amount of respect. The position "Your argument does not count if it involves God" is an unproved, *a priori* presupposition of philosophical materialism on Dawkins' part. He *thinks* God does not exist. However, once he begins to discuss ethics, he shifts to speaking as if he has *proven* that God does not exist.

Personally, I try to emphasize the nontheological, practical reasons for my position on homosexual rights and abortion when addressing

---

* Lest the argument of quote mining be turned back on me, I should mention my source is private correspondence directly with Mr. Wise.

unbelievers because I do not expect them to accept my worldview. Nor do I expect a nonbeliever to accept an argument from Scripture. However, I absolutely have a right to believe something for that reason until Scripture is proven false.

[original argument on page 213]

Summary

I found Dawkins' arguments unconvincing because they are founded on the logical fallacy of bifurcation. He creates a false dilemma: (A) Believe in evolution, or (B) believe in God. This summarily ignores valid options presented by prominent scientists, not Christian apologists.* He incessantly argues against the straw man of an evolved God, something even theists do not believe in, without ever interacting with the theist concept of the eternal God. He overstates the explanatory capabilities of science to such an extreme that *other atheist scientists* find fault. Why should any theist buy into his thinking when his arguments fail to convince even people who already share his worldview?

Dawkins commits categorical errors when he forces principles from biology upon anthropology and biogenesis, where they have no relevance. Yet he does not stop there. He goes as far as imposing biological principles onto cosmology and even ethics. Sam Harris wonders, and I agree, why anyone would believe God came to Earth solely on the basis of papal authority.[93] At the other extreme, the emphatic proclamations of an atheist biologist about the origins of the universe and ethics strike me as the atheist equivalent of papal infallibility.

On the issue of morality, like all of the New Atheists, Dawkins is guilty of Nietzsche's indictment: "Ultimately they all want English morality to be proved right."[94] He starts with the unproven assumption that English morality is superior, then builds a case after the fact to support his assumption. He neither acknowledges that the opposite case can be made from nature by simply looking at different species of

---

* The four major views are theistic creation, theistic evolution, naturalistic evolution, and naturalistic creation. Dawkins ignores theistic evolution and naturalistic creation entirely. He then pretends that young Earth creationism, which is just one subset of theistic creation, represents the entirety of the position.

birds nor justifies why his arbitrary morality should be adopted over Nietzsche's view of might makes right.

Finally, Dawkins holds an *a priori* commitment to philosophical naturalism on which he builds an argument demanding material proof of an immaterial God. He then feigns surprise that God cannot be proven within such narrowly defined constraints.

Dawkins presents false dilemmas, advances straw man arguments, relies heavily on the fallacy of overstated appeal to authority (his own when he presumptuously speaks for all scientists), and uses circular reasoning to support preconceived notions. For these reasons, I found Dawkins' arguments an ineffectual and inadequate basis for embracing atheism.

Dawkins' Key Concepts

Key Concepts	Source	Evidence Offered
Complex things (like God) come into existence only through gradual evolution.	Dawkins	In Darwinism, creative intelligence comes late in the evolutionary process (of biological beings).
Darwinism destroys the argument from design for God.	Russell	Talks about natural selection as a "consciousness raiser"
Religion is responsible for group hostilities.	Russell	9/11, Crusades, Israeli/Palestinian wars, the troubles of northern Ireland, etc.
Faith is belief "contrary" to evidence.	Russell	*None offered*—like Russell, he merely substitutes the definition of *fideism* for the definition of *faith*.
Religion gets undeserved respect.	Dawkins	Centro Espirita church members exempted from drug charges for drinking hallucinogenic tea at church. Easier for a Quaker to avoid a military draft than it is for a moral philosopher.
NOMA is wrong. Science and religion need to be integrated.	Dawkins	This is his personal opinion (which other atheist scientists disagree with).
There is no proof that prayer works.	Dawkins	Galton and STEP studies
God has not provided good evidence of his existence.	Russell	Russell's teapot analogy Dawkins' flying spaghetti monster analogy

Key Concepts	Source	Evidence Offered
Everyone has some god they do not believe in. Why not go one god further?	Dawkins	People do not believe in Zeus, Apollo, Ra, Thor, etc.
The cosmological argument is not a valid argument for God.	Russell	Our understanding of the Big Bang does not require a cause with biblical attributes.
The teleological argument is not a valid argument for God.	Dawkins	Evolution shows how natural causes can create the appearance of design, such as an insect that seeks heat like a guided missile.
Jesus may not have existed at all.	Russell	Quotes professor G.A. Wells
The proposition that God made the universe raises the bigger question, "Who made God?"	Russell	*None offered*—just an unproven philosophical assertion that all complex things have origins (i.e., ignores the possibility that something can be both complex and eternal).
Irreducible complexity is rubbish.	Dawkins	Half a wing is better than no wing. Cites eyes of various levels of complexity.
The God of the gaps theory leaves less room for God as science explains more.	Dawkins	Even Christian theologian Dietrich Bonhoeffer condemned it.
The anthropic principle is not an argument for God. It simply means we defied staggeringly improbable odds of being here by chance.	Dawkins	John Leslie's illustration of surviving a firing squad. The ant sitting on the needle has no problem finding the needle in the haystack.

Key Concepts	Source	Evidence Offered
The origin of religion is our slavish gullibility that helps us survive when we heed our parents' wisdom.	Dawkins	Parents tell their children not to swim in the crocodile-infested Limpopo river.
Believing in religion requires a predisposition to dualism.	Dawkins	Study by Paul Bloom that seems to indicate we are naturally predisposed to dualism.
We do not need God for morals. We can find examples of morals in nature.	Dawkins	Arabian babbler birds
Atheists and theists behave similarly in moral situations.	Dawkins	Marc Hauser's runaway trolley dilemma
The cargo cults show how new religions can start without anything supernatural happening.	Dawkins	Cults springing up in New Guinea when the natives were awed by seeing planes for the first time.
It matters not whether Hitler and Stalin were atheists, but rather, whether their atheism caused their actions.	Dawkins	Blames Marxism and eugenics theory respectively for Stalin's and Hitler's actions.
Religion is harmful.	Nietzsche	Subversion of science, homosexual and abortion rights
Raising children to be religious is tantamount to child abuse.	Russell	Story about a woman who feared hell into adulthood
Teaching about hell is unkind.	Russell	Hell houses

* NOMA stands for "non-overlapping magisteria," the idea that science and theism do not overlap and therefore can never contradict one another.

Replies and Rebuttals to Dawkins' Key Concepts

Arguments for Atheism/Against God	Rebuttal
Complex things (like God) come into existence only through gradual evolution.	Evolution has no relevance to spiritual entities. The suggestion that ghosts must evolve because animals do is absurd.
Darwinism destroys the argument from design for God.	Darwinism cannot explain either the design of the first living cell or the design of the universe that contains it.
Religion is responsible for group hostilities.	History gives ample evidence group hostility is inevitable with or without religion. Even when religion appears to be causal (i.e., Ireland), there are often underlying nonreligious causes.
Faith is belief "contrary" to evidence.	Confuses *fideism* and *faith*. The primary definition of faith in every major dictionary is "trust." In the words of Inigo Montoya from *The Princess Bride*, "You keep using that word. I don't think it means what you think it means."
Religion gets undeserved respect.	Possibly, but this is not an argument against God.
NOMA is wrong. Science and religion need to be integrated.*	Yes, there is some overlap, but theism fares better in the overlapping areas than Dawkins suggests.† Also, Dawkins subtly shifts from arguing that there is overlap (true) to the radical claim that science completely displaces religion (not true).
There is no proof that prayer works.	He ignores four studies showing that prayer does work and focuses exclusively on two which found the contrary. The Bible itself predicts that the STEP study would not work, but he conveniently ignores why.

Arguments for Atheism/Against God	Rebuttal
God has not provided good evidence of his existence.	"Good" evidence would be coercive for those who, like Dawkins, hate God and therefore is not consistent with a loving God's character.
Everyone has some god they do not believe in. Why not go one god further?	Just because I do not believe someone flew on crude wings of wax and feathers (Icarus) does not mean I should not believe someone flew on crude wings of wood and fabric (Orville Wright).
The cosmological argument is not a valid argument for God.	Logical fallacy of equivocation. Shifts from arguing the Big Bang does not demonstrate attributes of the *Christian* God, like forgiving sin and answering prayer (true), to arguing it demonstrates *no* attributes of God, like power and timelessness (false).
The teleological argument in not a valid argument for God	Non sequitur logical fallacy. He misapplies Darwin's explanation of design in biology to the nonbiological universe to which it does not apply.
Jesus may not have existed at all.	This was not even suggested for over 1800 years, and then only by people with an *a priori* commitment to materialism. It is a fringe view with minimal support among historians. Also, G.A. Wells is a professor of the *German language*, not a historian.
The proposition that God made the universe raises the bigger question, "Who made God?"	Category mistake fallacy—the question itself is illogical, like asking, "What color is the number nine?"
Irreducible complexity is rubbish.	A red-herring issue. Disproving evolution is not required to believe in God.[‡]

Arguments for Atheism/Against God	Rebuttal
The God of the gaps theory leaves less room for God as science explains more.	*Agreed*, which is why no Christian I know argues for God in the gaps. Every apologist argument I have ever heard argues for God on the basis of what we *do* know, not the gaps.
The anthropic principle is not an argument for God. It simply means we defied staggeringly improbable odds of being here by chance.	Atheist Bertrand Russell said defeating the odds of 1 in 36 (the odds of rolling sixes every time with a pair of dice) would be evidence of design. Dawkins says a universe defeating odds of 1 in 10^{138} is not evidence of design. Now who is deluded?
The origin of religion is our slavish gullibility that helps us survive when we heed our parents' wisdom.	Offers no explanation why people come to faith as adults. Also, based on the unproven (and offensive) assumption that people of faith have the mental aptitude of children.
Believing in religion requires a predisposition to dualism.	*Agreed*—in Dawkins' own position of monism/materialism, however, there can be no mind apart from the brain, so he must doubt whether his own conclusion was chemically predetermined.
We do not need God for morals. We can find examples of morals in nature.	He cannot justify why he extols the "good" actions of the Arabian babbler birds over the "bad" actions of frigate birds.
Atheists and theists behave similarly in moral situations.	Bait-and-switch logical fallacy—the issue is not whether both groups can follow social norms (they can), but whether they can determine correct social norms to begin with.

Arguments for Atheism/Against God	Rebuttal
The cargo cults show how new religions can start without anything supernatural happening.	The disparity between US military technology and the natives' technology made it *appear* that something supernatural had occurred. No such disparity in technology existed in first-century Israel when Christianity started.
It matters not whether Hitler and Stalin were atheists, but rather, whether their atheism caused their actions.	Logical fallacy of bifurcation—by phrasing the question whether Stalin committed atrocities in the name of atheism OR Marxism, Dawkins precludes the true answer of "both."
Religion is harmful.	History proves this wrong. See chapter for details.
Raising children to be religious is tantamount to child abuse.	Dawkins hypocritically supports Camp Quest, which teaches children about atheism while maintaining that religious parents do not have a similar right to teach their children theism.
Teaching about hell is unkind.	Fallacy of begging the question—it is unkind only if it is untrue, which he assumes without proving.

* NOMA stands for "non-overlapping magisteria" and is the idea that science and theism do not overlap and therefore can never contradict one another.

† One example among dozens is Dawkins' false dichotomy of evolution versus creation, which he alleges disproves Genesis. While evolution makes difficult (but does not technically disprove) *one interpretation* of Genesis by young Earth creationists, Dawkins does not even mention other interpretations, such as the one advanced by Augustine back in AD 426, which is perfectly compatible with evolution (Saint Augustine, *The City of God*, XI.6).

‡ As Dawkins himself points out, Kenneth Miller is both against Intelligent Design and, like Michael Behe, a devout Christian. I do not believe Dawkins refutes ID in *The God Delusion*. Although I have read some better challenges to it elsewhere, I remain undecided on the issue myself. For anyone wanting a deeper treatment, the touchstone book is Michael Behe's *Darwin's Black Box: The Biochemical Challenge to Evolution* (1996).

12

The Big Picture

*"Nobody talks so constantly about God as
those who insist that there is no God."*

HEYWOOD BROUN, AMERICAN JOURNALIST,
FROM *COLLECTED EDITION OF HEYWOOD BROUN*

In this book I undertook the ambitious task of explaining how someone could be truly open-minded to atheism and still find the corpus
of atheist writing unconvincing. There is an old saying, "He who stands
on neutral ground is likely to get shot by both sides." I know there will
be Christians who feel I conceded too much. Likewise, despite making every effort to be fair, there are bound to be atheists who question
my sincerity. Nevertheless, what I shared was my true story. Hopefully
in the course of sharing my journey, I have represented both sides fairly
and created some thought-provoking dialogue.

Tying It All Together

At this point, I would like to move beyond the trees to a vantage
point where we can see the forest. To me, Nietzsche seems to best articulate honest atheism. He is the only atheist I read who rejects Christianity without trying to hijack its moral system. He does not raise red
herrings like Dawkins, who argues for morality based on the behavior
of Arabian babbler birds but ignores less desirable behavior in frigate

birds. For Nietzsche, babbler altruism and frigate thievery are both natural behaviors. Neither is morally superior.

The disconnect between what New Atheists claim to believe about morality and how they actually live was conceded by Dawkins. In a televised interview, he said, "I don't derive my ethics when I am at home as a father and a husband from my Neo-Darwinism. *It doesn't work.* I believe it will one day. I believe we will find the answers but for now it doesn't and I can't derive what I believe at home from when I am in the science lab."[1] There are no such smoke and mirrors with Nietzsche: he lives by what he believes.

Nietzsche embraces the full implications of man being a hairless monkey—labels like "good" and "evil" are illusionary. Might makes right and you only get what you take. If I were to be an atheist, it would be Nietzsche's atheism. I appreciate its raw honesty and consistency with Darwinism. I could not embrace the Darwinian idea that we are animals yet live perpetrating a sham that we have some higher nobility, as if we were sons of God. However, Nietzsche's atheism, although sincere, is a nightmare. Were it true, I would have to reject it in the manner one wishes to wake from a bad dream.

While Nietzsche made sense to me, I found that atheists after him made assertions defying common sense. For example, Russell suggested that there is no moral difference between someone who defrauds me and someone who catches the flu, or that writing a poem is morally equivalent to committing a murder. I cannot see how I could subscribe to such nonsense. I simply could not assent to coffee-shop ethics that do not work in the real world.

Most people have the good fortune of not personally knowing someone who was murdered. My friend Jay was murdered in his own home. Russell claimed committing murder is no different than writing a poem,[2] and Harris asserts that murderers are just victims of "bad luck."[3] However, Jay gave people shelter when they were facing homelessness. They strangled him, stole his electronics and car, and left his body in the closet to rot. If Russell and Harris' worldview cannot afford them a moral basis to call such behavior "evil," then their worldview is fundamentally flawed.

At least Russell retains Nietzsche's understanding that in Darwinian evolution you simply cannot "make claims on behalf of man" that would not also hold true for a rat.[4] In that regard, he was still an honest atheist who was willing to grapple with the problems inherent to materialism—the problems of how materialism can be lived out in the real world outside the coffee shop.

After Russell, however, all of atheism's problems are neatly swept under the rug. The New Atheists play hide-and-seek with them. They refuse to admit that the foundation of man's dignity has been eroded, or that free will is doubtful in materialism, or that they are arguing backward to justify a predetermined set of morals that look suspiciously like Jesus' Golden Rule.*

In addition, the core definition of atheism gets changed from "There is no God" to "No evidence exists for God." Atheism is presented as a default position that can be held without evidence. It is incumbent on the other side to convince them otherwise. While that might be convenient for some, nothing about that was convincing for me. Perhaps the blame lies with me for expecting to hear a good argument for why God does not exist.

Broad Themes that Emerge Consistently

I have covered more than 50 points raised by atheists. The core arguments, however, really come down to just a few broad themes that keep reemerging with only slight variations. Here are the top ten:

1. Extraordinary Claims Require Extraordinary Evidence

"Extraordinary claims require extraordinary evidence" is probably the most repeated phrase in atheist literature. While it is repeated ad infinitum, the very people who profess it do not seem to live by it.

The September 11, 2001 terrorist attacks are arguably the most extraordinary news story of the twenty-first century. Terrorists flying

---

* Christopher Hitchens has attempted to argue that the Golden Rule did not originate with Jesus, because the code of Hammurabi dealt with reciprocity in ancient Babylon. However, Jesus himself acknowledged that the underlying principle came from ancient Mosaic Law and that he was merely identifying the principle as the second greatest duty of man after loving God (Matthew 22:36-40; Leviticus 19:18).

jumbo jets into skyscrapers had no historical precedent. Yet despite the extraordinary nature of the event, no atheist demanded extraordinary evidence before believing it. Not one of my atheist friends was more skeptical of the news networks because the story was extraordinary. Not one of them called a friend in New York to say, "Because this story is so extraordinary, please look out your window and confirm it, then I will believe it." Not one skeptic refused to believe what had happened because he had not seen the craters with his own eyes.

No atheists required any additional evidence despite the extraordinary nature of the event. They believed it on the same basis as theists—the same network news coverage that also informs us of ordinary events. What happened to all the rhetoric of extraordinary events requiring extraordinary evidence?

I understand that the resurrection is more extraordinary than the events of 9/11. Nevertheless, the observation remains that when skeptics heard of the most extraordinary event of our lifetime, they accepted it on the basis of the same evidence they accept for any other event.

It would appear the demand for extraordinary evidence is an argument of special pleading. Skeptics betray their bias when they apply it only to supernatural claims. There is clearly an underlying presupposition that the material world is all that exists. This foundational assumption is espoused by every writer except Harris. Materialism is an assumption because the claim that only matter exists cannot be observed through a microscope or a telescope. It is not something distilled from a beaker in a laboratory. It is not an empirical statement. It is a philosophical conclusion that must be accepted by faith despite atheists' strenuous efforts to pretend otherwise.

In the end, one's position may come down to the core choice of whether matter is or is not all that exists. Hume's argument against miracles, Harris' demand for extraordinary evidence, and other arguments are heavily biased by what we have previously concluded is the nature of the universe. The claim that a miracle has occurred is only *extra*ordinary to someone who has made a prior conclusion that the *ordinary* universe consists solely of matter. In either worldview, however, it is a presumption that cannot be empirically proven or disproven.

In hindsight, the reason I found atheist writing unconvincing may be because, although I had come to doubt God's existence, I was at least open-minded enough to allow the possibility he existed. It was an epiphany when I grasped how much the entirety of the argument rests on this core decision that both sides accept by faith. If someone presumes matter is all that exists, it takes significantly more evidence to convince him of God. Presumptions are nearly impossible to overcome. For example, it is exponentially more difficult to convince parents that their child has committed a crime than it is to convince anyone else in the general public who does not presume the child is innocent. As far as determining the nature of the universe, the faith that both sides place in the improvable hypothesis "matter is all that exists" may well be the hinge pin of the entire argument.

I am not suggesting a presuppositional argument for God. I am simply suggesting that an open-minded starting point would be "matter may or may not be all that exists." For example, someone willing to put all options on the table will almost certainly come to a different conclusion about the resurrection than the person who will only consider a materialistic answer. As we saw with Hume, vast amounts of evidence—like eyewitness testimony—can be summarily dismissed without serious consideration when we bring biased presuppositions into the inquiry.

2. Fallacy of False Dichotomy (Evolution or Theism)

Another strong theme is the fallacy of false dichotomy (a.k.a. fallacy of the excluded middle), wherein atheists create a false dichotomy between being a young Earth creationist on the one hand and believing in evolution and being an atheist on the other. There is allegedly no other alternative. This idea is especially pronounced in Dawkins, who argues exclusively against young Earth creationists. He offers no substantive argument for people who believe in both evolution and God. He writes as if he has never even heard of theistic evolution.

Just yesterday I was listening to a fascinating debate between Andy Macintosh, a professor of thermodynamics, and Robert Asher, a paleontologist at the Museum of Zoology in Cambridge.[5] Macintosh was arguing the scientific case for a young Earth,* while Asher was advocating that evolution occurred over millions of years. If you bought into Dawkins' oversimplifications, you would have assumed that Macintosh was a Christian and Asher was an atheist. The truth is, however, that both men have a deep faith in God. Asher finds no conflict between working in Dawkins' own field of paleontology and believing in God. Ignoring scientists like Robert Asher and Francis Collins, Dawkins effectively suggests that people must either take a strict, literal interpretation of Genesis or be an atheist. It is a fundamentally flawed false dichotomy that fails to even consider other viable alternatives.

3. Fallacious Conflict Between Science and Religion

A cousin of the fallacy of false dichotomy is the alleged conflict between religion and science, wherein the New Atheists falsely maintain that people must choose between religion and science. For example, atheist professor Jerry Coyne from the University of Chicago Department of Ecology and Evolution claimed in an editorial that "science and faith are fundamentally incompatible."[6]

I simply do not see this supposed conflict. I stand in good company on this position among intellectuals as diverse as H.G. Wells, Albert Einstein, Isaac Newton, Carl Jung, Max Planck, Freeman Dyson, Peter Higgs, and Stephen Jay Gould.[7] I would go as far as to make the accusation that the New Atheists do not even believe it themselves but just perpetuate it to sell books. I say that because when you catch Dawkins in a casual conversation, like the one he had with Jon Stewart on *The Daily Show*, his message changes. Stewart told Dawkins, "You seem to be the avatar for the dividing line of the incompatibility of religious beliefs and scientific beliefs." Dawkins smiled at this moniker and responded, "I will take that." Stewart then asked Dawkins if he was

---

* One by-product of the research done for this book was finding a surprising amount of scientific support for a young Earth. While I am not advocating that position, I was intrigued by some of the arguments. For example, Macintosh points out that Carbon-14 dating is useful only for objects up to about 60,000 years old because of the 5730-year half-life of ^{14}C. Yet it has been found in coal, which supposedly takes millions of years to form, though it should have all long since decayed into nitrogen-14. But whether the Earth is old or young has no bearing on whether God exists.

aware that there are religious individuals with a strong belief in God who also believe quite strongly in the scientific method. Surprisingly, Dawkins responded, "I am well aware of that."[8] You would never get that impression from his book.

4. Fallacy of Argumentum Ad Annis

The logical fallacy of argumentum ad annis ("argument because of age") comes up in some form with every author. This is the fallacious argument that older ideas are inferior simply because of their age, as if the truth was subject to aging. This fallacy is apparent when atheists use terms like "Bronze Age this..." and "Bronze Age that..." However, the age of something has nothing to do with whether it is true. The Pythagorean theorem ($a^2 + b^2 = c^2$) is every bit as true today as when the Greek mathematician Pythagoras discovered it in 500 BC. Like Pythagoras' teachings on math, the truth of whether Jesus did or did not rise from the dead 500 years after Pythagoras is not diminished by time.

5. Distorting the Nature and Role of the Old Testament

In addition to suggesting that timeless truths expire, the New Atheists also take the opposite tactic, selectively taking temporary Old Testament propositions and attempting to turn them into timeless truths. No author in this bunch appears to understand why the Old Testament is called "old." Nor do they know that its content specifically points out its interim status and predicts its replacement after the Babylonian captivity with a heart-based system of conscience based on Jesus. They are fond of comparing the standards of the Mosaic Law to those of modern society, but they dare not compare the Mosaic Law to the standards followed by surrounding ancient Near-Eastern neighbors, lest they be forced to acknowledge the advancement it represented in its day.

One would think a scientist like Richard Dawkins would understand that a scientific model could be a breakthrough today and yet, by the standards of science 4000 years from now, look rather stupid in contrast. Likewise, the Old Testament was a breakthrough for its time but its application today is limited. The New Atheists' continued love affair with it should be as embarrassing to them as a scientist who continues to extol the energy potential of atomic energy because he is ignorant of the discovery of the nucleus and the power of nuclear fission.

I have found great irony in the New Atheists' attempt to turn everything on its head. Any timeless truth they deem a Bronze Age superstition, but things which applied only during the Bronze Age they try to advance as timeless truth.

6. Distorting History

The New Atheists' dubious handling of history is a strong recurring theme. The way the New Atheists write about history reminds me of Paul Harvey's radio show from the 1980s, *The Rest of the Story*. His trademark style was describing a story, always accurately, yet minus some key detail. Then at the end, almost always after a commercial break intended to stir heightened suspense, he would supply the missing fact(s), always prefaced with his catchphrase "And now, the rest of the story." The rest of the story would completely alter your view about what had happened.

For example, he might describe a man who had climbed Mount Everest. He would describe how he and his guide had to trudge through blizzards for days and jump long ravines as certain death awaited thousands of feet below. Around the time you thought you understood the gravity of the situation, Harvey would go to a commercial break. Then he would come back on with, "And now, the rest of the story." The crucial bit of missing information was that the climber was a Vietnam veteran and a double amputee with no legs. He had climbed Mount Everest using his arms to pull himself on his belly. He had "jumped" deadly ravines clinging to the back of his Sherpa. Everything you thought you had known about the difficulty of his climb was radically altered.

When the New Atheists write about history, it reminds me of a Paul Harvey report minus "the rest of the story." Invariably, their anecdotes sound convincing until you do your research and discover that crucial bits of information have been excluded. Take Harris' denouncement of the Pope for not excommunicating Hitler. He gives the impression that the Pope made no response to Nazi atrocities. But "the rest of the story" is the Pope's strong denouncement of the Nazi movement in *Mit brennender Sorge,* in which he condemned the Nazis as pagans and denounced Hitler. Harris conveniently fails to mention that the Pope called on Catholics to not only pray against those who promoted racist ideologies but to take heroic action and sever ties with such groups. When you learn how widespread the Catholic opposition was and the tremendous costs its heroism incurred in the form of thousands of priests and parishioners who died opposing Nazism, the truth shatters Harris' extremely misleading portrait.

I found it very annoying that again and again I had to dig to find "the rest of the story" because the New Atheists consistently withheld the whole truth. It seemed they developed the ploy of selective fact-sharing together over a round of beers. I was profoundly disappointed with how often I found them to be misleading once all the facts were in. For example, Harris says "millions of Muslims" would like to see us live under Taliban rule.[9] According to *The London Times,* the actual number is closer to 36,000.[10] Such egregious errors cannot be accounted for by variance among sources. There can only be a deliberate intent to mislead or, at very best, gross negligence in fact-checking.

Granted, atheists' willingness to distort the facts does not disprove atheism. However, it does indicate a willingness to force history into their model. That is not an open-minded analysis of history. When attempts to prove a position require this degree of forced fact manipulation, there is almost certainly something wrong with the model.

7. Fallacy of Confusing Cause with Effect

Bertrand Russell acknowledged, "The question of the truth of a religion is one thing, but the question of its usefulness is another."[11] Regarding religion's usefulness, he extensively disparaged religion for what he perceived as its negative effect on free sexual expression and education. Harris deprecates religion for its alleged negative impact on politics, drug policy, medicine, and sex education. Dawkins criticizes religion for its impact on homosexual rights, abortion, and the alleged subservience of science.

As Russell himself pointed out, however, even if every one of the charges were true, they still say absolutely nothing about the truthfulness of religion. Even if Jesus coming to Earth were the worst thing that ever happened to humanity, that says absolutely nothing about whether he lived, died, and rose from the dead. Therefore, I found entire chapters of the New Atheists' books spurious because their endless complaints about religion contribute not one iota to whether God is real. It seems like the New Atheists have completely ignored the possibility that God could exist without meeting all their expectations of how he should be.

8. Fallacy of the Nonrepresentative Sample

Not only do the New Atheists mistakenly tie the truth of religion to its effect, they misrepresent the effect of religion using the logical fallacy of nonrepresentative sample. Also known as the cherry-picking fallacy, this misleading tactic selectively picks the worst of religion to represent its norms. Sometimes this is so blatant a schoolboy could spot it. An example is Russell's claim that religion's only contributions are the calendar and the prediction of eclipses. He claims religion has *never* contributed anything else useful to civilization at any time or any place.[12] Generally, the fallacy is more cleverly disguised by some token admission of a few of religion's meaningful contributions, like when Harris acknowledges that Muslim scholars invented algebra and essentially sparked the Renaissance in Western Europe by releasing forgotten classical Greek texts in Latin.[13] However, after conceding a trivial two sentences to what good religion does, Harris spends the entire remainder of a chapter trying to justify his claim that the roughly two *thousand* ISIS Muslim extremists currently laying siege to Baghdad are more representative of Islam than the nearly four *million* peaceful Muslim residents of Baghdad who oppose them.

Such fallacious arguments are not the least bit convincing because no belief, organization, or country could withstand such biased cherry-picking. If someone hates America, for example, there is no shortage of mistakes they could cherry-pick. America's blunders include slavery, child labor, mistreatment of the American Indians, war crimes, misogyny, racism, etc. However, selectively pointing out America's flaws does not accurately represent America as a whole, nor does it prove she is toxic. The gross distortion of focusing exclusively on religion's mistakes while ignoring its positive contributions speaks more to me about the personal bias of the New Atheist authors than about the need to eliminate religion.

By comparison, if some radical college professor were to spend considerable time in every class listing America's shortcomings without ever mentioning democracy, our role in World Wars I and II, the promotion of scientific research, the reduction of hunger, space exploration, or the promotion of home ownership and financially secure retirements, the majority of people, atheists included, would conclude there is a problem with the professor rather than with America.

9. Feuerbach's Argument (the Wishful Thinking Argument)

The wishful thinking argument was raised by every atheist except Nietzsche. He rightly dismissed it, citing the absurdity that anyone would believe something simply because it made them feel better.[14] The rest of the atheist writers, however, are all prepared to assume that religious people are willing to believe anything that makes them happy. However, this is like using a hand grenade to settle a knife fight. As C.S. Lewis and Alister McGrath have observed, atheists also have wishes (such as a desire for moral autonomy) that are threatened by the idea of an omniscient, moral law-giver. The wishful thinking is equally damaging to both sides.

10. Red Herring Fallacy/Appeal to Emotion

For Harris to point out the Catholic Church tortured people in the name of religion is a fair and rational criticism. But to spend entire pages pointing out every gruesome detail of how they did it, describing all the various implements of torture and how they worked, including in gory detail the agony of a hypothetical victim, is no longer an appeal to reason, in my opinion. It is a rhetorical appeal to emotion.

Judging by Harris' and Hitchens' book sales, some people evidently found the rhetoric persuasive. I found it hypocritical for the alleged champions of rational arguments to resort to such emotional tactics. I could easily do the same by describing how Romania's atheist government imprisoned, tortured, beat, and poisoned Father Calciu for simply speaking out against atheism. Yet after a long emotional harangue, such tactics establish nothing beyond the fact that both Christians and atheists have blood on their hands.

Areas of Disagreement Between Atheists

While it is interesting to note certain common themes, it is perhaps more interesting to note the widespread disagreement that exists amongst atheists. Dawkins openly admits he actively seeks to convert readers to atheism.[15] So it is worth noting that many of his arguments are not convincing even for other atheists!

Morality is the most divisive issue among atheists. Since the law of conscience seems to point to a law-giver, every atheist author feels incumbent, as they should, to explain morality without God. The fact that none of them have solved the problem of morality without God can be seen in how they disparage each other's solutions.

Dawkins looks for natural morality in the behavior of Arabian babblers. However, he simply ignores contrary examples in frigate birds, orangutans, sharks, lions, and other animals. He cannot explain why the behavior of one animal group is morally superior to another. The failure of his moral model is pointed out not by a theist but by a fellow atheist, Harris, who claims that "nature has not adapted us to do anything more than breed." The only natural moral good is lining up at a sperm bank to propagate our offspring.[16]

Harris claims to offer an absolute ethic based upon love. Russell points out he shares the same idea but claims, contrary to Harris, that it cannot be demonstrated to be anything more than personal opinion.[17] Nietzsche disagrees with all of them, claiming morality does not exist. According to him the very ideas of "good" and "evil" are illusionary, and mankind needs to embrace his animalistic instincts.

When their models are insufficient even to other atheists, it is empty hubris when they claim to have solved the problem of a Godless morality.

Amongst widespread disagreement, the majority of atheists I have talked to agree with Nietzsche and Russell's view that morality is merely a cultural invention. They would agree with Russell that, although undesirable, forgery is ultimately not any more "evil" than catching a cold.[18] When pressed to seriously consider it, occasionally I hear the concession that Russell was correct that there is no moral difference between writing a poem and committing a murder.[19] It would appear that Russell is right *if* atheism were true. It is just rare to find atheists who have Russell's courage to admit it.

Surprise Discoveries

Perhaps the most surprising revelation in all the atheists' books was that Sam Harris, one of the most famous names in New Atheism, is a closet Buddhist. Harris denies it, but he promotes a string of ideology in his final chapter that is essentially undistinguishable from Buddhist theology. Harris also questions the finality of death and claims some mysteries of the world can be as easily *experienced* through mysticism as *explained* through science. Far from proving theism or even deism, this does at least demonstrate how a highly rational and skeptical scientist can arrive at some spiritual truths without referencing a scrap of holy Scripture. This reminds me of Plato's belief in life after death absent any reference to divine revelation.

Nietzsche acknowledges that Plato arrived at the idea of soul and life after death through rational contemplation, not special revelation. While most of the hardcore New Atheists believe *any* spiritual claim can come only from irrational dogma, Harris and Plato clearly refute this and at least get us to the point where we can talk about which spiritual truths are worth believing instead of arguing over whether materialism alone explains reality. They demonstrate that it is possible for a highly intelligent, skeptical thinker to believe in spiritual truths.

Coming Full Circle

That is my story. I grew disenchanted with faith by first becoming emotionally disappointed with God. Questioning his goodness, as it often does, led to questioning his existence. However, when I sincerely investigated atheism, I found the "scientific" arguments of atheists like

Dawkins were directed almost exclusively at young Earth creationists and offered me nothing.* Authors like Harris and Hitchens proved to be phenomenal speakers and writers but horrible historians, damaging their credibility. Only Nietzsche seemed willing to be honest and consistent, but his model was a nightmare. Perhaps my biggest disappointment was that, with the exception of Dawkins, no atheist even attempted to prove that God does not exist. They mostly just attacked Christian apologists with logical fallacies or attacked the behavior of Christians. I kept searching for a good argument against God, but it simply never came.

In *An Enquiry Concerning Human Understanding,* David Hume wrote, "A wise man proportions his belief to the evidence."[20] I had weighed the evidence for Christianity and, in and of itself, it was not enough to prevent me from questioning my faith. But when I investigated the evidence against faith, I found the atheists' writings to be so completely devoid of evidence that faith seemed to be the only wise belief.

---

* I lean toward theistic evolution. While I do not believe the young Earth position is indefensible, that discussion is far beyond the scope of this book.

Notes

Chapter 1: My Journey into Disbelief

1. Job 23:3,8 (NIV).

2. Words and music by William Berry, Peter Buck, Michael Mills, and Michael Stipe. Copyright © 1991 Night Garden Music (BMI). All rights administered by Warner-Tamerlane Publishing Corp. (BMI). All rights reserved. Used by permission of Alfred Music.

3. See http://www.huffingtonpost.com/2012/06/26/young-adults-losing-faith-americans-under-30-doubt-god-exists_n_1627333.html.

4. See http://en.wikipedia.org/wiki/Ice_core. Since I do not answer these questions in the book itself, for those who are curious, ice core dating is similar to dating a tree by counting its rings. Each year when the snow thaws, melts, then refreezes, it produces detectable rings, which can then be counted to date the age of the core sample. Personally, I am inclined to believe the dating taken from these cores is accurate. However, it is not a significant problem for young Earth creationists. The best explanation I have heard is, "Suppose, hypothetically, that God created a tree yesterday and you, being unaware of that, cut it down today and counted the rings. How old would you think the tree was?" In similar manner, if God created the Earth 6000 years ago and you drilled an ice core today and counted the rings, how old would you think the Earth is?

5. Once again, since the question deserves an answer, the answer given by *Answers in Genesis* is that there was a land bridge between Asia and Australia that is no longer there. It was similar to the land bridge believed to have existed between what is now the former Soviet Union and Alaska, by which the ancestors of American Indians are believed to have entered the Americas. While I think *Answers'* president, Ken Ham, is right about a lot of things, personally I find the idea of such a massive land bridge implausible. The problem is not merely the absence of evidence of such a massive land bridge but that, by Ham's account, kangaroos, wombats, and Tasmanian devils made the daunting migration without any of them dying along the way. We have no fossils of these mammals outside of the Australian mainland. My personal view is that the flood was local in nature. In other words, when Genesis talks about "every living thing on the face of the earth was wiped out" (Genesis 7:23), it is talking about every *known* living thing but not necessarily animals on a continent that was entirely unknown to the original audience of Genesis. Before attacking this as a play of semantics, consider how we use words today. The Seattle Seahawks were declared "world" champions on Super Bowl Sunday, February 2, 2014, even though they played no teams outside of America and not a single other country of the "world" participated in the event.

6. See http://www.youtube.com/watch?v=oVZnwZdh-iM&list=FLtxzoawJX0NXbQ9f29r3f2w&index=26.

7. See http://www.boston.com/bostonglobe/ideas/articles/2010/07/11/how_facts_backfire/.

8. Ibid.

9. Bill Bright *Have You Heard of the Four Spiritual Laws?* (San Bernardino, CA: Here's Life, 1993).

10. Van A. Harvey, *Feuerbach and the Interpretation of Religion* (Cambridge: Cambridge University Press, 1995).

11. Sigmund Freud, *Future of an Illusion* (Claremont, Canada: Broadview Press, 2007).

12. Richard Dawkins, *The God Delusion* (New York: Bantam Press, 2006), 353.

13. See http://www.mountainman.com.au/essenes/thesis.pdf.

14. C.S. Lewis, *Surprised By Joy: The Shape of My Early Life* (New York: Harcourt Books, 1955).

15. Bertrand Russell, *Why I Am Not a Christian* (New York: Simon & Schuster, 1957), 50.

16. Private correspondence with Richard Dawkins, July 9, 2014.

Chapter 2: The Early Skeptics

1. George Santayana. *Reason in Common Sense* (New York: Scribner, 1905), 284.

2. See http://www.historyofphilosophy.net/thales.

3. John Martiall, *A Replie to Mr Calfhills Blasphemous Answer Made Against the Treatise of the Cross: Volume 203 of English recusant literature, 1558–1640* (Ilkley: Scholar Press, 1566).

4. Colin Buchanan, *Mixed Blessing: The Motor in Britain* (London: L. Hill, 1958).

5. Will Durant, *The Story of Civilization* (New York: Simon & Schuster, 1954).

6. Ibid.

7. Sarvepalli Radhakrishnan, *A Sourcebook in Indian Philosophy* (Princeton, NJ: Princeton University Press, 1957, 1989), pp. 227–249.

8. See http://vedda.org/primitive.htm.

9. Ibid.

10. Bertrand Russell, *The History of Western Philosophy* (New York: Simon and Schuster, 1945).

11. Charles Singer, *A Short History of Science to the Nineteenth Century* (Oxford: Oxford University Press, 1941).

12. See http://www.historyofphilosophy.net/thales.

13. Diels-Kranz, *Die Fragmente der Vorsokratiker* (Berlin: Weidmannsche Buchhandlung, 1903).

14. See http://www.egs.edu/library/xenophanes/quotes/.

15. See http://www.historyofphilosophy.net/xenophanes.

16. Deepak Sarma, *Classical Indian Philosophy: A Reader* (New York: Columbia University Press, 2011).

17. Eugene F. Bales, *A Ready Reference to Philosophy East and West* (Landam, MD: University Press of America, 1987), 211.

18. See http://plato.stanford.edu/entries/xunzi/.

19. Edward Machle, *Nature and Heaven in the Xunzo: A Study of the Tian Lun* (Albany, NY: State University of New York Press, 1993), 119.

20. See http://www.hooverradio.com/garin%20hoover%20radio%20show%20archive.htm (5/1/2014 episode).

21. Friedrich Nietzsche, *Beyond Good and Evil* (New York: Random House, 1989), 2.

22. See http://en.wikipedia.org/wiki/Christian_philosophy.

23. See http://www.iep.utm.edu/epicur/.

24. Nietzsche, *Beyond Good and Evil*, 14.

25. Titus Lucretius Carus, *On the Nature of Things* (London: Henry G. Bohn, 1851).

26. Monica R. Gale, *Myth and Poetry in Lucretius* (New York: Cambridge University Press, 1994), 213, 223-24.

27. Bertrand Russell, *Why I Am Not a Christian* (New York: Simon & Schuster, 1957), 24.

28. Robert Wilken, *The Christians as the Romans Saw Them* (New Haven, CT: Yale University Press), 2003, 100.

29. See http://www.ccel.org/ccel/schaff/anf01.viii.ii.v.html.

30. "Bertrand Russell >Quotes >Quotable Quote," *Goodreads*. Goodreads Inc, n.d. Web. February 24, 2015.

31. Sam Harris, *The End of Faith* (New York: W.W. Norton, 2005), 14.

32. Dio Cassius, *Dio Cassius: Roman History, Volume VIII, Books 61-70* (Cambridge, MA: Harvard University Press, 1925).

33. Suetonius Tranquillus, *The Lives of Twelve Caesars* (London: George Bell and Sons, 1890).

34. See http://en.wikisource.org/wiki/The_Annals_%28Tacitus%29/Book_15#44.

35. Richard Dawkins, *The God Delusion* (New York: Bantam Press, 2006), 345.

36. Alleyne Nicholson Reynold, *A Literary History of the Arabs* (New York: Routledge, 1962), 318.

37. Cyril Glasse, *The New Encyclopedia of Islam* (Lanham, MD: Rowan & Littlefield, 2001), 313.

38. Samar Attar, *The Vital Roots of European Enlightenment: Ibn Tufayl's Influence on Modern Western Thought* (New York: Lexington Books, 2007).

39. Ibid.

40. See http://plato.stanford.edu/entries/kant-hume-causality/.

41. Christopher Casey, "Grecian Grandeurs and the Rude Wasting of Old Time," *Foundations*, Volume III (Fall 2008).

42. See http://www.britannica.com/EBchecked/topic/508675/Romanticism.

43. See http://www.ncbi.nlm.nih.gov/pmc/articles/PMC2745620/.

44. Hugh Ross, *The Creator and the Cosmos* (Colorado Springs: NavPress, 1995), 57.

45. See http://www.arn.org/docs/odesign/od172/cosmos172.htm.

46. Francis Collins, *The Language of God* (New York: Free Press, 2006), 1.

47. See http://www.premierradio.org.uk/listen/ondemand.aspx?mediaid={95B21082-F4E4-42C2-BA29-A38448080D34}.

48. See http://www.truthinscience.org.uk/tis2/index.php/evidence-for-evolution-mainmenu-65/51-the-miller-urey-experiment.html.

49. See http://latimesblogs.latimes.com/world_now/2012/01/kim-jong-il-death-new-north-korean-leader-kim-jong-un-crackdown-on-defectors.html; http://www.dailynk.com/english/read.php?cataId=nk03600&num=8669, http://www.dailynk.com/english/read.php?cataId=nk01500&num=8668.

50. See http://www.strangenotions.com/flew/.

51. Antony Flew, *There Is a God: How the World's Most Notorious Atheist Changed His Mind* (New York: HarperCollins, 2007), 88-89. John Pasquini, *Atheist Persona: Causes and Consequences* (Lanham, MD: University Press of America, 2014), 95.

52. See https://www.youtube.com/watch?v=jrXf8KCJLMg.

53. Mark Oppenheimer, "The Turning of an Atheist," *The New York Times Magazine* (November 4, 2007).

Chapter 3: Friedrich Nietzsche—Enlightenment Atheism

1. Bertrand Russell, *The Mysteries of Life and Death* (New York: Simon & Schuster, 1957), 92.

2. See http://www.ncbi.nlm.nih.gov/pubmed/18575181.

3. Ibid.

4. Christian Emden, *Friedrich Nietzsche and the Politics of History* (New York: Cambridge University Press, 2008), 35.

5. Jörg Salaquarda, "Nietzsche and the Judaeo-Christian tradition," *The Cambridge Companion to Nietzsche*, (Cambridge: Cambridge University Press, 1996), 99.

6. Julian Young, *A Philosophical Biography: Friedrich Nietzsche* (New York: Cambridge University Press, 2010), 239.

7. Ibid.

8. Joachim Köhler, *Zarathustra's Secret: The Interior Life of Friedrich Nietzsche* (New Haven: Yale University Press, 2002), 106.

9. See http://www.nytimes.com/2002/07/06/books/is-there-a-gay-basis-to-nietzsche-s-ideas.html?src=pm&pagewanted=1.

10. Young, *A Philosophical Biography*, 399.

11. Peter R. Sedgwick, *Nietzsche: The Key Concepts* (New York: Routledge, 2009).

12. See http://en.wikipedia.org/wiki/Nietzsche#CITEREFNietzsche2004.

13. See http://en.wikipedia.org/wiki/Nietzsche.

14. Steven E. Aschheim, *The Nietzsche Legacy in German: 1890–1990* (Los Angeles: University of California Press, 1992), 135.

15. See http://www.nytimes.com/2002/07/06/books/is-there-a-gay-basis-to-nietzsche-s-ideas.html?src=pm&pagewanted=1.

16. William L. Shirer, *The Rise and Fall of the Third Reich* (New York: Simon & Schuster, 1959), 100.

17. Ibid.

18. Friedrich Nietzsche, *Beyond Good and Evil* (New York: Random House, 1989), 15.

19. See http://en.wikipedia.org/wiki/Epicurus.

20. Ibid., 2.

21. Nietzsche, *Beyond Good and Evil*, 20.

22. Ibid., 26.

23. Ibid., 15.

24. Ibid., 21.

25. Ibid., 45.

26. Ibid., 38-39.

27. Ibid., 49.

28. Ibid., 54.

29. Ibid., 48.

30. Ibid., 47.

31. Ibid., 68.

32. See http://www.buddhist-quotes.com/buddhist-quotes/mistaking-a-rope-for-a-snake.html.

33. Nietzsche, *Beyond Good and Evil*, 69.

34. Ibid., 72 (emphasis added).

35. Ibid., 116.

36. Ibid., 72.

37. Ibid., 73-76.

38. Karl Marx, *Critique of Hegel's "Philosophy of Right"* (New York: Press Syndicate of the University of Cambridge, 1970), 132.

39. See http://www.nybooks.com/articles/archives/2011/mar/10/hitler-vs-stalin-who-killed-more/.

40. Ibid., 88.

41. Ibid., 86.

42. Richard Dawkins, *The God Delusion* (New York: Bantam Press, 2006), 51.

43. Ibid., 58.

44. Nietzsche, *Beyond Good and Evil*.

45. Ibid., 112-13.

46. Ibid., 115.

47. Ibid., 68.

48. Ibid., 98-99.

49. Ibid., 157.

Chapter 4: A Response to Friedrich Nietzsche

1. Bertrand Russell, *History of Western Philosophy* (New York: Simon & Schuster, 1945), 697.

2. Russel, *History of Western Philosophy*, 773.

3. Peter Boghossian, *A Manual for Creating Atheists* (Durham, NC: Pitchstone Publishing, 2013), 16.

4. Ibid.

5. Francis Crick , *The Astonishing Hypothesis* (New York: Touchstone, 1994).

6. See http://www.tere.org/assets/downloads/secondary/pdf_downloads/ALevel/ConscienceNotes.pdf.

7. See https://www.youtube.com/watch?v=oVZnwZdh-iM&list=FLtxzoawJX0NXbQ9f29r3f2w&index=25.

8. See http://www.wingia.com/web/files/news/14/file/14.pdf; also https://www.cia.gov/library/publications/the-world-factbook/fields/2122.html#xx.

9. See http://www.pewresearch.org/daily-number/number-of-christians-rises-but-their-share-of-world-population-stays-stable/.

10. See http://www.stephenjaygould.org/ctrl/schafersman_nat.html.

11. Ibid.

12. See http://www.

13. Ibid., 72.

14. Ibid., 73.

15. Ibid., 76.

16. See http://www.archives.gov/exhibits/charters/declaration_transcript.html.

17. See http://plato.stanford.edu/entries/locke-political/.

18. Friedrich Nietzsche, *Beyond Good and Evil* (New York: Random House, 1989), 72.

19. Ibid.

20. Ibid.

21. See http://en.wikipedia.org/wiki/Demographics_of_the_Soviet_Union#Population.

22. Ibid., 99.

23. Ibid.

24. Friedrich Nietzsche, *The Portable Nietzsche*, trans. Walter Kaufmann (New York: Penguin Books, 1954).

25. Bertrand Russell, *Why I Am Not a Christian* (New York: Simon & Schuster, 1957), 92.

26. Nietzsche, *Beyond Good and Evil*, 167.

27. Ibid., 108.

premierradio.org.uk/listen/ondemand.aspx?mediaid={258253D8-DE26-45AE-A3E1-0E57C29488CA}.

Chapter 5: Bertrand Russell—Classical Atheism

1. Nicholas Griffin, *The Cambridge Companion to Bertrand Russell* (Cambridge: Cambridge University Press, 2003).

2. Bertrand Russell, *Why I Am Not a Christian* (New York: Simon & Schuster, 1957), 14.

3. Ibid., 6.

4. Bertrand Russell, *The Autobiography of Bertrand Russell* (New York: Simon & Schuster, 1969), 35.

5. Ray Monk, "Russell, Bertrand Arthur William, third Earl Russell (1872–1970)," *Oxford Dictionary of National Biography* (Oxford University Press, September 2004; Web March 14, 2008).

6. Bertrand Russell, "The Future of Pacifism," *The American Scholar* (March 1944): 7–13.

7. Bertrand Russell, "Love, Bertie: The Selected Letters of Bertrand Russell: The Public Years, 1914-1970," *The Economist* (July 19, 2001).

8. See http://en.wikipedia.org/wiki/Bertrand_Russell#cite_note-108.

9. See http://www.asl-associates.com/einsteinquotes.htm.

10. Ibid., vi.

11. Friedrich Nietzsche. *Beyond Good and Evil* (New York: Random House, 1989), 69.

12. Ibid., vi.

13. See http://en.wikiquote.org/wiki/Richard_Dawkins.

14. Russell, *Why I Am Not a Christian*, vii.

15. Richard Dawkins, *The God Delusion* (New York: Bantam Press, 2006), 85.

16. Russell, *Why I Am Not a Christian*, 5.

17. Ibid., 6.

18. Ibid., 7.

19. Ibid., 8.

20. Ibid., 10.

21. Dawkins, *The God Delusion*, 151.

22. Russell, *Why I Am Not a Christian*, 11.

23. Ibid., 14.

24. Ibid.

25. Ibid., 16.

26. Ibid., 17.

27. Ibid.

28. Ibid., 24.

29. Ibid.

30. Ibid., 25.

31. Ibid., 27.

32. Ibid., 28.

33. Ibid., 29.

34. Ibid., 30.

35. See http://en.wikipedia.org/wiki/Theodicy.

36. Russell, *Why I Am Not a Christian*, 33.

37. Ibid., 38.

38. Ibid.

39. Ibid., 38, 48.

40. Ibid., 38.

41. David Hume, *An Enquiry Concerning Human Understanding* (Oxford: Oxford University Press, 2007), 114.

42. Ibid., 83.

43. David Hume, *Of Miracles* (introduction by Antony Flew) (La Salle, IL: Open Court Classic, 1985).

44. Russell, *Why I Am Not a Christian*, 41.

45. Ibid., 71.

46. Ibid., 43.

47. Dawkins, *The God Delusion*, 130.

48. See http://www.nytimes.com/2002/05/11/arts/so-god-s-really-in-the-details.html.

49. See http://64.62.200.70/PERIODICAL/PDF/SaturdayRev-1974feb23/27-29/.

50. See https://theweeflea.wordpress.com/tag/bertrand-russell/.

51. Russell, *Why I Am Not a Christian*, 50.

52. Ibid.

53. Ibid.

54. Ibid.

55. Ibid., 174.

56. Ibid.

57. Ibid., 178.

58. Ibid., 194.

59. Ibid., 195.

60. Ibid.

61. Ibid., 197.

Chapter 6: A Response to Bertrand Russell

1. "Bertrand Russell >Quotes >Quotable Quote." *Goodreads.* Goodreads Inc, n.d., Web, February 24, 2015.

2. Sam Harris, *The End of Faith* (New York: W.W. Norton, 2004), 64.

3. Ibid., 75.

4. Richard Jenkins, *Rethinking Ethnicity: Arguments and Explorations* (London: SAGE Publications, 1997), 120-21.

5. Ibid., 32.

6. Simon Blackburn, *The Oxford Dictionary of Philosophy* (Oxford, UK: Oxford University Press, 1994), 58.

7. See the explanation at http://mathcentral.uregina.ca/QQ/database/QQ.09.06/s/matt1.html. The odds are 1/6 per die so 1/6 x 1/6 = $(1/6)^2$ for the first pair rolled, 1/6 x 1/6 x 1/6 x 1/6 = $(1/6)^4$ = 1/1296 for rolling double sixes twice, $(1/6)^6$ for three consecutive rolls, etc. The point being you would roll a whole lot of double sixes before approaching the 1 in 10^{138} odds of a naturally occurring universe.

8. Hugh Ross, "Why I Believe in Divine Creation," in Norman Geisler and Paul Hoffman, eds., *Why I Am a Christian* (Grand Rapids, MI: Baker, 2001), 138-41.

9. Elgar G, Vavouri T., "Tuning in to the signals: noncoding sequence conservation in vertebrate genomes," *Trends Genet,* July 2008, http://www.ncbi.nlm.nih.gov/pubmed/18514361.

10. See http://www.sciencemag.org/content/337/6099/1159.summary.

11. See http://www.premierradio.org.uk/listen/ondemand.aspx?mediaid={95B21082-F4E4-42C2-BA29-A38448080D34}.

12. J.R. Ellis, "Tackling unintelligent design," *Nature 463* (January 14, 2010).

13. Friedrich Nietzsche, *Beyond Good and Evil* (New York: Random House, 1989), 49.

14. Albert Schweitzer, *The Quest of the Historical Jesus* (Mineoloa, NY: Dover, 2005), 146.

15. See http://www.aha.org/research/rc/stat-studies/fast-facts.shtml.

16. See http://www.newadvent.org/cathen/11322b.htm.

17. See http://www.salvationarmy.org/ihq/statistics.

18. See http://www.huffingtonpost.com/2012/04/13/marriage-sex_n_1422644.html.

19. See http://www.stateofourunions.org/2012/SOOU2012.pdf.

20. See http://marriageandfamilies.byu.edu/issues/2001/January/cohabitation.htm.

21. See http://psychcentral.com/archives/tragedy_provides.htm.

22. C.S. Lewis, *Mere Christianity* (New York: HarperCollins, 1952), 38.

23. Steven Anzovin, *Famous First Facts, International Edition: A Record of First Happenings, Discoveries, and Inventions in World History* (New York: H.W. Wilson, 2000). The first life insurance company known of record was founded in 1706 by the Bishop of Oxford and the financier Thomas Allen in London. The company, called the Amicable Society for a Perpetual Assurance Office, collected annual premiums from policyholders and paid the nominees of deceased members from a common fund.

24. Nietzsche, *Beyond Good and Evil,* 203.

25. Robert M. Young, "The mind–body problem," in RC Olby, GN Cantor, JR Christie, MJS Hodges, eds., *Companion to the History of Modern Science* (New York: Routledge, 1990).

26. See http://www.thelancet.com/journals/lancet/article/PIIS0140-6736%2808%2961009-0/fulltext.

27. Bertrand Russell, *Why I Am Not a Christian* (New York: Simon & Schuster, 1957), 50.

28. Pew Research Center, *The decline of marriage and rise of new families,* 2010, http://

pewsocialtrends.org/files/2010/11/pew-social-trends-2010-families.pdf, accessed January 16, 2015.

29. Mark Branschick,, *The High Failure Rate of Second and Third Marriages*, 2012; retrieved January 16, 2015 from http://www.psychologytoday.com/blog/the-intelligent-divorce/201202/the-high-failure-rate-second-and-third-marriages.

30. Pew Research Center, *The decline of marriage and rise of new families*.

31. Ibid., 169.

32. See http://en.wikiquote.org/wiki/Robert_Fulghum.

33. See http://psycnet.apa.org/journals/fam/24/6/766/.

34. See http://yourlife.usatoday.com/mind-soul/doing-good/kindness/post/2011/03/with-17-million-children-going-hungry-in-the-us-al-roker-says-its-time-to-act/148571/1.

Chapter 7: Sam Harris—New Atheism

1. Richard Dawkins, "Coming Out Against Religious Mania," Huff Post Politics, *Huffington Post* (May 25, 2011), http://www.huffingtonpost.com/richard-dawkins/coming-out-against-religi_b_5137.html, accessed February 25, 2015.

2. See http://www.patheos.com/blogs/friendlyatheist/2007/06/07/how-well-are-the-atheist-books-selling/.

3. See http://www.amazon.com/The-End-Faith-Religion-Terror-ebook/dp/B000VUCIZE.

4. See http://www.latimes.com/opinion/op-ed/la-oe-morrison-sam-harris-spirituality-without-religion-20140924-column.html#page=1.

5. See http://www.newsweek.com/rationalist-sam-harris-believes-god-73859.

6. Ibid.

7. Sam Harris, *The End of Faith* (New York: W.W. Norton, 2004).

8. See http://rationalist.org.uk/855.

9. See http://www.washingtonpost.com/wp-dyn/content/article/2006/10/25/AR2006102501998_pf.html.

10. See https://www.youtube.com/watch?v=OSBaAT6WPmk, comment occurs at 1:00.

11. Harris, *The End of Faith* , 129.

12. Ibid., 53.

13. See http://www.theguardian.com/commentisfree/2007/may/07/comment.religion.

14. See http://www.samharris.org/about.

15. Harris, *The End of Faith*, 13.

16. Ibid., 14.

17. Ibid., 13.

18. Ibid., 15.

19. Ibid., 17.

20. Ibid., 19.

21. Ibid., 21.

22. Ibid.

23. Ibid.

24. Ibid., 41.

25. See http://www.philosophynews.com/post/2012/05/15/An-Analysis-of-Sam-Harris-Free-Will.aspx.

26. Harris, *The End of Faith*, 62.

27. Ibid., 65.

28. Ibid., 82.

29. Ibid., 83.

30. Ibid., 100.

31. Ibid., 102.

32. Ibid., 103.

33. Ibid., 104.

34. Ibid., 123.

35. Ibid.

36. Ibid., 133.

37. Ibid.

38. Ibid.

39. Ibid., 134.

40. Ibid., 111.

41. Ibid., 115 (emphasis added).

42. Ibid., 125.

43. See http://www.mediamonitors.net/mosaddeq16.html.

44. Sarah Oates, *Terrorism, Elections, and Democracy: Political Campaigns in the United States, Great Britain, and Russia*, Palgrave (New York: Macmillan, 2009), 101.

45. Harris, *The End of Faith*, 147.

46. See http://www.theatlantic.com/politics/archive/2013/12/if-a-drone-strike-hit-an-american-wedding-wed-ground-our-fleet/282373/.

47. Harris, *The End of Faith*, 153.

48. Ibid., 153-54.

49. Ibid., 170.

50. Ibid., 172.

51. Ibid., 171.

52. Ibid., 173.

53. Ibid., 180.

54. Ibid., 182.

55. Ibid., 183.

56. Ibid., 185.

57. Ibid.

58. Ibid.

59. Ibid.

60. Ibid., 186.

61. Ibid.

62. Ibid., 190.

63. Ibid., 191.

Chapter 8: A Response to Sam Harris

1. See http://archive.today/JjPR7.

2. See https://www.youtube.com/watch?v=OSBaAT6WPmk, comment occurs at 1:00.

3. See http://www.pewresearch.org/fact-tank/2013/06/07/worlds-muslim-population-more-widespread-than-you-might-think/.

4. See http://en.wikipedia.org/wiki/List_of_terrorist_incidents,_January%E2%80%93June_2013.

5. See http://www.nytimes.com/2011/01/22/world/africa/22sidi.html?_r=1&pagewanted=2&src=twrhp.

6. See http://www.thenational.ae/news/world/bouazizi-has-become-a-tunisian-protest-symbol.

7. Sam Harris, *The End of Faith* (New York: W.W. Norton, 2004), 13.

8. See http://www.newyorker.com/reporting/2014/03/17/140317fa_fact_solomon?currentPage=all.

9. See http://en.wikipedia.org/wiki/Sandy_Hook_Elementary_School_shooting#Perpetrator.

10. See http://www.politico.com/story/2013/12/newtown-shooting-police-file-101561.html.

11. See http://www.nytimes.com/2012/12/15/nyregion/adam-lanza-an-enigma-who-is-now-identified-as-a-mass-killer.html?smid=tw-share&pagewanted=all&_r=0.

12. See http://www.livescience.com/16585-psychopaths-speech-language.html.

13. Harris, *The End of Faith*, 18.

14. See http://en.wikipedia.org/wiki/Moloch.

15. See http://www.samharris.org/site/full_text/response-to-controversy2.

16. See http://rationalist.org.uk/855.

17. C.S. Lewis, *Mere Christianity* (New York: HarperCollins, 1952).

18. Alister McGrath, *The Dawkins Delusion*

(Downers Grove, IL: InterVarsity Press, 2007), 34.

19. See http://www.continuetolearn.uiowa.edu/laborctr/child_labor/about/us_history.html.

20. See http://en.wikipedia.org/wiki/Native_Americans_in_the_United_States#Removals_and_reservations.

21. William M. Osborn, *The Wild Frontier: Atrocities During The American-Indian War from Jamestown Colony to Wounded Knee* (Garden City, NY: Random House, 2001).

22. See http://viewmixed.com/top-7-us-massacres-in-history/1890/4.

23. See http://www.fordham.edu/halsall/mod/1920womensvote.html.

24. See http://en.wikipedia.org/wiki/African-American_Civil_Rights_Movement_%281954%E2%80%9368%29#Race_riots.2C_1963.E2.80.9370.

25. Ibid.

26. See http://www.alexandrmen.ru/english/demokratizatsia/Father_Aleksandr_Men_and_the_Struggle_to_Recover_Russia.html.

27. Paul Froese. "Forced Secularization in Soviet Russia: Why an Atheistic Monopoly Failed," *Journal for the Scientific Study of Religion*, Vol. 43, No. 1 (March 2004), 35-50.

28. See http://icl.nd.edu/assets/84231/the_demographics_of_christian_martyrdom_todd_johnson.pdf.

29. See http://en.wikipedia.org/wiki/Spanish_Inquisition#cite_note-81.

30. Henry Kamen, *Inkwizycja Hiszpańska* (Warszawa, Poland: Państwowy Instytut Wydawniczy, 2005), 62. Helen Rawlings, *The Spanish Inquisition* (Malden, MA: Blackwell Publishing, 2006), 15.

31. Vera Alexander. *Father Arseny, Priest, Prisoner, Spiritual Father* (New York: St. Vladimir's Seminary Press, 1998), vi-1.

32. Adrian Cioroianu, *Pe umerii lui Marx. O introducere în istoria comunismului*

românesc ("On the Shoulders of Marx. An Incursion into the History of Romanian Communism"), *Editura Curtea Veche*, 2005.

33. See http://www.washingtonpost.com/wp-dyn/content/article/2006/11/25/AR2006112500783.html.

34. Guenter Lewy, *The Catholic Church and Nazi Germany* (New York: McGraw-Hill, 1964).

35. William L. Shirer, *The Rise and Fall of the Third Reich* (London: Secker & Warburg, 1960), 240.

36. Ibid.

37. See http://en.wikipedia.org/wiki/Nazi_persecution_of_the_Catholic_Church_in_Germany.

38. John S. Conway, *The Nazi Persecution of the Churches, 1933-1945* (Vancouver, BC: Regent College), 1997.

39. Shirer, *Rise and Fall of the Third Reich*.

40. See http://en.wikipedia.org/wiki/Nazi_persecution_of_the_Catholic_Church_in_Germany.

41. Stéphane Courtois and Mark Kramer, *The Black Book of Communism* (Cambridge, MA: Harvard University Press, 1999).

42. See http://en.wikipedia.org/wiki/Mit_brennender_Sorge.

43. Frank Coppa, *The Papacy, the Jews, and the Holocaust* (New York: CUA Press, 2006).

44. Eamon Duffy, *Saints and Sinners, a History of the Popes* (New Haven: Yale University Press, 1997), 343.

45. Thomas Bokenkotter, *A Concise History of the Catholic Church* (New York: Doubleday, 2004), 389-92.

46. Carlo Falconi, *The Popes in the Twentieth Century* (Deltrinelle Editore. 1997), 230.

47. See http://www.pewresearch.org/fact-tank/2013/06/07/worlds-muslim-population-more-widespread-than-you-might-think/.

48. Fareed Zakaria, *The Future of Freedom:*

Illiberal Democracy at Home and Abroad (New York: W.W. Norton, 2003), 138.

49. See http://en.wikipedia.org/wiki/ List_of_terrorist_incidents,_ January%E2%80%93June_2013.

50. Harris, *The End of Faith*, 126.

51. See http://carnegieendowment.org/ experts/?fa=435.

52. See http://carnegieendowment. org/2009/10/22/who-are-taliban/161#why.

53. Dawkins, *The God Delusion* (New York: Bantam Press, 2006), 92.

54. See http://www.pewglobal. org/2006/05/23/where-terrorism-finds- support-in-the-muslim-world/.

55. Ibid.

56. See http://www.aasc.ucla.edu/ cab/200708230009.html.

57. See http://www.gallup.com/poll/17677/ majority-supports-use-atomic-bomb- japan-wwii.aspx.

58. Harris, *The End of Faith*, 126—53 percent is the average rate of support for suicide bombings among the 12 countries he cites.

59. Ibid.

60. See http://www.gallup.com/poll/148763/ muslim-americans-no-justification-vio- lence.aspx.

61. See http://www.gallup.com/poll/148763/ muslim-americans-no-justification-vio lenceaspxp.com/poll/157067/views-vio lence.aspx#4.

62. See http://www.salon.com/1998/09/23/ news_114/.

63. Harris, *The End of Faith*, 147.

64. See https://www.youtube.com/ watch?v=rKffGOHLPOo.

65. Harris, *The End of Faith*, 137.

66. Ibid., 132.

67. See http://news.bbc.co.uk/2/hi/middle_ east/2888989.stm.

68. See http://www.appgkurdistan.org. uk/?p=116.

69. See http://www.alternet.org/story/49864/ how_george_h.w._bush_helped_saddam_ hussein_prevent_an_iraqi_uprising.

70. See http://history1900s.about.com/od/ saddamhussein/a/husseincrimes.htm.

71. See http://www.oxforddictionaries.com/ definition/english/terrorist.

72. See http://www.webcitation. org/5wovK3hIw.

73. Harris, *The End of Faith*, 137.

74. See http://www.theguardian.com/ world/2001/jun/11/mcveigh.usa4.

75. US Naval War College Analysis, p.1; Jona- than Parshall and Anthony Tully, *Shattered Sword* (Washington DC: Potomac Books, 2005), 416-30.

76. See http://en.wikipedia.org/wiki/ Kamikaze#Recruitment.

77. See http://www.japan-101.com/history/ kamikaze.htm.

78. See http://en.wikipedia.org/wiki/ Kamikaze#Recruitment.

79. See http://en.wikipedia.org/wiki/ Imperial_Rescript_on_Education.

80. See http://en.wikipedia.org/wiki/ Leonidas_Squadron.

81. See http://home.comcast.net/~christine_ fair/pubs/Fair_Shepherd.pdf.

82. Albert Schweitzer, *The Quest of the His- torical Jesus* (Mineola, NY: Dover, 2005), 13-26.

83. Dominic Crossan, *The Historical Jesus: The Life of a Mediterranean Jewish Peasant* (New York: HarperCollins, 1991).

84. Harris, *The End of Faith*, 185.

85. Robin Higham, ed., *Bayonets in the Streets: The Use of Troops in Civil Disturbances* (Manhattan, KS: Sunflower University Press, 1989). Robert Coakley, *The Role of Federal Military Forces in Domestic Disor- ders, 1789–1878* (Washington, DC: Center of Military History, 1988).

86. Friedrich Nietzsche, *Beyond Good and Evil* (New York: Random House, 1989), 38-39.

87. Ibid., 54.

88. Ibid., 48.

89. Ibid., 73-76.

90. Ibid., 206.

91. Ibid., 203.

92. Bertrand Russell, *Why I Am Not a Christian* (New York: Simon & Schuster, 1957), 38, 48.

93. Ibid., 56.

94. Nietzsche, *Beyond Good and Evil*, 112-113, 115. For Russell's view see his article "Can Religion Solve Our Troubles" published in a Stockholm newspaper in November 1954, wherein he argues there are two bases for morality, religious dogma, and social utility.

95. Harris, *The End of Faith*, 187.

96. See http://www.brainyquote.com/quotes/quotes/l/leobuscagl150293.html.

97. Harris, *The End of Faith*, 189.

98. Ibid., 185.

99. See http://en.wikipedia.org/wiki/Distribution_of_wealth#mediaviewer/File:World_distributionofwealth_GDP_and_population_by_region.gif.

100. See http://en.wikipedia.org/wiki/Distribution_of_wealth#mediaviewer/File:Wdpiechartexchangerates2000.gif.

101. See http://www.bbc.com/news/magazine-17512040.

102. Harris, *The End of Faith*, 191.

103. Ibid., 16.

104. Ibid., 43.

105. See http://www.nytimes.com/2010/10/16/us/16beliefs.html?_r=3&.

106. See http://www.samharris.org/site/full_text/response-to-controversy2.

107. See http://news.uk.msn.com/world/scientist-held-over-terror-plot.

108. Harris, *The End of Faith*, 27.

109. Charles Phillips and Alan Axelrod, *Encyclopedia of Wars*. as cited in Vox Day, *The Irrational Atheist* (Dallas, TX: BenBella Books, 2008), 104-5.

110. See http://carm.org/religion-cause-war#footnoteref2_bfjbeid.

111. Gordon Martel, *The Encyclopedia of War* (New York: Wiley, 2012).

112. Harris, *The End of Faith*, 186.

113. Ibid., 191.

114. See http://rationalist.org.uk/855.

Chapter 9: Sam Harris and Buddhism

1. Sam Harris, *Killing the Buddha*. March 2006, http://www.samharris.org/site/full_text/killing-the-buddha/.

2. Sam Harris, *Waking Up: A Guide to Spirituality Without Religion* (New York: Simon & Schuster, 2014).

3. Ibid., 208.

4. Ibid., 209.

5. Ibid., 210.

6. Ibid., 214.

7. Ibid.

8. Ibid.

9. Ibid., 215.

10. Ibid.

11. Ibid.

12. Ibid., 207.

13. Ibid., 217.

14. Ibid.

15. Ibid., 218.

16. Ibid., 219.

17. Ibid., 220.

18. Ibid.

19. Ibid., 221.

20. See http://www.shambhalasun.com/index.php?option=content&task=view&id=2903&Itemid=244&limit=1&limitstart=1.

21. Harris, *Killing the Buddha.*

22. Ibid.

23. See http://www.watkinsbooks.com/review/ top10-people-on-spiritual-power-list.

24. Ibid., 235.

25. Eckhart Tolle, *The Power of Now* (Vancouver, BC: Namaste Publishing, 1999), 200.

26. Ibid., 187.

27. Ibid., 137.

28. Sam Harris, *The End of Faith* (W.W. Norton, 2004), 220.

29. Ibid., 208.

30. Ibid., 221.

Chapter 10: Richard Dawkins—New Atheism

1. ShirleyFilms, "Something from Nothing? [official] Richard Dawkins * Lawrence Krauss [HD] 02-04-12," online video clip, YouTube, February 12, 2012 accessed February 24, 2015.

2. See http://www.beliefnet.com/columnists/scienceandthesacred/2009/08/ why-i-think-the-new-atheists-are-a-bloody-disaster.html.

3. See https://www.prospectmagazine. co.uk/magazine/dawkinsthedogmatist/#. UzoMEFceUQE.

4. Private correspondence with Richard Dawkins. July 9, 2014.

5. See http://www.prospectmagazine. co.uk/magazine/world-thinkers-2013/#. U3Qolyh-MQE.

6. See https://www.youtube.com/ watch?v=sOMjEJ3JO5Q.

7. Nick Pollard, "High Profile," *Third Way* (Harrow, England: Hymns Ancient & Modern Ltd), April 1995.

8. Simon Hattenstone, "Darwin's Child" (London: The Guardian), February 10, 2003.

9. Richard Dawkins, *The God Delusion* (New York: Bantam Press, 2006), 141.

10. "Sean Faircloth joins RDFRS (US) as Director of Strategy and Policy," The Richard Dawkins Foundation for Reason and Science, October 1, 2011, http://old.richarddawkins.net/ articles/643044-sean-faircloth-joins-rdfrs-us-as-director-of-strategy-and-policy.

11. "The Out Campaign," RichardDawkins. net, July 30, 2007.

12. Dawkins, *The God Delusion,* 33.

13. Ibid., 39.

14. Ibid., 34.

15. Ibid., 52.

16. Ibid.

17. Ibid., 78.

18. Ibid., 79.

19. Ibid., 125.

20. See https://itunes.apple.com/us/podcast/ debategod-rss-feed/id367717543?mt=2 DebateGod Podcast #17, "Conversation between Richard Dawkins and John Lennox," November 2, 2011. Upon John Lennox informing Dawkins of two prominent scientists who believe in Jesus' resurrection, Dawkins responded, "Really? I rather thought better of them than that."

21. Ibid., 85.

22. Ibid., 87.

23. Private correspondence with Richard Dawkins, July 9, 2014.

24. Dawkins, *The God Delusion*, 73.

25. Ibid., 75.

26. Ibid., 76.

27. Ibid., 77.

28. See http://www.youtube.com/ watch?v=p5_0Fx_RICI.

29. Dawkins, *The God Delusion*, 101.

30. Ibid.

31. Ibid., 103.

32. Ibid., 122.

33. Ibid., 151.

34. Ibid., 173.

35. Ibid., 163.

36. Ibid.

37. Ibid., 164.

38. Ibid., 168.

39. Ibid.

40. Ibid., 170.

41. Ibid., 173.

42. Ibid., 166.

43. Ibid.

44. Ibid., 172.

45. Ibid., 169.

46. Ibid., 180.

47. Ibid., 251.

48. Ibid.

49. Ibid., 258.

50. Ibid., 239.

51. Ibid., 309.

52. Ibid.

53. Ibid., 316.

54. Ibid., 309.

55. See https://www.youtube.com/watch?v=oVZnwZdh-iM&index=26&list=FLtxzoawJX0NXbQ9f29r3f2w.

56. Dawkins, *The God Delusion*, 311.

57. Ibid., 312-13.

58. Ibid., 313.

59. Ibid.

60. Ibid., 315.

61. Ibid., 316.

62. Ibid., 318.

63. Ibid., 321.

Chapter 11: A Response to Richard Dawkins

1. See http://www.strangenotions.com/flew/.

2. Pablo Jauregui, "Peter Higgs Criticises Richard Dawkins Over Anti-Religious 'Fundamentalism,'" *The Guardian* (December 26, 2012), http://www.theguardian.com/science/2012/dec/26/peter-higgs-richard-dawkins-fundamentalism.

3. Ibid., 194.

4. See http://www.nsf.gov/od/nms/recip_details.jsp?recip_id=5300000000451.

5. See http://nihrecord.od.nih.gov/newsletters/2007/11_30_2007/story4.htm.

6. Richard Dawkins, *The God Delusion* (New York: Bantam Press, 2006), 52.

7. Bertrand Russell, *Why I Am Not a Christian* (New York: Simon & Schuster, 1957), 7.

8. Dawkins, *The God Delusion*, 136.

9. Simon Blackburn, *The Oxford Dictionary of Philosophy* (Oxford: Oxford University Press, 1994), 58.

10. Dawkins, *The God Delusion*, 78.

11. See http://royalsociety.org/awards/darwin-medal/.

12. Library of Congress, "Living Legend: Stephen Jay Gould," http://www.lcweb.loc.gov/about/awardshonors/livinglegends/bio/goulds.html.

13. Allan Bullock and Stephen Trombley, eds., *The New Fontana Dictionary of Modern Thought* (London: HarperCollins, 1999), 775.

14. See http://www.churchofengland.org/prayer-worship/worship/texts/psalter,-collects-and-other-resources/litprayr/prayers.aspx.

15. See http://download.journals.elsevier-health.com/pdfs/journals/0002-8703/PIIS0002870306006405.pdf.

16. *American Heart Journal*, October 2006, 152 (4): 41–42.

17. John A. Astin, et al. "The Efficacy of 'Distant Healing': A Systematic Review of

Randomized Trials," *Annals of Internal Medicine* (June 6, 2000), 903-10.

18. Dawkins, *The God Delusion*, 73.

19. Ibid., 51.

20. Ibid.

21. Ibid., 19.

22. C.S. Lewis, *Screwtape Letters* (New York: Macmillan, 1961), 128.

23. Ibid., 131.

24. Ibid., 101.

25. Ibid., 174.

26. Ibid., 103, emphasis added.

27. Stephen W.A. Hawking, *A Brief History of Time* (New York: Bantam, 1988).

28. See Hugh Ross, "Why I Believe in Divine Creation," in Normal Geisler and Paul Hoffman, eds., *Why I Am a Christian: Leading Thinkers Explain Why They Believe* (Grand Rapids, MI: Baker, 2001), chapter 8.

29. Dawkins, *The God Delusion*, 252.

30. Ibid., 121.

31. The literacy levels of ancient Mediterranean societies are fully explored in William V. Harris' *Ancient Literacy* (Cambridge, MA: Harvard University Press, 1989). His conclusions for the period I am discussing can be found in chapter 7 of his book (pages 175-284).

32. John Dickson, *The Christ Files: How Historians Know What They Know About Jesus* (Grand Rapids, MI: Zondervan, 2005), 51.

33. Ibid., 53.

34. Dawkins, *The God Delusion*, 118.

35. F.F. Bruce, *The New Testament Documents: Are They Reliable?* (Grand Rapids, MI: Wm. B Eerdmans, 1943), 9.

36. Dickson, *The Christ Files*, 46.

37. Dawkins, *The God Delusion*, 122.

38. Ibid.

39. James Beilby and Paul Eddy, *The Historical Jesus: Five Views* (Downers Grove, IL: InterVarsity, 2010), 62.

40. Ibid., 86.

41. Dickson, *The Christ Files*, 25.

42. Henry Drummond, *The Lowell Lecture on the Ascent of Man* (London: Hodder and Stoughton, 1904), 426.

43. Dietrich Bonhoeffer letter to Eberhard Bethge, May 29, 1944, *Letters and Papers from Prison*, ed. Eberhard Bethge (Old Tappan, NJ: Touchstone, 1997), 310-12.

44. Hugh Ross, "Why I Believe in Divine Creation," in Norman Geisler and Paul Hoffman, eds., *Why I Am a Christian* (Grand Rapids, MI: Baker, 2001), 138-41.

45. Russell, *Why I Am Not a Christian*, 8.

46. See the explanation at http://mathcentral. uregina.ca/QQ/database/QQ.09.06/s/matt1.html. Obviously the odds start to go up exponentially when you consider the odds of getting double sixes every time. For example, the odds of getting double sixes back to back jumps to 1/1296. Nevertheless, this is still far short of approaching the 1 in 10^{138} odds of a naturally occurring universe.

47. See http://hyperphysics.phy-astr.gsu.edu/hbase/forces/funfor.html.

48. Frank Turek and Norman Geisler, *I Don't Have Enough Faith to Be an Atheist* (Wheaton, IL: Crossway Books, 2004), 102.

49. Ibid.

50. Dawkins, *The God Delusion*, 165.

51. Ross, "Why I Believe in Divine Creation," 138-41.

52. Turek and Geisler, *I Don't Have Enough Faith to Be an Atheist*, 106.

53. Hawking, *A Brief History of Time*.

54. Paul Davies, *Other Worlds* (New York: Penguin, 1990).

55. Dawkins, *The God Delusion*, 173.

56. Dawkins, *The God Delusion*, 169.

57. Elizabeth A. Schreiber and Joanne Burger, *Biology of Marine Birds* (Boca Raton, FL: CRC Press, 2001).

58. See http://www.iucnredlist.org/details/22697733/0.

59. See http://en.wikipedia.org/wiki/Frigatebird.

60. From a letter to Oskar Pfister, February 24, 1928. Cited in H. Meng and E. Freud (eds.), Psycho-Analysis and Faith: The Letters of Sigmund Freud and Oskar Pfister (London: The Hogarth Press, 1963), 123.

61. Mary Koss, "Hidden Rape: Sexual Aggression and Victimization in a National Sample of Students in Higher Education," Rape and Sexual Assault (New York: Garland Publishing, 1988).

62. Dawkins, The God Delusion, 122.

63. Ibid.

64. Ibid., 235.

65. Ibid., 309.

66. Ibid., 23.

67. See https://www.youtube.com/watch?v=oVZnwZdh-iM&index=26&list=FLtxzoawJX0NXbQ9f29r3f2w.

68. Dawkins, The God Delusion, 313.

69. Ibid., 22.

70. See http://www.cnn.com/2013/09/18/world/asia/north-korea-human-rights-kirby/.

71. Dawkins, The God Delusion, 313-16.

72. Emphasis added; see http://atheists.org/.

73. See http://www.huffingtonpost.com/2013/06/30/atheists-monument_n_3523762.html.

74. See http://en.wikipedia.org/wiki/American_Atheists#Court_cases.

75. See http://newyork.cbslocal.com/2014/03/06/american-atheists-work-to-keep-wtc-cross-out-of-911-museum/.

76. See http://www.politico.com/story/2014/02/cpac-2014-american-atheists-103917.html.

77. Martin Beckford, "Atheist buses denying God's existence take to streets," The Daily Telegraph (January 6, 2009).

78. See http://www.iep.utm.edu/n-atheis/.

79. Ibid.

80. Peter J. Bowler, Evolution: The History of an Idea (Berkeley: University of California Press, 2003).

81. Eugenie Samuel Reich, "Edwin Hubble in Translation Trouble," Nature (June 27, 2011).

82. Michael E. Bakich, The Cambridge Planetary Handbook (New York: Cambridge University Press, 2000), 198.

83. See http://podbay.fm/show/267142101/e/1369497600?autostart=1.

84. See http://en.wikipedia.org/wiki/Angelo_Secchi.

85. Man of science-and of God from The New American (January 2004) via TheFreeLibrary.com.

86. See http://books.google.com/books?id=J4TZPlihVUoC&pg=PA451#v=onepage&q&f=false.

87. See http://en.wikipedia.org/wiki/List_of_Christian_thinkers_in_science.

88. Sarah E. Gabbott, "Exceptional Preservation," Encyclopedia of Life Sciences (New York: John Wiley, 2001).

89. See http://www.stephenjaygould.org/ctrl/gould_darwin-on-trial.html.

90. Jauregui, "Peter Higgs Criticises Richard Dawkins."

91. John F. Ashton, In Six Days: Why 50 Scientists Choose to Believe in Creation (Green Forest, AR: Master Books, 2001).

92. Alister McGrath and Joanna Collicutt McGrath, The Dawkins Delusion: Atheist Fundamentalism and the Denial of the Divine (Downers Grove, IL: Intervarsity, 2007). Andrew Wilson Deluded by Dawkins? (Lottbridge Drove, England: Kingsway, 2007).

93. Harris, The End of Faith, 73-77.

94. Friedrich Nietzsche, Beyond Good and Evil (New York: Random House, 1989), 157.

Chapter 12: The Big Picture

1. See https://player.fm/series/unbelievable/ unbelievable-3-nov-2007-the-new-athe ism-03-november-2007.

2. Bertrand Russell, *Why I Am Not a Christian* (New York: Simon & Schuster, 1957), 38.

3. Sam Harris, *The End of Faith* (New York: W.W. Norton, 2004), 157.

4. Russell, *Why I Am Not a Christian*, 38.

5. See https://player.fm/series/unbelievable/ does-the-rock-and-fossil-record-point-to-noahs-flood-or-evolution-unbelievable-02-august-2013.

6. See http://usatoday30.usatoday.com/ news/opinion/forum/2010-10-11-col umn11_ST_N.htm.

7. Harris, *The End of Faith*, 15.

8. Richard Dawkins on *The Daily Show*, New York (September 24, 2013).

9. Harris, *The End of Faith*, 203.

10. See https://login.thetimes.co.uk/?goto Url=http%3A%2F%2Fwww.thetimes. co.uk%2Ftto%2Fnews%2Fworld%2F.

11. Ibid., vi.

12. Ibid., 24.

13. Harris, *The End of Faith*, 108.

14. Friedrich Nietzsche, *Beyond Good and Evil* (New York: Random House, 1989), 49.

15. Richard Dawkins, *The God Delusion* (New York: Bantam Press, 2006), 141.

16. Ibid., 186.

17. Russell, *Why I Am Not a Christian*, 56.

18. Ibid., 41.

19. Ibid., 38.

20. David Hume, *An Enquiry Concerning Human Understanding* (Oxford, New York: Oxford University Press, 2007), 80.

To learn more about Harvest House books and
to read sample chapters, visit our website:

www.harvesthousepublishers.com

HARVEST HOUSE PUBLISHERS
EUGENE, OREGON